The Invention of Religions

The Invention of Religions

Daniel Dubuisson

Translation by Martha Cunningham

SHEFFIELD uk   BRISTOL ct

Published by Equinox Publishing Ltd.

UK: Office 415, The Workstation, 15 Paternoster Row, Sheffield,
        South Yorkshire S1 2BX
USA: ISD, 70 Enterprise Drive, Bristol, CT 06010

www.equinoxpub.com

First published in French as *L'Invention des religions* by CNRS *Éditions* 2019.
This first English edition published by Equinox Publishing Ltd. Translation
Martha Cunningham.

British Library Cataloguing-in-Publication Data

A catalogue record for this book is available from the British Library.

ISBN-13   978 1 78179 812 6 (hardback)
          978 1 78179 813 3 (paperback)
          978 1 78179 814 0 (ePDF)

Library of Congress Cataloging-in-Publication Data
Names: Dubuisson, Daniel, 1950- author.
Title: The invention of religions / Daniel Dubuisson.
Other titles: Invention des religions. English
Description: Bristol : Equinox Publishing Ltd., 2019. | Includes
   bibliographical references and index.
Identifiers: LCCN 2018032326 (print) | LCCN 2018052650 (ebook) | ISBN
   9781781798140 (ePDF) | ISBN 9781781798126 (hb) | ISBN 9781781798133 (pb)
Subjects: LCSH: Religion--Methodology. | Religion--History. | Religions.
Classification: LCC BL41 (ebook) | LCC BL41 .D82513 2019 (print) | DDC
   200.72--dc23
LC record available at https://lccn.loc.gov/2018032326

Typeset by S.J.I. Services, New Delhi, India

Contents

Part Three: What to Do with "Religions"?

It is the study of religion that invented "religion".
(Jonathan Z. Smith, 1988, 234)

My argument is that there cannot be a universal
definition of religion, not only because its constituent elements
and relationships are historically specific, but because that
definition is itself the historical product of discursive processes.
(Talal Asad, 1993, 29)

Following Smith, I contend that the category of religion
is a conceptual tool and ought not to be confused with an
ontological category actually existing in reality.
(Russell T. McCutcheon, 1997, viii)

[I]s Western anthropology, religious anthropology in
particular, in its quest for the Other and for our very humanity,
capable of discovering anything but itself—that is, anything
other than its own categories and its own ways of conceiving
the world?
(Daniel Dubuisson, 2003 (1998), 6)

I am simply wanting to acknowledge the sense in which
the "religious" and the "political" are not separate realms in
reality.
(Richard King, 1999, 14)

So what can we do? Is it even worth talking about
"Christianity," "Hinduism," or "Buddhism," or is it all so
relative that there's nothing to even hang words on?
(Craig Martin, 2012, 158)

Too often in the study of Islam—and, I think it is fair to
say, the academic study of religion more generally—we
reproduce the narratives that people we study want us to tell
about them.
(Aaron W. Hughes, 2015, 190)

With the Darwinian theory of evolution, [...] history
attained for the first time a real possibility of being nothing but
meandering tracks of fortuitous events, patterns of change as
pointless as the results of a game of chance, or a case of the
proverbial tale told by an idiot... signifying nothing.
(Tomoko Masuzawa, 2015, 134)

Introduction

For just short of thirty years, a veritable scientific revolution has been taking place in the departments of "Religious Studies" in many North American universities along with some of their British counterparts. The results obtained are so considerable that one must here and now envisage new ways to think of the History of Religions. This re-examination will include the ensemble of its privileged themes, its favorite arguments, and its long Western pre-history at the heart of Christian culture; but also, it must be said without skirting, of its numerous ethnocentric *a prioris*.

From among the remarkable works that have laid out these often radical, always iconoclastic and polemical theses,[1] one must point to *Imagining Religion: From Babylon to Jonestown* (Jonathan Z. Smith, 1982); *Genealogies of Religion: Discipline and Reasons of Power in Christianity and Islam* (Talal Asad, 1993); *Savage Systems: Colonialism and Comparative Religion in Southern Africa* (David Chidester, 1996); *Manufacturing Religion: The Discourse on Sui Generis Religion and the Politics of Nostalgia* (Russell T. McCutcheon, 1997); *Orientalism and Religion: Postcolonial Theory, India and "The Mystic East"* (Richard King, 1999); and *The Ideology of Religious Studies* (Timothy Fitzgerald, 2000).[2]

In order to take a rather exact measure of the amplitude and originality of this intellectual revolution, it suffices to consider the situation in the French academic world. The latter, perhaps too obscured by the importance it accords to Franco/French questions such as the most prudent teachings of religion as a phenomenon and of secularism,[3] seems for the moment to have missed out on this crucial rendez-vous.[4] It would be hard to imagine in France such lively polemics as those that have taken place in the United States around a subject as delicate in the eyes of our public powers as the university's teaching of Islam.[5] When it does exist, the contribution of French universities is rather orientated toward "religious history" — that is, the history of Catholicism and French Catholic populations of the modern (and especially contemporary) eras. As it is, this historiography appears to be part and parcel of the decline of Catholicism in French society today.[6]

The present work wishes to present a clear, if sometimes critical, synthesis of the principal themes, controversies, and works that have fed into and continue to nourish this vast current.

Part One proposes two objectives. On the one hand, it intends to recall the history of Christian notions, but especially that of the notion of religion, with its simultaneous controversies and turbulence. This constitutes an indispensable chapter, since too often we project retroactively upon the distant past what amounts to *post facto* clarity, since these were not our convictions at the time. On the other hand, it will allow for the discovery of the topics that have been circumscribed via the main questions of specialists since the mid-nineteenth century — that is, since the appearance of the History of Religions as an academic discipline. (Note that using capital letters here allows me to distinguish the academic discipline from the simple succession of historical facts.) This creation was characterized, as is proper, by the establishing of university chairs, specialized journals, and scholarly collections. For indeed, one must never assume that questions, especially in the social sciences, arise in and of themselves from how we view their importance (which is often merely the product of a retrospective illusion, tainted with ethnocentrism). In reality, these questions are always the result of a historical process, often long and complex, that has imposed itself upon the conscience of its contemporaries. That is why it will be necessary to examine the *aporias*, impasses, and contradictions that the History of Religions, as an academic discipline anchored in European and Christian cultural compost, has navigated through up to now — that is, up to the appearance of this radical movement that has so profoundly secularized (or neutralized, if preferable) the study of religions.

Strengthened by this preliminary support, the first three chapters of Part Two are devoted to the presentation of the theses, authors, and methods — but also the institutions and controversies — that today form the main substance of the vast current of Critical Studies of Religion (henceforth, Critical Studies). These Critical Studies clearly show that the current has a critical orientation, both held and asserted, whose arrows are, for the most part, directed toward a certain type of History of Religions — that which was in practice up to then and whose ecumenist and *religionist* orientation was personified by Mircea Eliade (who died in 1986). In the American university milieu, the term "religionist" serves to designate with clear irony the works and colleagues specializing in the History of Religions, who, to put it concisely, considered that a universal matrix of "religions" existed, and that as a consequence the only explanations for them were *sui generis* — that is, what was religious could only be explained by, or in terms of, what was also religious.[7] This wave, therefore, does not look at past philosophical criticisms of materialist or atheist inspiration (D'Holbach, Sade, Marx, Nietzsche, Freud, etc.) addressed to religions in order to reconsider or develop their thought,[8] because only the academic discipline itself is concerned. A fourth chapter follows immediately, containing three internally related contributions, devoted respectively to "colonialism and cultural imperialism," the "invention" of two Oriental religions (Hinduism and Shinto), and, finally, the emergence of approximately ten World Religions over the course of the nineteenth century.

Finally, in Part Three, some of the paradoxes, lacunae, and *aporias* of this current will be examined, as have already been collected during its brief existence, but also the fruitful paths that it has opened up for the future. In under 30 years, and while the History of Religions tended to doze in the shade of the powers who guard the defenders of *religion*[9] and The Sacred (Rudolf Otto, Gerardus van der Leeuw, Joachim Wach, Mircea Eliade), the current has made use of a large number of ideas, theses, and arguments that themselves are far from having passed through the crucible of … *meta-criticism*. Once they have gone through this test, they will probably provide the material for major future paradigms, much needed by the discipline in order to be recast and able to pursue renewal.

Yet another point to be refined in this regard, and which the reader should ever keep in mind, is that the History of Religions is not a university discipline comparable to the other human sciences, nor even to the other historical sciences. The reason for this is clear enough, and one that certainly ought not to be minimized or masked. Among the objects it treats, several constitute *at the same time*, in the mind of certain specialists, immutable articles of faith and, also at the same time, manifestations (images, symbols, hierophanies, etc.) of a supernatural revelation — that is, of transcendence in some form or other. In its eyes, therefore, it is impossible to reduce religious facts to a dimension that is merely human, social, psychological, cultural … which science, for its part, requires. Nothing indicates that this profound discord, related to a major conflict, is on the point of being resolved. After all, it has run through the History of Religions since its origins, as will be seen from Chapter One below. One may say that this very discord has supplied Critical Studies with a good part of its inspiration and *raison d'être*.

My translator, Martha Cunningham, would like to thank the following persons for their help in procuring texts and addressing translation-issues: Teresa and Matt Edwards (U/Toronto); David Smith (U/Toronto); Donald Wiebe (U/Toronto); Bronwen Neil (Macquarie U.); Timothy Quigley (The New School U.); and Robert Wicks (U/Auckland). As for myself, besides Martha for her remarkable work, I warmly thank Russell McCutcheon, Aaron W. Hughes, Richard King, and Kocku von Stuckrad for their help and support.

Part One

The History of Religions: A Western Science

Chapter One

Christian Culture and the History of Religions

1.1 Links: Numerous and Diffuse

I have just raised a major and, in fact, unsolvable problem, the influence of which is impossible to minimize whatever the method or point of view adopted. In one form or another—be it allusive, implicit, or clearly stated—this problem presents itself in all the ideas, theses, and arguments expressed within the domain of the History of Religion. And it will accompany us all the way through this book. I summarize it here by two emblematic expressions: "Christian Culture" *and* "History of Religions". The former, which includes theology, aims at eternal, timeless truths, in conformity with the designs of the chosen divinity. The latter, however, to be faithful to its vocation, must on the contrary place emphasis solely on the historical and anthropological dimensions of its "objects" — that is, on the processes and elements that have nothing to do with transcendence or supernatural teleology. The former finds its *raison d'être* fully in the Beyond, whereas the latter belongs entirely to our human world. This rather healthy distinction should be present and respected everywhere. Unfortunately, however, innumerable, often subtle threads are woven between Christian Culture, in its broad sense, and the History of Religions. And between the two there lies a vast grey area occupied by works of erudition (text editions, translations, philological tools, historical monographs, ethnographic research, etc.) that do not necessarily presuppose a specific philosophical engagement on the one side or the other. Thus, for example, the preparation of a critical edition of an ancient Buddhist text in Sanskrit or Tibetan is first and foremost—indeed, exclusively—philological. Yet this No Man's Land between the two is in fact a place of transactions, interferences, and incessant exchanges from which has emerged a literature that is equally "grey" (popularized works, encyclopaedias, reports, documentaries, journalism, etc.). Now this literature, for its part, has played and still plays a determining role in the establishment and diffusion of a largely dominant, and indeed conservative, *doxa*, little concerned with rethinking the tradition that preceded it.

This situation, if not too difficult to sum up quite generally, contains numerous causes of confusion and misunderstanding. The main cause I am tempted to evoke is the following: the situation is linked to the most intimate fabric of Western culture, since the fundamental questions that we raise are based on its materials (accumulated and fashioned for centuries, especially around the topics associated with the notion of *religion*), as well as the corresponding responses that we formulate. Neither the questions nor the answers have any existence outside of their own history. Contrary to many received ideas, they do not correspond to any form of timelessness or universality.[1]

Thus, when asking if God exists or if all human beings possess an immortal soul, we are not asking universal questions—that is, questions that people—all people—would have asked at some time or other in their history. On the contrary: we are posing questions whose horizon is tightly circumscribed, since they are in a certain way the exclusive products of Western Christian Culture. One must therefore be quick to come back down from the universal, which is the claimed object of these questions, to the local, indigenous level. This means that, seen exactly this way, these questions contain their entire meaning and value only when in this delimited and specific frame. And the same goes for the corresponding answers to the questions. The circularity between the questions and the answers is complete; it is a circle both vicious and hermeneutic, and impossible to exit. No culture can conceive of the "truths" that another culture has imagined and upon which the latter has constructed its world and developed its conception of man. This quite general remark is valid for all cultures. How could I immediately—that is, without any long initiation coupled with an *in-situ* immersion—deal with the questions of an expert in Haitian voodoo or a Buryat shaman, each being a fully integrated member of their respective cultures?

As with every topic, that which in our culture is associated with the term *religion* defines or rather contains a vast repertoire of knowledge, commonplaces, arguments, notions, and specific hypotheses, all of which permit, with perfect circularity, the investigation of the domain—any domain—with the religious label. This simple operation of labelling is usually enough to shackle the terms of the debate, for it defines *a priori* the choice of questions and arguments that will precede the responses.

Now — and this point is crucial — beginning in the mid-nineteenth century, several elements of this topic played a part in the securing and developing of the History of Religions as an academic discipline. The "sliding" here from one genre to another was especially frequent and easy. And is so still today. And it is thus that many debates give the impression of taking place on terrain occupied by theology and its philosophical offshoots, the most famous of these being, in contemporary times, the phenomenology of *Religion*. Borne along by Western triumphant imperialism, the most banal and most narcissistic error consisted in considering as universal and immutable elements borrowed from Christian Culture, beginning with the very idea of *religion*. This behavior is at the base of an incalculable number of misunderstandings and controversies encountered constantly when scholarly anthropology confronts the certainties of "popular" anthropology.

Nevertheless, there is a crucial difference between cultures — more specifically, between all cultures and our culture. The domination exerted by the West since the era of great discoveries, but especially since the grand conquests of the European colonial enterprise of the nineteenth century, has modified (sometimes profoundly) all local and traditional cultures under its influence. By contrast, one would agree with me that the influence of Buryat shamanism and Haitian voodoo on Western culture can be seen as negligible. The Catholic and Protestant missions (and with them, administrators, scholars, explorers, military, bankers, merchants, entrepreneurs, etc.) over the centuries moved from the West in the direction of other continents. This profound and durable influence was seen in particular in the area that interests us here. The European scholars, in fact, discovered (or rather, "invented") *religions* everywhere, whose Western and Christian version evidently represented to them the ideal prototype. But in that case, what does the verb "invent" mean? What complex processes does it summarize? And what games (political, economic, military, etc.), which have nothing spiritual about them, did it conceal? We will see what answers to these questions have been provided by Critical Studies.

With regard to a single example aimed at illustrating this mechanism (since we could bring in hundreds of others), it is fascinating to see how José de Acosta, in his *Natural and Moral History of the Indies*[2] written in the second half of the sixteenth century, comes to "translate" into Christian, thus religious, terms (*cult, confession, communion, priests, female convents, unction, penitence,* and so on) the facts pertaining to all of the orders he observed among the Incas and the Aztecs. At no point did he think to understand these cultures as something in and of themselves, proceeding from their own identity or personality. For Acosta, this question does not even arise. It is true that this translation is coupled with a fairly clear ideological and political objective. It never forgets to point out — each time, and in a quasi-obsessive manner — that these "religious" traditions, practices, institutions, ceremonies (etc.) are presented in the West Indies in a deviant and thus degenerate way, as if the natives had lost or forgotten the meaning of original revelation. At the end of this transcultural translation, the superiority of the monotheistic and Christian West is somehow reaffirmed in the eyes of our Jesuit Acosta, the inferiority of the Aztecs is demonstrated, and the Christian norm is confirmed in its role as unsurpassable universal reference. In addition, accusing the other of idolatry is a subtle but terribly twisted way of confirming, in spite of everything, its place in humanity, for whom the possession of a religion is the most indisputable sign, all the while maintaining its subaltern rank.

The problem I raised at the beginning, and which I summarized by the concise formula "Christian Culture and History of Religions," is written into the current of a very long history that began well before the mid-nineteenth century, and whose principal characteristics it would be fitting to retrieve now. But without forgetting that this historical dimension goes against the immutability and timelessness that the Christian religion claims for its own creations. Over this precise point, philosophical in nature, there reigns a discord that is as deep as could possibly be.

1.2 The Invention of "Religio"

The word "religion" is derived, as we know, from the Latin word *religio,* which existed before the birth of Christianity (as witnessed by Cicero and Lucretius). And it evidently had a different acceptation from what was later communicated by Christian thinkers in Latin (e.g., Arnobius, Tertullian, Lactantius, Augustine). But this process was neither sudden nor immediate.[3] Augustine, for example, noted as early as the beginning of the fifth century that the use of the word *religio* did not remove all ambiguities, "yet in Latin usage, and that not of the ignorant but of the most cultured also, we say that religion is to be observed in dealing with human relationships, affinities and ties of every sort."[4]

From these first remarks we must keep in mind that the Romans themselves had no religion—no more than had the Greeks, incidentally—in the later, Christian sense of the term. John Scheid clarifies with respect to the Romans: "This was a religion without revelation, without revealed books, without dogma and without orthodoxy. The central requirement was, instead, what has been called 'orthopraxis,' the correct performance of prescribed rituals."[5] Now, unlike orthodoxy, orthopraxy (driving on the right side, eating with a knife and fork, doffing one's hat to a lady, etc.) is neither right nor wrong. These things are carried out as exactly and as scrupulously as possible. Thus, the Romans or the Greeks could not look on other *religions* as false, but the Christian tradition cannot imagine any religion other than itself as the true one. The Greeks and Romans in fact did not doubt the existence of other cities' gods, as is proven, in Rome, by the explicit *euocatio* rite, during which the Romans invited the gods of an enemy city about to be conquered to come and join them.[6]

And a Jew, as Jesus was, who thought and expressed himself in Aramaic, would have been unable to conceive of this concept, which did not gain prominence until a few centuries after him, at the end of a long maturation process punctuated with numerous controversies. If this reasoning were pushed to its paradoxical end, in order to better understand it one could say that Jesus could not have had a "religion" nor *a fortiori* have created one, since the thing itself and the word that accompanied its future Christian acceptance did not exist at the beginning of our era. It is thus that Ignatius of Antioch, who died at the beginning of the second century, did not need the word *religion* or any of its modern equivalents (spirituality, faith, belief, etc.) to speak about Christians and Christianity.[7] These facts are located at the antipodes of the orthodox point of view, such as that developed by Jacques-Bénigne Bossuet, for whom *the* religion, the only *true* religion, has existed since the origin of the world, with hardly any change since.[8]

In this same philological register, it must also be added that the word *religion* is abused in order to translate into French or English such Greek terms as *eusébia* and *thrêskeia*, terms that are not synonymous with *religion* and which it would be preferable to translate by cultural observances and practices. These two Greek words could only have a different acceptation, since Greek also has no exact equivalent for the word "religion". This is seen, for example, in French as well as English translations of the Greek New Testament, and in that of the *Praeparatio Evangelica* (*The Preparation of the Gospel*) by Eusebius of Caesarea (ca. 265–339).[9] The word *threskêia* is translated by the word *religio* three times in the Latin version of the New Testament (James 1:27; Acts 26:5; Colossians 2:18). Elsewhere, the word *eusébia* (piety) is rendered by *religio*, at the price of another inexactitude and an additional anachronism.

Whether the New Testament or the texts of Eusebius of Caesarea (who invented the Church History genre in that he was the historian who first provided the narrative framework into which the official history of the first centuries of Christianity would be fitted and piously re-written), what must be understood are the strategies, via biased translation, that hide this retrospective re-writing of history. In both cases, the anachronism suggests that Christianity was born, endowed with all of its attributes, in the New Testament—that is, from the beginning and not as a result of a complex and turbulent historical process.[10] Moreover, translating the Greek term by the word "religion," derived anyway from the Latin and not from the Greek, the translator of Eusebius was following the work of his author in a particular manner. In effect, from the beginning of the fourth century he inserts a notion into this text that did not yet exist with the acceptation that has since become traditional. The modern reader, French or English, doubtless does not ask about it, and, if confronted with the question, would answer that the religion spoken of in the Greek text is indeed the Christian religion. Doing this, the "helping hand" of the translator reinforces to some degree the demonstration that Eusebius wishes to make, but in a way that the latter could not have foreseen, much less enunciate. It is not easy to account accurately for this small mechanism of extreme precision whose semantic couplings and tendentious translations, associated with subtle narrative anachronism, deform historical reality by covering it with a uniform teleology whose origin is self-ascribed as the New Testament. The New Testament, which itself experienced a rocky history, was located at the opposite extreme of the mollified story entertained and transmitted by the Church.[11] The establishing of the collection of New Testament texts ultimately — thus retro-spectively — considered canonical is inseparable from the unending struggle of the Church against its innumerable heretical adversaries. In any event, the strategy lies not only in the strict definition of orthodoxy, which would in the end be considered solely valid, but also in the sacralization of that orthodoxy. The source for the orthodoxy must therefore lie as closely as possible to the person and activity of Jesus *as presented by the myth*.

Jennifer Eyl,[12] Paul Robertson,[13] and Todd Klutz[14] have arrived at fairly comparable conclusions regarding terms that are no less essential for theology and the history of Christianity (i.e., *ekklêsia*, *pneuma*, and *christianos*). Eyl, for example, is right to recall that the simple fact of not signaling these problems of translation and thus deviations or resultant anachronisms contributes to a transformation of historical fact into ideal account. Any solution of continuity and all ideas of evolution are suppressed. In this sense, these translations fulfill an entirely essential ideological function. This fundamental semantic instability, incompatible with the idea of eternal and immutable dogmas, equally affected the ontological bases of the person of Jesus from the beginning. How many Ecumenical Councils were necessary for theologians to agree upon a definition of the person of Jesus? This of course means that, contrary (once again) to pious legend, the figure of Jesus did not emerge by itself from the onset; it was the object of numerous discussions and rivalries before a satisfactory compromise could be arrived at. Concerning these *reinventions of Jesus* that were contemporaneous with the troubled history (which was anything but linear), I gladly refer to William Arnal. For Arnal, the causes of the historical development of Christianity cannot be found *in nucleo* in what is the mythical person of Jesus, but rather in the vicissitudes and jumping back and forth of the historical movement, which, I do not hesitate to add, is indeed responsible for the *reinventions* of the myth.[15]

It is not always easy to avoid anachronisms when translating old texts, but one should at least refrain from exploiting the ambiguities that inevitably spring from them. The use of these forced translations and anachronisms does not stop with the Greek. The Sanskrit *dharma*, as we will soon see,[16] was also enrolled in this vast, deliberate enterprise of abusive translations that tend to imply that "religion" as a phenomenon is universal, since every great culture possesses an equivalent of the Christian term. The reader who does not have a solid training in philology would imagine in good faith that religions exist everywhere, since words exist everywhere that are translated by and correspond to our indigenous term. At the same time, the originality of every culture is erased in favor of a uniform, fundamental "religious" vision of humanity that conforms to the unique and universal model imposed by the West. Originality is not always easy to recover when it has been transfigured or metamorphosed by centuries of Western and Christian acculturation. Another phenomenon can be added to this which must also be attributed to our Western intellectual history, and to which Arnal, again, has very recently drawn attention.[17] The central argument developed by Arnal, a specialist in the history of early Christianity, consists of saying that New Testament Studies should not enjoy special status, living in a sort of autarchy apart from all other academic departments. In particular, he reproaches such studies for not integrating the givens and problematics of anthropology, but rather, too often, those of theology. This rhetorical artifice allows them not to be placed (and certainly not to do it themselves) on the same footing as studies of other so-called religious traditions. And this even in American university departments specializing in Religious Studies. Thus, to give just one revealing example of this double standard, there is talk of the myth of Vishnu or of Zeus in these departments, but not that of the Christian god. This means implicitly that the latter belongs to a theology but not a mythology. One could say the opposite of Greek or Indian divinities: in general, they possess a rich mythology but no theology worthy of the name. Now if one considers that the Indian divinities have a mythology, there is no reason to refuse one for the Christian divinity.

In New Testament Studies, the accent is placed on a certain number of themes that imply a tacit recognition of the superiority and unique character of Christianity. To arrive at this, Arnal continues, it suffices in effect to privilege the approaches that imply notions of faith and belief, central in Christianity but ignored everywhere else; also, to accept only themes limited to Christianity and whose responses are found in the New Testament; to assume the identity and continuity of Christianity throughout history as a homogenous block faithful to its origins; to recall its favorite foundational myth; to subordinate the historical explanation to the rhetoric of the New Testament; and especially to avoid engaging these studies in overt comparisons with other traditions and based on lines of questioning that have nothing specifically Christian about them (such as those of comparative anthropology). In erecting this wall around it, in isolating itself in the refuge, it wishes to be inexpungable. In defining the topic as it suits it, New Testament Studies is trying to avoid any promiscuity with other "religions". This situation allows it to preserve more easily a type of exegetical and hermeneutical approach (rather than comparative, historical, or critical) that is very specialized and that is habitually only found in faculties of theology. It is thus Arnal's wish that, outside of these faculties, New Testament Studies be normalized — that is, examined in the same way as non-Christian traditions, so that they may lose the privilege that is unjustly self-accorded and that is not justified from a scientific point of view. From this first development, what must be kept in mind particularly is that "religion" — that is, the word itself in its Latin form, the corresponding concept and theme (in other words, the ideas, notions, and arguments associated with it), as well as the social institution itself (the world of the faithful and the believers) placed under the aegis of the Church — is initially a creation and a construction[18] that progressively made itself in the Latin world at the end of Antiquity, and whose development has continued since. "Religion" thus did not emerge in its definitive and ideal form from the New Testament and the teaching of Jesus, as if having to do with the incarnation of a timeless essence. On the contrary, several centuries were needed in order to establish the elements (dogmatic, intellectual, ritual, sacramental, institutional, political, etc.) that would end up constituting the Christian religion.

This original situation also permits us to understand that, up to now, an intellectually satisfying definition has never been found for the word "religion". In fact, this fundamentally Christian term, although coming from paganism and being fairly imprecise at the beginning of the Christian era, was then fashioned over the centuries to be adapted as best as possible to Christian culture and institutions. How could this term be fit for describing each of the configurations observed in the infinitely mottled ensemble of all human cultures? Its uneven historical destiny countered such theoretical ambitions. The insurmountable gaps and *aporias* were inevitable: what do our Buryat shaman, ancient haruspex, Haitian mambo priestess, and cardinal of the Roman curia have in common? And this list could be lengthened very easily to make it even more heteroclite. If the provincial term "religion" had not accompanied Western domination (imposing it more or less everywhere), who would have thought to choose it to make of it today one of the best-known concepts of the unity of the human race? A unity that must be credited for this domination. It was essential to have an overview of these controversies and discussions situated as closely as possible to the origins—let us say the Christianity of the first centuries—since they condition the (pre-)understanding of each of us and, especially, that of the specialists in the History of Religions when they utilize the notion of religion.

Two other characteristics of this long history are worth stressing, for they have exerted, and still exert, a decisive influence on the birth and development of the History of Religions as an academic discipline.

1.3 The Intellectual Hegemony of Christianity

Some situations appear clearly with sufficient distance, as their dimensions lack perspective. Thus, if one considers the intellectual history of Western Europe from the end of the Roman Empire up to today, one particular fact immediately comes to mind: during two-thirds of these fifteen centuries, if not for a good millennium, the quasi-totality of the intellectual production was concentrated in the hands of the Catholic Church and its specialized clerics. Their principal function consisted, in fact, in tirelessly exposing and defining Christian orthodoxy, its dogmas, and its institutions. And, very often, they did so by the use of scholarly language (Latin) and rhetorical procedures inspired by the poets of pagan antiquity not understood by the majority of the population. These practices made them members of a fraternity as mysterious as it was feared. This fear was due to, among other reasons, their claim to hold the keys to immortality or eternal damnation in the next world.[19] How many secular works and, dare we say it, pagan works during these thousand years were composed outside of the Church, that is, independent of its influence? And how many have survived? I see only a small handful of texts, written in Old Icelandic, Welsh, or Middle Irish—texts from the Western periphery of old Europe. The totality of these pagan literatures would occupy only a few volumes. Thus, for centuries the intellectual hegemony of the Church knew no rival. It is true that the latter never hesitated to suppress its adversaries, most often after having tortured them.

On the other hand, it would be impossible to count the number of essays, works, commentaries, exegeses, theses, and articles published under the authority of the Catholic Church for more than fifteen centuries. This impressive mass of documents was not merely composed and diffused *urbi et orbi*; the contents were methodically and systematically controlled *a priori* during the same period — that is, before dissemination and, after the invention of the printing press at the end of the fifteenth century, before publication. This practice of censorship is ancient. Gelasius I, Pope from 492 to 496, was the author of what is considered the first list of indexed texts (*De libris recipiendis et non recipiendis*), texts whose reading and proliferation were forbidden to the faithful. As I recall in my *Religion and Magic*:[20]

> [T]he current (1983) *Code of Canon Law*[21] still describes quite minutely the incredible system of control and censure put in place by the Catholic Church in order to ensure a complete grip on its members' expressing their opinions. It is thus, in particular, that this code frames all publications haughtily.
>
> Canon 823 §1 specifies, for the laypeople who may have had illusions:
>
> "In order to safeguard the integrity of faith and morals, pastors of the Church have
> the duty and the right to ensure that in writings or in the use of
> the means of social communication there should be no ill effect on
> the faith and morals of Christ's faithful. They also have
> the duty and the right to demand that where writings of the
> faithful touch upon matters of faith and morals, these be submitted to
> their judgment.
> Moreover, they have the duty and
> the right to condemn writings which harm true faith or good morals."

It is understandable that those responsible in the Church would often have preferred to speak of the "Little Flowers" ("*Fioretti*") of Saint Francis than of the particularly implacable system of control and surveillance.

No Western equivalents would be found for this exorbitant power that consists of trying at all costs to control the content and exercise of all human thought, with the exception of modern absolute monarchies and contemporary dictatorships. Perhaps the latter found there a model of fearsome efficacy that responded to their wish to break all intellectual resistance and hostile opinion as it arose.

This situation has only been possible, and has endured for so long, because it was in the hands of a centralized and powerful institution that itself culminates in the absolute power accorded its unique head, the sovereign pontiff:

> [W]e do not keep silent what the whole Church throughout the world knows: that the See of Saint Peter, the Apostle, has the right to loose what the sentences of any pontiffs have bound, since, though it has the right to judge of every church, no one may judge of its judgment, even as the canons allow appeals to it from any part of the world, though no one is allowed to appeal from it.[22]

This theocratic institution tirelessly defends a strict orthodoxy, and does so with all the more zeal since the latter was laboriously acquired and was always hard to protect from heresies:

> Is there on earth a power that was given the mission to direct thought with infallible rectitude? Yes: the Catholic Church, the unique repository of the religious life. All thought that deviates from the ways it has prepared is in error. And all opinionated error that it rebukes as contrary to its divine teaching and its revealed dogmas is heresy... The Church does not have to justify the condemnation of heresy other than by the fact of its priority and by the opposition to its teaching.[23]

The author of these lines is relying, as do those like him, on the foundational myth of the Church, ritually called upon for every occasion: that of an uninterrupted, supernatural tie, according to which the "members of the sovereign tribunal of the Catholic Church go back to the Apostles, and from the Apostles right back to Jesus Christ."[24] This amounts to their enjoying an absolute authority, since this comes in a direct line from the Son of God. The recalling of this true myth of origin is one of the most frequent clichés in the production of ecclesial ideology. It is found, of course, in Bossuet, speaking of Christian institutions.[25] In the same vein, he adds that the holy books were all published from the time of the apostles — that is, as close as possible to the original divine root-place.

For centuries, all those who opposed the Church or distanced themselves from it (heretics, sorcerers, free thinkers, atheists, or even the merely indifferent) were chastised without pity, starting with the first of them, Priscillian of Avila, who in 385 was condemned as a heretic and burned alive for his crime. Europe lived this way over several centuries, crushed under an authority that was as absolute as it was implacable.

In order to apply all of its weight against the intellectual life of its time, the Church needed a specialized body of clerics subject to its authority alone. The *Code of Canon Law* allows for no doubt on this crucial point. The same obedience is of course demanded of the simple faithful.[26] The Church and its specialized corps of clerics did not just exert implacable censorship; they also fashioned a good part of Western culture around their values and their own vision of the world. On the one hand, they looked to suppress any word that ran contrary to their teaching; on the other, they defined and imposed the constraining framework of a Christian anthropology. For in these texts, in addition to innumerable questions relative to the ecclesial institution itself, its dogmas, its sacraments, its rules, its governance (etc.), all aspects of human life and of the history of the world, from its genesis to its final apocalypse, have been methodically entered into the repertory, defined, and normalized. No aspect of the human condition, down to the most intimate (which the practice of the confession was there to track, in any case…) escaped them. The objective conformed to the designs of any absolute power — that is, any power that has as its ambition to model the individual in the image of its demiurge-ideal. It involved pursuing the divine work of fashioning "Christian" souls, bodies, and spirits — men and women whose existence would, from that point on, conform in all respects to this ideal world. But attaining this result presupposed as much abnegation from those who submitted their lives to this strict discipline as it did intransigence on the part of those guiding them.

1.4 Power, Church, and Religion

The second characteristic that needs mentioning — or, rather, simply recalling, since it is in everyone's mind — has precisely to do with this power that has been repeatedly alluded to above.[27]

The influence of the Church did not in fact limit itself to its role as schoolmaster of the West, director of conscience, or author of consoling supernatural mythology. A spiritual power endowed with an ultra-centralized organization, the Church was also an organ of incomparable power that used accusations of blasphemy and sacrilege to protect the ideological content of its propaganda.[28] As I recall in *Religion and Magic*,[29] whether it be in terms of masses of people to dominate and subjugate, of pleasures to be experienced, riches to accumulate, mechanisms for self-celebration, or consciences to mold, "spiritual power" (even if purely spiritual, which is rarely the case) is, as a power, no less efficacious or determined than the power that rests on the use of physical restraint alone. Indeed, this is rarely the case: the most brutal powers in operation in modern times never ceased to entertain belief in their own mythology, be it communist, fascist, or Aryan. The history of contemporary sects proves that we would be wrong to think of spiritual power as naturally inoffensive and benevolent, with absolute political power being the only merciless power, especially when, as the Church has done methodically, this spiritual power has been accompanied over the centuries by the use of corporal punishment, all the while instilling, day after day, a weighty feeling of guilt in the consciences of the faithful. But at the same time, it entertains a consoling mythology and imagery that culminates in the dual promise of immortality and eternal happiness, a mythology that, as Timothy Fitzgerald recognizes,[30] diverts attention from real questions relative to the construction of values and the legitimation of power. This radical alternative — the paradisiacal existence promised for tomorrow, in contrast to the punishments endured today in this world due to disobedience — doubtless represents a Machiavellian mechanism, for it entraps the individual in a pseudo-alternative. In effect, one has no choice between the quite hypothetical promise of happiness for the morrow and a very real punishment inflicted now.[31] This alternative, the carrot (eternal life) versus the stick (eternal damnation), is found at the base of how all powers function. These powers may exploit all resources, using a mixture of brutality and persuasion.

In every case, and if one places oneself for a moment on the side of the powerful, what matters is to obtain as complete a subjugation of the individual as possible. And this submission is only truly complete when accompanied by adherence to the values that defend the institution holding the power. To arrive at this, the powers (whatever or whoever they are) entertain costly mythologies that console, reassure, exalt, and so on. They are "costly," in effect, because they assume the existence of institutions and specialized personnel permanently charged with transmitting and glorifying the mythology but also with defending it at any cost.

In all the history of humanity, one will not find many examples of this ecclesial power not only in terms of its breadth, duration, and *omnipotentia*, but also in the fact that it has come to be associated with, and even to melt into the heart of, the same strictly hierarchical and centralized institution. It is a temporal power, an absolute political power as well as a spiritual and intellectual power that for a long time had no rival. For this reason alone, and if at the same time a rapid, circumambient glance is cast over the great civilizations of humanity, it would no doubt be possible to say that this constitutes an original creation.

Since religion is a matter of power, and indeed absolute power, one must invert the direction of the usual explanation and not take the effect for the cause. It is not religion that, fallen down from Heaven where it usually dwelt in ethereal form, was itself able to create an institution with as immeasurable powers as those held by the Catholic Church. On the contrary: it is the power of the Church (and of the quite real men who hold and enjoy this power) that has allowed it to develop and, especially, to impose a culture of religion which, for its part, had as a priority the responsibility for justifying its powerful position. Together, the progress of the Church and its imposed culture over the course of history ran in parallel and, here again, the circularity is perfect, because power defined the idea that, along with its mythological baggage, had to justify its existence. But those who carried out this work that was at the same time ideological, theological, and mythological are the same people who held and used this power. There is no visible contradiction; one finds nothing in the idea of religion that might weaken the institution it serves. Nor can anything be found in the institution that can weaken in any way the idea it needs so very badly. Incidentally, it is revealing that this religion lends itself with no problem at all to the service of temporal powers, monarchs, aristocrats, and business people, bringing and offering to them unhoped-for security. Here, again, in a spiritual definition of religion we would look in vain for the reasons behind the complicity that has perpetuated itself for centuries and that was expressed in sinister fashion even in the twentieth century.

It nevertheless appears evident that, even in the depths of this very Christianity, the notion of religion presents great complexity and is not easily understood. Moreover, who can say what figure best incarnates a center of gravity in this image: the apostle Paul? Augustine? Julius II? Saint John of the Cross? Torquemada? Bossuet? Schleiermacher? It is enough to raise the question in order to realize that there is no such nucleus or, rather, that it changes according to the context—that is, according to need. The notion of religion thus cannot be reduced to a space with a simple essence, disembodied as some people would wish. On the contrary, it must be accepted complete with the density of its turbulent history and the multiple dimensions of the ecclesiastical institution that created it and then firmly perpetuated it over the centuries. Its complexity renders it impossible to recognize within it the expression of an innate need that would characterize a timeless, and just as phantasmagoric, *homo religiosus*. This complexity is more prosaically — as every creation in this world — a human work and, in this case even more, the work of an institution that was *par excellence* the heir of the Roman *imperium*.[32]

The characteristics that have been brought out in the first part of this book will be found again winding their way through the chapters to follow. In putting them together now, I have particularly hoped to underline the extreme singularity of the Western situation dominated by the omnipresence and architectonic role of the notion of religion in Western history and culture. But what makes the situation even more paradoxical is that, for historical reasons that we will soon examine, this absolutely unique configuration has served as a reference, norm, and model for the West alone in its invention and inventory-taking of others' "religions". This *religion*, rich with incomparable and overwhelming intellectual heritage, with deep plough-lines traced and dug into Western history for centuries, would become the inevitable reference point for the History of Religions from its beginnings; a confrontation, although the word is doubtless not the most exact, since what was happening was much more often a veritable epistemological complicity between *religion* and the History of Religions.

Chapter Two

Two Major Paradigms

2.1 *Idealism* versus *Materialism*

In the middle of the eighteenth century, the grand aristocrat, Melchior de Polignac, who was also one of the French princes and Cardinal of the Catholic Church, published (posthumously) a Latin work in two volumes, entitled *Anti-Lucretius sive de Deo et Natura*. As the title reveals, the work presented itself as a refutation of the unfinished poem by Lucretius (*De rerum natura*) written seventeen centuries earlier, that is, in the course of the first century before Christ.[1]

What is astonishing in this history can be perceived by asking some very simple and almost evident questions. For what reasons did Polignac, Bossuet's successor at the *Académie française*, apply his talents to, and occupy his time with, the ten-thousand-line Latin refutation of arguments of an ancient text—and a pagan one, at that? During that Enlightenment century, would he not have had more dangerous, and especially contemporary, enemies to fight? And why choose Lucretius? To answer these questions, one must, as so often, step back slightly and modify the focus of our scrutiny before returning to where we started off.

From the point of view of the history of ideas and of the great philosophical theories, one must recognize that the history of the Christian *religio*(n) inscribes itself into an intellectual context that is much more vast and more ancient, a context that I consider to be one of the major polemical paradigms, indeed the dominant paradigm of the history of Western thought: idealism *versus* materialism.[2] This explains how a cardinal in the eighteenth century can still consider as urgent and sacred the task of refuting an author from antiquity. In fact, in my view, despite the seventeen centuries that separate the two men, they occupy antithetical and therefore structurally close positions on opposite sides of the paradigm. From this point of view, seen achronically, they are in some ways contemporaries. Or, put another way, if indeed one considers the history of Western thought, philosophy, and theology as a homogeneous ensemble, the notable positions that individuals and works occupy therein are not subject to the constraints of chronology. Influences such as those of Plato or Aristotle can exert and perpetuate themselves even when separated by centuries. And the same goes for antithetical positions that can reveal themselves or reappear after long periods. This result has been made possible by the quasi uninterrupted presence of intellectual corporations and clerics (philosophers, professors, theologians, etc.) who have devoted, and still devote, a large part of their existence to reading and commenting upon the texts of their predecessors. Thanks to these institutional mechanisms (ancient schools, monasteries, modern universities) and to the weight of these conservative traditions based on glosses and commentary, the *great* texts to a certain extent remain alive and contemporary within the long memory of Western thought. It is for this reason that we feel nothing strange or exotic when reading Plato, Augustine, or Cicero, to which I gladly add that the same phenomenon is observable, the same conservatism, in all of the great civilizations that had at their disposal the writing and the uninterrupted presence of colleges of specialized clerics (Chinese mandarins, Jewish rabbis, or Indian Brahmins, for example). In the present case, the two sides of this paradigm place in opposition, on the one hand (Lucretius), materialist theses, and on the other hand (Cardinal de Polignac), those theses that I here call (for convenience) *idealist*. In fact, this idealist side contains several expressions from European culture. It regroups, in effect, all of the theses — idealist in the Platonic sense of the word, but also spiritualist, religious, theist, deist, mystic[3] — that recognize the existence of a transcendent level; that is, one that escapes the laws of reality and matter. It is a level that can be occupied by God, The Sacred, Absolute Ideas, Symbols, or Eternal Essences. For this reason alone, these theses can quite easily be "inter-paraphrased". On the other side, materialist theses, thus atheistic, defend the contrary idea. According to the latter, there is no transcendent level, since everything that exists arises from a combination of atoms, be they from Epicurus or from modern physics. This opposition therefore is accompanied by another trait that finds all of its meaning in the case of the Christian religion. These materialist theses, which preclude the existence of an immortal human soul, also deny any divine intervention. They are hostile to all forms of providence and teleology. For them, the creation of our world as it is does not respond to a project by a superior intelligence who would have conceived of it with a predetermined end in mind.

However, as I have already mentioned, materialist works have been, at least up to the eighteenth century (Sade, D'Holbach, Diderot, La Mettrie), not just extremely rare but also tirelessly chased down and put onto the *Index Librorum Prohibitorum* by the Church. It is for this reason that a manuscript of the Lucretius poem did not appear until the beginning of the fourteenth century, and this only by chance (not to say here "miraculously"). It thus almost disappeared definitively during the course of the High Middle Ages.[4] With this in mind, one must look on Lucretius as the one who, for centuries, was the paradigmatic representative of materialism in the West (alongside the few letters and fragments of Epicurus). This entirely explains why, for Cardinal de Polignac, Lucretius would have been the ideal adversary of the providentialist, idealist Christian theses that required defending. On the other hand, works that are hostile to materialism, whether overtly so or not, are innumerable, because they bring together all of the Platonizing philosophies and all of the Christian works (the latter forming perhaps only a single section). Augustine realized, in fact, that the Platonic philosophers were the philosophers of choice for the Christians.[5] Indeed, could Christianity not be seen, from a certain philosophical and slightly ironic point of view, as a late-arriving theist and Platonizing sect?

2.2 *Religious* versus *Profane*

Despite appearances, the major paradigm just summarized is not to be confused with another (*religious versus profane*) to which I must also draw attention, for the latter is the product of a more recent evolution. This evolution has contributed to making *religion*, in our modern era, a singular domain, fundamentally original, and one which is distinct from all others that bring together secular activities (art, politics, medicine, economics, and so on). Under this new framework, far from being able to assimilate in the society of human relations and institutions, religion possesses a specific field and enjoys its own autonomy. This concerns one of the most original evolutions to attach itself to the Christian notion of *religion*. In the second half of the nineteenth century, it resulted in the institutional-ization and considerable influence of the History of Religions in the heart of the nascent Human and Social Sciences. Quite prosaically, one might observe that if a "History of Religions" exists, it is in fact because in the eyes of its founders it was possible to isolate discrete units called "religions". In its wake, encyclopedias, popular (vul-garized) works, and journals have expanded this movement within popular culture. Therefore, this academic discipline was not content with reviewing and studying its "objects," as it contributed to their hypostasis. This movement would lead to the invention of the Great World Religions that we will encounter below.

In order, once again, to take a precise measure of things, it is impor-tant to specify that the couple "religious/profane" is also something unique. Outside of the Western Christian world, this distinction and this opposition do not exist and indeed are inconceivable. Where would one make the separation between the two in ancient Chinese civilization or in post Vedic India? For us, Westerners, these oppo-sitions seem so indisputable that we would easily, and do, assign them universal value.

But the religious and the profane do not oppose each other in the same way as materialism and idealism, that is, as a pair of adversar-ies. They can coexist quite well, and in fact most often do so in our modern societies.[6] Profane activities do not set themselves in oppo-sition to "religious" activities in order to take their place, even for those who consider the latter as sacred. And that is made possible because the religious remains a domain apart, separate from oth-ers. And our contemporaries, be they Catholic or Protestant, are not wrong in this; they may say in all certainty, "this is part of religious practice and that, of profane."

The invention of the profane domain which, in contrast, has strengthened the place of the religious, is a recent creation in Europe. It resulted from the convergence of several factors leading to a profound reorganization of public space and the intellectual sphere, beginning with the eighteenth century.

The heritage of the Enlightenment,[7] the progress of atheism and philosophical materialism, and the end of the reign of theology as the discipline crowning the ensemble of human knowledge, could have dealt a fatal blow to religion, especially in its Catholic form. The same goes for the defense of the legal state populated with citizens equal before the law, the fruit of collective will, and the installation of a political life based on democratic principles, which placed the public space under the rule of human rationality alone.

But, by one of those twists of fate whose secret is known to history, two factors contributed to redefine the domain of religion, both on the side of believers and on that of scholars, allowing religion to adapt to this new situation.

On the one hand, the progress of introspection and the examination of the conscience, of the attention given to the least mental stirring, accentuated the interior and personal dimension of Christian religious life at the expense of its dogmatic, public, and solemn expressions. I have noted elsewhere[8] that texts such as essays, memoirs, and confessions centered on écriture *de soi* — writings of the self (Louis Marin), the most intimate for the individual — were entirely inconceivable in civilizations as prestigious as those of ancient India or China. This also means that our modern conceptions of the internal self or of the personality are not immediate, congenital "givens". They are also the result of complex historical evolutions entered into by numerous indigenous factors. It is therefore an illusion to think that the mystic experiences of a John of the Cross or of a Francis de Sales can be found anywhere else. Furthermore, the diffuse influence of a liberal Protestantism went the same way; it became a version of Christianity that was or is plucked clean, purified, and reduced to the essential, the relation based on the faith that unites the creature to its Divinity.[9] This evolution opened the way to a more ecumenical conception of religion. Paraphrasing Chidester,[10] I would say that the less this latter idea spreads out, the more it concentrates on the essential, on the kernel to which a superior ontological density is attributed. And it is this bare, ecumenical version that numerous contemporary thinkers, new disciples of Natural Religion, gladly ascribe to the fundament of all religions. They think to have discovered there the original kernel — ideal, timeless, and thus universal — of a religion free of all revelation, all naive mythology, all superfluous dogma, and all superstition,[11] that is, a religion free of all historical accretion that would have particularized it overmuch. I have already had occasion (and will have again) to denounce the naive and ethnocentric illusion driven by the latter conception of religion. We are loath to imagine the stones of the Greek monuments as they were originally, covered with garish painting, because the austerity of the naked stone exposed to the sun seems to conform better to the spiritual elevation of the Greek genius. And in the same way, Lutheran austerity and Cistercian stripping-down seem to many of our contemporaries to be closer to what could be a timeless and disincarnate version of religion. This austere concept runs contrary to all of the cults and ceremonies that use music, dance, intoxication, possession, bloody rituals, etc., that have long been deemed savage or primitive.

Chapter Three

A Nineteenth-Century Science

I have already had occasion to recall, in the introduction to this book, that the History of Religions as an official academic discipline endowed with the traditional institutional tools — university chairs,[1] specialized journals, collections of reference works[2] — developed from the mid-nineteenth century in Western Europe. This indeed flourished during the 1870s and 1880s, in terms of the first creation of university chairs: Geneva in 1873; Leiden and Amsterdam in 1877; the Gifford Lectures[3] delivered by the great Max Müller in 1888; in Paris *the Collège de France* in 1879 and the Fifth Section of the École Pratique des Hautes Études in 1880; Brussels in 1884; Germany in 1910, and so on.

Faced with these converging facts, the question that immediately comes to mind is: why in Western Europe, at that precise moment, and in such a brief period of time? To answer this, or, rather, in an attempt to solve this apparently simple question, a certain reflection arises that implies several aspects of European intellectual history and which, from this, additionally prompts numerous discussions and controversies. In these circumstances, the least unsatisfactory solution might be to review the indisputable factors that contributed to this genesis.

3.1 The Discovery of the Indo-Europeans

At the end of the eighteenth century, a considerable event took place. It would hardly be an exaggeration to say that this event changed the way of seeing the history of humanity, which had, up until that point, been solely a tributary of the biblical story (at least in countries of Christian culture). It is also true that elsewhere (China, India, Japan, pre-Colombian Mexico, etc.) the notion of such a "history of humanity," conceived as a whole movement, simply has no meaning.

Indeed, at the beginning it had to do with a discovery of a philo-logical and grammatical nature; from these areas one did not expect modifications of general knowledge or the triggering of profound intellectual upheaval. It was in fact at the end of that century that light was cast for the first time on the family relations between lan-guages that later would be called Indo-European. Thanks in par-ticular to Franz Bopp,[4] the idea took root quite quickly that Sanskrit, Greek, Latin, Old Persian, and ancient Germanic belonged to the same family and that they must therefore have had an ancestor in common: the Indo-European language. This language would have been spoken[5] some thousand years previously, before its users sep-arated and populated the European continent, part of the Middle East (Anatolia, Iran, Afghanistan), and the Indian subcontinent (the modern Indo-Aryan languages belong to this vast family as well). Further, the Indo-European family was completed (Celtic language, Slavic, Baltic, Armenian, Albanian, Hittite and Tocharian) thanks to the systematic discoveries permitted by the rapid progress of com-parative grammar throughout the nineteenth century, the century one could no doubt call "the Century of the Philologists". At the same time, critical and historico-philological exegesis of biblical texts, especially in the Protestant universities (Tübingen, Lausanne, Geneva), was making progress[6] that the Catholic world would take a good deal longer to recognize.

From this comparative grammar, one must bear in mind that, beyond the punctual lexical resemblances that can always be explained as borrowings, we find sophisticated mechanisms con-cerning the subtle rules of verbal and nominal morphologies: processes as special as vowel alternation (still found today in the so-called irregular verbs of English and German) or the construction of the perfect tense by reduplication in Greek, old Irish, and Sanskrit. Such processes, equally intimate to the economy of every language, cannot be borrowed; they evolve from their deepest functional structures. Further, the discovery of the Indo-Europeans yielded at least two supplementary, considerable repercussions in areas other than the language-sciences.

First of all, this discovery upset biblical chronology, for it became impossible to hold fast to linguistic evolutions and slow Indo-European migrations within a history as brief as the one defended by the Bible (four thousand years from Genesis to the New Testament era).[7] And, at the same time, it offered a credible alternative to the equally biblical tale that saw in Noah and his three sons (Shem, Ham, and Japheth [Genesis 9:18–10:7]) the sole ancestors of humanity. A substitution would need to be made subsequent to this monogenist vision (where all humanity emerged from a single ancestor): polygenism, according to which humanity possesses at least a second branch among its distant ancestors, independent of the first branch—that of the Indo-Europeans or "Aryans".[8] In this way, an ideological theme was established, founded on the opposition between Aryans and Semites, that would contribute so greatly to darkening the history of Europe in the twentieth century. As concerns France and the latter end of the nineteenth century, one may recall, among those historians of religion who shared this anti-semitic and anti-judaic prejudice, Ernest Renan,[9] Émile Burnouf, and Salomon Reinach. Burnouf wrote, for example, on the eve of the Belle Époque:

> It is fair to attribute this scientific barrenness in religions founded upon the Koran, less perhaps to the particularly moral character of the Musulman religion than to the nature of the Semitic spirit, always inferior, in the matter of science, to the genius of Aryan peoples. This opinion, long since diffused among scholars, confirms itself more and more each day, and tends towards becoming an incontestable point of doctrine. It is a sure fact that there is scarcely any theoretic philosophy in the Semitic books which preceded the Koran, that is to say, in the Bible and in other Hebrew writings. If we had under our notice only the succession of religions proceeding exclusively from the Mosaic, the law demonstrating to us religions which only assume a definite practical character after having alienated themselves, as it were, from morals, would lose its weight; but certain it is, that purely Aryan religions were developed by means of this law.[10]

As for Reinach:

> It is quite in vain to have wished to find in Christianity merely an aggrandized Judaism, a Jewish sect. Judaism alone, with its exclusionary spirit and its strict rites, could not have conquered nor regenerated the world. Christianity is born of Graeco-Roman philosophy infused, as new blood, in the simplest forms of the noblest religion of the Orient, Judaism. Aryan by the spirit that animated it, it is also Aryan from its foundation.[11]

But, as is known, the Christian West did not wait for these scholars before distinguishing itself for its anti-Judaism, as Léon Poliakov shows in his irreplaceable *History of Antisemitism*.[12]

3.2 Charles Darwin and Herbert Spencer

So, it is the past of the history of humanity that was considerably enlarged, while at the same time the discoveries regarding pre-history by Jacques Boucher de Perthes (1847) and the evolution of the species by Charles Darwin (1859) made their own contributions to the profound upheavals that shook the Christian foundations and touchstones of European culture as they had been recognized for centuries. What was substituted for the narrow horizon restrained by the chronology and immutable world of the Bible was a much older, dynamic universe, in which geological formations, plants, animal types, languages, and man himself lost their primary immu-tability as had been conceived up to then, in conformity with a providential and benevolent divine plan. Just as three centuries ear-lier astronomic discoveries had proven that the Earth was not at the center of the universe, from the nineteenth-century period evoked here the certain biblical conception of man and the world lost its central and unique position. Freudian psychology would several years later come to confirm this diagnostic, in its way, by mining the ontological foundations of Descartes's subject and unveiling the obscurity of the human soul.

The influence of Darwin, or, more exactly, the influence of his ideas, had in time a profound resonance on the domain of the History of Religions, whereas at the beginning these ideas sprang only from the natural sciences. This was doubtless because they were con-torted along the way by the interference of the ideas of Darwin's contemporary and compatriot, Herbert Spencer. Translated in terms of natural selection that favors the triumph of the most adept (the survival of the fittest), and not in terms of capacity for adaption in a given environment, the ideas were in fact easily transposed in the contexts of the history of societies, of races, cultures, and religions of humanity into the ambiguous notions of progress and evolution (going from the simplest or most primitive, such as "the savage," to the most evolved: Western man). The use of the word "race" was banal in the nineteenth century, just as with the word "savages"! In the middle of the century, for example, A. W. Schlegel wrote:

> Many facts of ancient and modern history seem to prove the existence of indestructible differences in the natural dispositions of human races; that there have been wise and inventive peoples who became spontaneously 'humanized' or were never savages; other people who

were docile and capable of educating themselves by the legislative and industrial instruction that their first members brought with them; and finally, people who rebuff all better organized social order as an intolerable bother. Contact with civilization seems to them even pernicious, because they only lay hold of its bad side.[13]

These arguments are to be found in the colonial era, the convenient alibi for the civilizing work of the West, serving to justify the intervention of great powers more evolved and more humanized than the other, inferior ones (so they claimed).

The confusion between the naturalist theses of Darwin and of Spencer's "social Darwinism" goes back to this era. They are found in, and attached without difficulty to, the feelings of superiority that without the least remorse or doubt were shared by most Europeans when they compared themselves with the members of other, exotic societies. And the scholars of the time were not the last to share them and thus to look for scientific justification. For example, at the beginning of his work on *Primitive Culture*, the great Edward B. Tylor wrote:

> But even those students who hold most strongly that the general course of civilization, as measured along the scale of races from savages to ourselves, is progress towards the benefit of mankind, must admit many and manifold exceptions. Industrial and intellectual culture by no means advances uniformly in all its branches, and in fact excellence in various of its details is often obtained under conditions which keep back culture as a whole. It is true that these exceptions seldom swamp the general rule; and the Englishman, admitting that he does not climb trees like the wild Australian, nor track game like the savage of the Brazilian forest, nor compete with the ancient Etruscan and the modern Chinese in delicacy of goldsmith's work and ivory carving, nor reach the classic Greek level of oratory and sculpture, may yet claim for himself a general condition above any of these races.[14]

At the same time, John A. Lubbock, another of the founding fathers of modern anthropology, expressed this thought:

> I have felt doubtful whether this chapter should not be entitled 'The Superstitions' rather than 'The Religion' of savages, but have preferred the latter, partly because many of the superstitious ideas pass gradually into nobler conceptions, and partly from a reluctance to condemn any honest belief, however absurd and imperfect it may be. It must, however, be admitted that religion, as understood by the

lower savage races, differs essentially from ours; nay, it is not only
different, but even opposite.[15]

Raising the name of Tylor allows us to remember that three major
disciplines of modern human sciences were born during his time:
sociology, ethnography, and anthropology.[16] But, rather curiously,
if Spencer's theses open up immense horizons for the studies whose
objects were human cultures and societies, they did not yet play a
decisive role (in the critical development of the History of Religions)
in attacking, for example, the unflinching analysis of its foundations
and its indigenous *a prioris*. Most often they limited themselves to
the habitual elements of a general *doxa* (of Christian inspiration)
that still dominates today, and which, without malice or (usually)
partisan spirit, sees in man a religious animal and in human societies organisms generating religion mechanically,[17] just as surely
as relations of domination. This is why we continue today to cite
the names and works of Edward B. Tylor, James G. Frazer, Marcel
Mauss, and Émile Durkheim in particular.

Indeed, Durkheim illustrates this position quite well. In his
Elementary Forms of the Religious Life, for example, Durkheim recognized: "If we have taken [archaic religion] as the subject of our
research, it is because it has seemed to us better adapted than any
other to lead to an understanding of the religious nature of man, that
is to say, to show us an essential and permanent aspect of humanity."[18] The "religious nature of man" and religion as an "essential
and permanent aspect of humanity" are expressions that can only
be written into the Western Christian tradition. In fact, they take up
one of its favorite themes; that is, that man is, by nature, religious,
since God himself willed it so:

> [I]n creating us God could give us no other ultimate end than himself.
> Acting otherwise he would have failed in what he owes to his perfec-
> tion and sanctity, and it would have betrayed his love in not giving as
> terminus for our destiny and our efforts the sovereign as he indeed is,
> par excellence. It is thus necessary that in creating the human soul he
> made it religious, able and apt to know and love him.[19]

Once again, we find here the procedure that consists in justifying
a current institution of the Church—here, "religion"—by inventing for it a divine origin, either turning to the imagery of a mythological foundation or, as here, to the argument of authority. The
essential thing is to hide the true process of historical creation by

directly hooking the human *hic et nunc* to its supposed divine origin. The major Durkheimian paradox consists in the following: the great scholar certainly recognizes that society is the "universal and eternal objective cause of these sensations *sui generis* out of which religious experience is made,"[20] except that this Durkheimian society, itself fundamentally humanist and pacific, "is found [in the religion] only in an enlarged, transformed and idealized form. In this respect, the most primitive religions do not differ from the most recent and the most refined."[21] In other words, the "materialism" of Durkheim is tainted with such a dose of benevolence with regard to religions and idealism that his materialism ceases to be authentic, as Durkheim himself hastens to clarify: "In showing that religion is something essentially social, we do not mean to say that it confines itself to translating into another language the material forms of society and its immediate vital necessities."[22] And since these religions, once created, "obey laws all their own,"[23] but without quite knowing which ones, they free themselves definitively from the material infrastructures that at any rate hardly occupy much of a place in Durkheim's sociological conceptions.[24] There we see all that sets them in opposition to Marxist materialism and atheism. For Durkheim, at no moment is religion considered an opiate of the people, prepared by the Machiavellian hands of their exploiters.

3.3 The Founding Fathers

If now we turn to the scholars who are considered to be the founding fathers (and uncles) of the History of Religions between the mid-nineteenth century and World War One, a series of shared characteristics stands out immediately. Let us begin by establishing a list of the persons unanimously considered the most influential: Herbert Spencer (1820–1903); Max Müller (1823–1900); Albert Réville (1826–1906); Cornelis P. Tiele (1830–1902); R. H. Codrington (1830–1922); Edward B. Tylor (1832–1917); John A. Lubbock (1834–1913); Andrew Martin Fairbairn (1838–1912); Auguste Louis Sabatier (1839–1901); William James (1842–1910); Andrew Lang (1844–1912); William Robertson Smith (1846–1894); Eugène Goblet d'Alviella (1846–1925); Pierre D. Chantepie de la Saussaye (1848–1920); James G. Frazer (1854–1941); and Robert R. Marett (1866–1943).

All of the members of this list are Protestants,[25] and, with the exception of the two Frenchmen (Réville and Sabatier) and the one

American (James), all originate in Northern Europe (Great Britain, Belgium, Netherlands). *A contrario*, there are no Catholic scholars in the list from any country in southern Europe (Spain or Italy). Two who appear even more notable in this context are Marcel Mauss (1872–1950) and his uncle, Émile Durkheim (1858–1917), both French, and from Jewish families established in Alsace. This exceptional situation can in no way be considered a coincidence; it is also found in the following generation, with Lars O. J. Söderblom (1866–1931); W. Brede Kristensen (1867–1953); Rudolf Otto (1869–1937); and Gerardus van der Leeuw (1890–1950).

Roman Catholicism thus does not figure in this paragraph devoted to the founders. Its complex and intransigent orthodoxy, rich ritualism, abundant cult of the saints, implacable centralism, ceaselessly repeated claims to be the one and only true religion, strict intellectual control exerted over its clergy and faithful, and, indeed, its immemorial intolerance, doubtless could not permit the study of other "religions" in any way other than by prefacing it with condemnation without recall. No great Catholic thinker therefore has distinguished himself in the History of Religions. In contrast, Protestantisms were being spread over several Churches, thus preventing any one of them from becoming a new papacy; they were attached to paring-down in all areas (theological and ritual); they placed faith alone at the center of their interior life (that is, what they considered its quintessence); and they frequently boasted an openness of spirit and a liberal attitude. In other words, these Protestantisms set themselves up to be a much more presentable way of beginning the study of other cultures: with curiosity and a certain benevolence. This does not mean that, in their time, these men did not share several of its prejudices, primarily of which was a hierarchical vision of individuals and cultures. Rather, they simply succeeded in envisioning for the first time an ecumenical conception of (the history of) religions that would be touted later, in the twentieth century, but which had been announced at the end of the eighteenth, with the capital and innovative work of Friedrich Daniel Ernst Schleiermacher's *On Religion: Speeches to Its Cultured Despisers*.[26] In this work, Schleiermacher develops many themes (the fundamentally religious nature of man; the universality and innateness of religious feeling; the common sources of all religions; but also, significantly, the superiority of Christianity) that are frequently raised even today, to the point of having become commonplace.

After all, where others launched anathemas and condemnations with no appeal, Schleiermacher was able to appear more judicious to certain enlightened spirits, in looking to reduce differences, overcome prejudices, and find points of convergence, especially when the latter aimed at demonstrating in what they thought was an indisputable manner that man—all men, whoever they were—possessed an identical religious foundation, and that Christianity —but a Christianity stripped down and reduced to its essentials—represented man at his most noble and most perfect.

3.4 The Classification of Religions

For good measure, I must add right away to what has just been said. If one were looking for a theme through which the ethnocentric prejudices of the scholars of the second half of the nineteenth century could be seen with the greatest transparency, this would surely be found in the classifications they elaborated to evaluate what for them represented the greater or lesser degree of perfection of each religion or group of religions.

I addressed this matter in 1998 in a short chapter of *The Western Construction of Religion*, entitled "Arbitrary Typologies,"[27] in order to show that the idea of their hierarchy demonstrates evident historiographical interest. The same year, Jonathan Z. Smith took up the same question in his article "Religion, Religions, Religious,"[28] illustrating his point, as I also did, with particular reference to a text of Tiele (which will be summarized in a moment). One must remember that, up to the beginning of the nineteenth century, the most habitual conception was of four religions:[29] the three monotheistic ones (Christianity, Judaism, and Islam) and all the others being indiscriminately grouped under the label "idolatry". Among the three monotheisms, indisputable superiority is accorded to Christianity by European scholars. In conformity to the opposition "Aryans *versus* Semites" that we have already mentioned, Islam—just as with Judaism for Schleiermacher, Hegel, Spencer, Renan,[30] Burnouf, Reinach, W. D. Whitney, and so many others—is thus considered a Semitic, ethnic,[31] rigid, and immutable religion.[32]

Over the course of the nineteenth century this four-part model was profoundly modified. Discoveries that were made by European scholars and missionaries were integrated and quickly baptised in the name of religions—at least the most important of them. (We will see this in Part Two, Chapter Seven, below, under the subheading "The Invention of Religions.") But the upheavals never led to a declassification of Christianity, nor to a promotion of other religions to its level. On the contrary, I wish to state that these classifications are all hierarchies and inevitably culminate in affirming the superiority of the monotheism stemming from the New Testament. Far from weakening it, these pseudo-scientific creations were put to the service of Christianity and the West. It is certain they had all been conceived with this goal in mind.

Two images dominate at the heart of these classifications. First of all is one based on a simple opposition that recalls the "*nostra religio versus vestrae religions*" of Arnobius (*Adversus nationes* II, 71–73) or the "*vera religio versus falsa religio*" of Lactantius (*Divinae Institutiones* I, 1; V, 19) — canonical opposition if ever there was one, and an opposition that has survived to today. Conforming with the fundamental principle of this multi-century model, one of its two opposing poles bears only positive terms (true, ethical, revealed, monotheistic, universal, civilized, historic, prophetic, etc.), whereas the other is entirely negative (false, vulgar, superstitious, natural, polytheistic, mythological, ethnic, etc.). Auguste Louis Sabatier, for example, put into opposition religions of the spirit and religions of authority,[33] whereas, more recently, Paul Ricoeur no doubt thought he was modernizing this old scheme in opposing (with a fair bit of ambiguity) religions of manifestation and religions of proclamation.

The second image rests on a model that is more frankly evolutionist,[34] crowned by Christian monotheism by whatever name. From the most famous defenders of this opinion, one may mention: animism, ancestor cult, fetishism, idolatry, totemism, polytheism, monotheism (Tylor); naturist, animist, mythological, polytheistic, legalistic and monotheistic religions (Réville); religions of nature, religions of morality, religions of redemption (Siebeck); natural religions (themselves subdivided into three groups: polydemonistic, therianthropic polytheisms [organized or not], and anthropomorphic polytheisms) and ethical religions (here of two families: national religious communities and universal religious communities). The first family includes Taoism, Confucianism, Brahmanism, Jainism and primitive Buddhism, Mazdaism (Zoroastrianism), Mosaism, and Judaism. The second has only three members: Islam, Buddhism, and Christianity (Tiele).[35]

What is remarkable is that, reduced to the expression of a simple opposition or prompting a sophisticated construction such as Tiele's that was summarized above, all of these classifications culminate, whatever their internal criteria, in an affirmation of the indisputable superiority of Christian monotheism.

3.5 Break? Or Merely Evolution?

Before going any further, it must also be asked to what extent the birth of the History of Religions in the second half of the nineteenth century represented an epistemological break rather than simply evolution, carrying on from what had preceded in the seventeenth and eighteenth centuries. To answer this legitimate question, one may choose and compare three authors who were representative of their respective times, each separated by approximately a century: Bossuet for the seventeenth century, Jean-Jacques Rousseau for the eighteenth century, and Tylor for the end of the nineteenth century.

To speak very schematically, but nonetheless not necessarily inexactly, over the course of this period one may observe a passing from Catholic theology to the philosophy of religion, and then on to the modern science of religions. Hans Gerhard Kippenberg, in his book on religious history,[36] refers to the above-mentioned second stage as "From the Philosophy to the History of Religions" (choosing as his representative of the eighteenth century David Hume, with the 1757 work *The Natural History of Religion*). By contrast, Guy G. Stroumsa places the birth of this new paradigm within the two previous centuries (the seventeenth and eighteenth).[37] One may certainly admit, with Stroumsa, that the first emergence and initial formation of the modern study of religions indeed took place at this time, but it seems clear to me that Tylor's text (which will be quoted in a moment) could never have been written a century — or, *a fortiori*, two centuries — earlier. Tylor, with the breadth of his views, his anthropological perspective, his comparative approaches, his openness of spirit, and the correct intuition that animated him, was foretelling quite clearly the best of the History of Religions in our time. The impression of a rupture and change of paradigm wins out over the idea of continuity, even if his anthropological aim remains profoundly ethnocentric and nestled within his century.

This does not mean, however, that each stage expunged its predecessor. Theology still exists today, as does the philosophy of religion. Nevertheless, it is impossible not to recognize something more than mere evolution, an ultra-neat transformation over the two centuries.

Bossuet speaks of what is inside the Catholic religion: its dogmas, its holy history, its Church, its certainties. He belongs to a world where the Catholic religion still dominates absolutely (especially in France). For him, everything else is superstition and idolatry. Moreover, he has no tool or concept that would allow him to inspect his definitive certainties. Nor does he have the ethnographic knowledge that will be prevalent and consistent by the end of the nineteenth century.

As for Jean-Jacques Rousseau, like his contemporaries Voltaire and Hume, the central reference point is Christianity and its monotheism. He imagines no other form of religion worthy of interest (or of criticism…) or that stands at the same level. But, in contrast to Bossuet, Rousseau is not entirely an "insider". He observes and judges from the outside. In particular, for him the dogmas, mysteries, and revelations only obscure what he is after, what he calls, along with others (Herbert of Cherbury,[38] Joseph Butler, Diderot, Hume, Voltaire), "natural religion" — that is, a religion born spontaneously in the heart of every man, fascinated as Rousseau was by the admirable order regnant in nature and the cosmos. But what all of these men do not see, nor could they have, is that "natural religion" is at its base nothing but a sort of stripped-bare Christianity, rid of everything the Roman Church would have added on (primordial revelation, dogmas, sacraments, rituals). Here is where we doubtless find the major illusion described above, and that we would find again in other authors of the nineteenth and twentieth centuries.[39] According to this illusion, a purified and bare version of Christianity would approach (as much as possible) the essence of *religion*, of all religion, thus opening the path to an ecumenism that is still not perceived to be just as ethnocentric as the baroque and Catholic version of Religion. This Rousseauist position, according to which there is a "natural religion" at the foundation of all religions, is thus quite close to that of Schleiermacher's Liberal Protestantism[40] and to his Francophone spiritual heir, Benjamin Constant:

> If, therefore, there is in the heart of man a sentiment not found in the rest of living beings which always occurs, whatever the condition in which he finds himself, is it not plausible that this sentiment is a fundamental law of his nature?

> In our judgment, such is the religious sentiment. The primitive hordes, the barbarous tribes, the nations which have attained the social state, those that languish in the decrepitude of civilization – all experience the power of this indestructible sentiment.
>
> It triumphs over all interests. The primitive for whom fishing or a difficult hunt provides bare subsistence will devote a portion of the catch to a fetish. A bellicose people will lay down their arms to come together in front of an altar. Free nations will interrupt their deliberations to call upon the gods in their temples. Despots will grant their slaves days of respite. [...]
>
> Yes, to be sure, there was a revelation, but this revelation was universal, it is constant, it has its source in the human heart. Man needs to listen only to himself. He needs to listen only to that nature that speaks to him in a thousand voices in order to be brought irresistibly to religion.

To be sure, external objects influence beliefs, but they only modify the forms, they do not create the internal sentiment that serves as their basis.[41]

This idea is illusory as well, because it rests on the eminently disputable idea that there are certainly numerous religions around the world but that they possess a common kernel or essence. If belief in the universality of religious attitudes is a Christian idea, the idea of things possessing an immutable essence that transcends history and material conditions is a good deal earlier, since it rather rests on a Platonic type of idealist notion.[42] The other illusion Rousseau cultivated consisted of thinking that men experienced the same impressions (in the face of grand natural phenomena, for example) and the same intuitions, and that for this reason they drew the same metaphysical conclusions. Cultural and historical relativism at the time of Rousseau is unthinkable, since it contradicts too sharply the idea of an intelligible cosmos desired by God.

With Tylor, the horizon expands considerably thanks to the entrance on the scholarly scene of primitive religions and Oriental religions that at the time were increasingly known and documented (and particularly thanks to the innumerable missionaries, Catholic and Protestant, that were fairly active in exotic lands). From then, the chronological and spatial limits of humanity are attained, and comparativism sprouts up almost inevitably, since it alone allows for a treatment of this documentary and impressive mass accumulating on the desks of European and American scholars at the end of the nineteenth century. Although Protestant and, as has been seen, sharing a certain number of inveterate prejudices of the time, Tylor, one of the fathers of modern anthropology, nonetheless writes the following, which is a plea in favor of man and of science:

> Notwithstanding all that has been written to make the world acquainted with the lower theologies, the popular ideas of their place in history and their relation to the faiths of higher nations are still of the mediaeval type. It is wonderful to contrast some missionary journals with Max Müller's Essays, and to set the unappreciating hatred and ridicule that is lavished by narrow hostile zeal on Brahmanism, Buddhism, Zoroastrism [sic], beside the Catholic sympathy with which deep and wide knowledge can survey those ancient and noble phases of man's religious consciousness; nor, because the religions of savage tribes may be rude and primitive compared with the great Asiatic systems, do they lie too low for interest and even for respect. The question really lies between understanding and misunderstanding them. Few who will give their minds to master the general principles of savage religion will ever again think it ridiculous, or the knowledge of it superfluous to the rest of mankind. Far from its beliefs and practices being a rubbish-heap of miscellaneous folly, they are consistent and logical in so high a degree as to begin, as soon as even roughly classified, to display the principles of their formation and development; and these principles prove to be essentially rational, though working in a mental condition of intense and inveterate ignorance.[43]

All of the ambiguities and contradictions of the nineteenth century are present in the above quotation. It is not certain that they have all disappeared today, as they are clothed in hypocrisy and political correctness. If the History of Religions represented a profound break with all that preceded it, it nevertheless remained, in its nascent phase, a science of the nineteenth century. It shared the nineteenth-century prejudices with regard to an optimistic conception of progress written into the history of humanity. And in particular it touted an unshakeable belief in the superiority of Western man and his works (a superiority that had as corollary the inferiority of savages, primitives, blacks and, indeed, of Semites). In this kind of sentiment, if part of it is ridiculous presumption, another large part is always naivety; and neither of these serves the interests of science. These theories melted in the twentieth century but without completely disappearing — at least as concerns the general public and certain political currents.

The next phase of the History of Religions, from the 1920s to the 1980s, was dominated by a different current, inspired by phenomenology, in which several scholars shone. In the first ranks of these were Otto, van der Leeuw, and Eliade, in particular. For the moment, I will hold back my analysis of these, as this will follow in detail in Part Two when we take a solid look at the theses involved in Critical Studies. Phenomenology, in its widest acceptance, without any doubt represented the perfect antithesis and remained the ideal adversary of Critical Studies. It is indeed against phenomenology and the idealism it promoted that Critical Studies was drawn up as a priority, since phenomenology is indeed the only approach to propose a (meta-)theory of religion that transcends eras and cultures no matter how different. In this sense, it distinguishes itself from numerous sociological, historical, and ethnographic monographs that, no matter how precious and instructive, approached the religions they observed with a tacit acceptance of the very general framework and format of dominant definitions. In contrast, phenomenology began by asking what *religion* is—that is, what it is in and of itself, in its essence, behind its differing historical manifestations.

Part Two

Autopsy of a Critical Paradigm

Chapter Four

Religious Studies in the United States

Up to now we have come across only a few characteristics, and only intermittently, of the type of analyses currently conducted by the most active partisans of Critical Studies. But before examining the favored targets of this trend, it would be useful to take a collective view of the American institutional and intellectual context in which Critical Studies was born and has developed, for it is fundamentally different from, for example, the French system. No extrapolation is possible, proceeding from here (France) and to understand there (the United States), which would probably not be the case with other academic areas/fields, such as the physical or medical sciences. One can say that, as soon as the theme of Religious Studies is approached, the French reader, as a citizen of a secular state where university departments specializing in the History of Religions are rare, finds themselves confronted with the profound particularity of American culture, both academic and popular.

4.1 Notable Statistics

A French observer, or perhaps any European, cannot but be struck at first by the statistics relative to American higher education (colleges and universities) in the field of Religious Studies.[1]

Here, I need to make a crucial clarification concerning this last statement. To emphasize the word *studies* preceded by the word *religious* seems preferable, in my view, to the frequent use of the singular noun of *religion*, as in "Introduction to Religion," "Philosophy of Religion," "American Religion," and "Comparative Religion," that one encounters endlessly in the documents to be cited presently and that emanate from the American Academy of Religion. In every case, the plural form would seem preferable, for what meaning should be given to this singular? I fear that what is understood by it is a significance clear to those who use it, and that it is therefore possible to situate oneself sufficiently "above" it so that one can extract a concept from the diverse "religions" that would summarize an ideal prototype, indeed a unique essence: that of *religion*. What is being researched under this singular? Is it not a type of broad, ecumenical consensus, in favor of a religious vocation as part of all people and of human society? Since it appears in categorical expressions or titles, one must exclude the possibility that it could concern a heuristic concept—that is, following the lesson of Emmanuel Kant, that any affirmation in this area is only provisional and is thus only valid "to a certain degree," "as far as is possible," accompanied by an "as if" or a "by analogy" (expressions all borrowed from Kant).

> In this way, the idea is properly a heuristic, and not an ostensive conception; it does not give us any information respecting the constitution of an object, it merely indicates how, under the guidance of the idea, we ought to investigate the constitution and the relations of objects in the world of experience.[2]

With this in mind, it is revealing that the same documents make parallel use of the plural in an expression such as "Introduction to World Religions" (compared with "Introduction to Religion" just cited). This malaise is also reinforced by the French translation, since one is obliged to add the definite article: "Introduction à *la religion*." But what *is* this mysterious "*religion*"? And what connections does it have with the different "religions"? At what conceptual level of abstraction is it located, relative to them? In a word, what is its nature? The answer to these questions, however crucial, will not be found in the sources mentioned above. This would tend to prove that the pair "essence/manifestation" (religion/religions) is spontaneously associated with the study of religions, whereas in fact it is a product of the phenomenological movement that did so much in the twentieth century to idealize and essentialize "*religion*,"[3] that is, to make of the latter something that exists both on the concrete level of human reality (through its historical manifestations: "religions") and on the transcendent level of incorruptible, eternal essences ("*religion*"). What we have here is an excellent example of the popularized version, among the broad public, of a philosophical thesis, facilitated by the fact that in that context it meets up with a banal structure that has been learned and absorbed by so many by means of catechism (if so experienced). This structure sets in opposition the idea of a superior world (divine, eternal, immutable, incorruptible, immaterial…) with an earthly world; but, in fact, the two are complementary. In its simplest form, the structure appears in the cosmogonic myth, with Heaven and Earth or Time and Eternity in opposition. This example offers me the chance to recall that our most familiar cosmological models travel about in the form of commonplaces encountered in conversation, echoing each other, with so many figures coming from the Christian tradition.

So as to avoid needless perplexity on the reader's part over the next few pages, I must also recall that the First Amendment of the United States Constitution makes a clear separation between Church and State, which quite logically should prevent the latter from promoting in its institutions any instructional activity that presents confessional or religious finality. Nevertheless, in these same public schools, "teaching *about* religion," if non-confessional (which would in this case be "teaching *of* religion"), has been constitutionally permitted in the States since 1963[4] – in the name of the very distinction cited. But it is quite certain that this fragile distinction can be easily transgressed by religious thinkers (religionists or theological universities, "theologically minded scholars") who are tempted to introduce into their teaching *about* religion a bit of "*religion*". And this is that much easier to do since the courses, readers, and textbooks "about religion," as we will see, are based on a theme and framework furnished by Christian religion(s). The choice of topics selected for the courses, the editorial choices for the manuals, the ideological dressing and laxity conformant to the dominant opinions (etc.) all seem to converge to assure these teachings of the maximum "right-thinking" conformity and political correctness.

It remains that the statistics furnished by research and surveys conducted in the United States are impressive. Under the topics summarized below, they concern the years 2005 or 1999–2000 (for the *Survey of Undergraduate Religion and Theology*) and 2007–2008 (for the *Humanities Departmental Survey*, or *HDS*).[5] At the undergraduate level alone, in 2005 there were 885 departments and programs, of which 150 and 320 were in Catholic or Protestant institutions (respectively).[6] Out of the 885 departments, 477 were autonomous, or "free-standing" departments. Of the 885, 56% required that the students take a specialization in an area within the department if they wished to obtain a graduate diploma; and for 90% of the students, 90% saw Religion as a central discipline. There were 782

Religion-majors and 740 Religion-minors awarded, of which 442 and 404 respectively were from Catholic and Protestant institutions. The number of majors varies considerably according to the establishment, from 130 by McMaster University, Hamilton, Canada, to 6 by Beloit College, Wisconsin, USA. More than 31,000 courses would have been given in 1999–2000 by close to 9000 instructors (whose categories are mixed, from tenured professors to part-time instructors). Of these, 3451 courses were classified as "Introduction to the Bible"; 3292 were on the New Testament; 2958 on Christian Theology; 2727 as "Introduction to Religion"; 2627 on the Old Testament; 1720 as "Introduction to 'World Religions'"; 1689 on the History of Christianity; and so on. None of these course-titles evoke an approach that is in any way critical; moreover, more than half of them concern Christianity and its biblical sources. Comparatively, however, only 397 courses concerned Islam: a mere 1.3%. At this same time, 31,190 bachelor students took a major in Religion.

More recently, according to the second *HDS*,[7] in 2012–2013 there were 502 departments and 4860 specialized instructors in the field of Religion. 4780 students earned a minor in Religion, and 9150 a major. That same year there were 3030 graduate students in Religion. According to the same study, close to 50 universities and colleges offered majors in Religion, of whom over half offered all three levels (Bachelor, Master, Doctor).[8] We must keep in mind that these institutions are principally public, private non-sectarian, and confessional (principally Catholic or Protestant). They demonstrate a diversity that is entirely unknown to the uniform French situation. Certain universities, such as Birmingham (Alabama), have a Department of Theology and Religion. Others, such as the Catholic University of the Incarnate Word (Texas), recognize that, as they are, their objective is to have students learn about the Catholic tradition while exposing them to the interdisciplinary methods used in the Religious Studies field. One cannot easily see, however, how one can marry these two objectives, other than by softening the methodological principles to make them conform to the dominant *doxa*.

At first reading, these crude figures do have something impressive about them. But if one looks at them with a certain incredulity, certain singular aspects become apparent. First of all, as has been noted, in 2005 more than half of the institutions required that their students follow courses in Religion. This figure is an average, and the percentage is higher in both the Catholic universities (94%) and

Protestant universities (88%). This may be compared to the mere 4% in public institutions. But if one puts all of the categories together, almost 90% considered that Religion was an important subject, indeed a central focus, in their instruction. Next, among the courses offered, a very large proportion in fact concerns Christianity, in the broadest acceptance of the term — and this even in public establishments. Of the latter, the top ten of the courses offered bear the following titles (and all of these are present in more than half of the schools):

1. Introduction to World Religions;
2. Christianity (New Testament);
3. Christianity (Old Testament);
4. Introduction to Religion;
5. Introduction to the Bible;
6. History of Christianity;
7. Introduction to Oriental Religions (headed up by Buddhism and Hinduism);
8. Introduction to Western Religions;
9. Judaism;
10. Philosophy of Religion.

For their part, private, non-confessional establishments offer six identical "Christian" subjects, to which they also add "Introduction to World Religions" and "Introduction to Religion". All that is missing to complete the list are "American Religion" in tenth place and "Comparative Religion" in eighth.

Those who expected to see a close relation between the nature of the courses offered and the orientation of the establishment were mistaken. Surprisingly, at least for the French observer, the difference between public and private-confessional is in fact a lot less clear. In a global sense, overall one finds the same course-offerings, as is seen in the results regarding classes in Catholic and Protestant schools:

Catholic institutions	*Protestant institutions*
1) Christianity (New Testament)	1) Christianity (New Testament)
2) Christianity (Theology)	2) Christianity (Old Testament)
3) Christianity (Old Testament)	3) Christianity (Theology)
4) Christianity (Ethics)	4) Christianity (History)

5) Christianity (History)	5) Introduction to the Bible
6) Introduction to Religion	6) Introduction to World Religions
7) Introduction to the Bible	7) Christianity (Ethics)
8) Introduction to World Religions	8) Philosophy of Religion
9) Ethics	9) Ethics
10) Comparative Religion	10) Comparative Religion

This means that a high percentage of young Americans having completed studies in public schools as well as private schools (confessional or not) have been made familiar, outside of any religious instruction that they may have received in the family circle, with the world of religions as it can be conceived by adopting the reading plan provided by the dominant *doxa* in matters of religion. But what kind of a "familiarity" is this?

Unfortunately, these statistics do not tell us if the way these themes are treated differs fundamentally from one institution to the next, or, if so, how. Nor do they tell us what attitudes are adopted (or could be adopted) by the course-instructors (which, in France, would no doubt give rise to endless polemics). But would American public and non-confessional institutions devote five or six of their top ten subjects to different aspects of Christianity (and Religion) for any other reason than to align themselves with the dominant *doxa* that is quite naturally imposed in confessional institutions? In other words, we see an abundance of courses, but concentrated on a very small number of themes. For the majority, the latter deal with Christianity following a standard, ecumenical model that tends to be imposed as the dominant norm.[9] These courses, which in fact are very general, consensual introductions, hardly represent a pronounced critical and theoretical dimension.[10] No course from these top ten imagines presenting that dimension, which is no doubt considered far too polemical. In most cases, under the crushing domination of very conventional versions of the different Christianities, originality seems to be limited to summarily presenting the other religions, principally Oriental, according to a stereotypical plan inspired by the Christian model. This presentation is cloaked, in its most philosophical part, in an idealist and ecumenical approach (witness the titles: Introduction to Religion and/or Philosophy of Religion) that is related to what we find in the broad current of phenomenology. Inversely, and since the existence of the discipline, it may be affirmed that neither the Orient nor Africa has ever been requested to furnish such a model or such an archetype. Once again, it must be stated that it is impossible to speak of Religion without referring one way (explicitly) or another (more implicitly) to the historical model that conceived it. A simple school-hypothesis: if such courses were organized by putting not the idea of *religion* in the center, but rather Oriental notions such as the Hindu *dharma* or Buddhist *nirâtmaka*,[11] according to which all of the others order themselves, it is clear that one would provoke an upheaval that would question the foundations upon which all of these courses are built. And this upheaval would go far beyond the questions traditionally seen as religious at the heart of the Christian culture; this idea, as we have seen, has played an architectonic role in the development of Western civilization. In modifying one of the pillars of the traditional *Weltanschauung* of *homo occidentalis* (if indeed such a thing is realizable or even conceivable in the context of a human life), what would be disorientated would probably be some of its most archaic points of reference—and also the most frequently evoked.

I would therefore be tempted to add that we speak of religion or religions, but no doubt from a place deep inside—that is, while accepting *a priori* a certain number of presuppositions that come directly from the Christian tradition, such as are conceived by a certain tolerant, ecumenical, and liberal Protestantism. The simple fact that religions are recognized *a priori* as indisputable evidences is a valuable indication of this. Such a considerable number of courses would not be devoted to them if the prevailing intention were to submit them to a Marxist or Lucretian reading. The critical examination of textbooks and readers that are conceived and edited to accompany students will confirm this impression.

4.2 The American Academy of Religion and the North American Association for the Study of Religion

We have just encountered a much softened form of the dominant paradigm presented in Part One, and which McCutcheon summarizes, in his way, by opposing "naturalistic approaches" with "non-reductive approaches."[12] In fact, in teachings and in textbooks, the materialist and scientific—note we are not saying 'atheistic'—dimension is marginalized in favor of a religious point of view that is certainly liberal and ecumenical (one might at least hope) but nonetheless religious. However, the other side of the paradigm is never far off; it is even part of a major paradigm in a given culture when, as here, it is based on an antithesis. Its two sides are structurally interdependent. The intelligibility of the one depends on that of the other. Thus, they are always there, present and ready to be re-actualized, even if one of the two terms is explicitly evoked; the atheist and the believer, in our culture, form an indissociable couple, and one cannot think of the one without conjuring up the other. To prove this, it is enough to change points of reference and to move, for example, from the undergraduate teaching level, where we had stopped, up to the superior level of research institutes. There, we will immediately see our initial paradigm and, I venture to add, endowed with all of its polemic power.

This paradigm has in fact played a considerable structuring role from the time of the introduction of the History of Religions in the United States at the end of the nineteenth and beginning of the twentieth centuries. And it has experienced quite a lively rejuvenation in the debates that have taken place from the middle of the 1990s—that is, at the end of the long period that began in the 1940s and 1950s that had seen the absolute domination of theses globally qualifiable as religionist and/or phenomenological. Now, these debates do not concern a marginal academic discipline, of interest merely to a few erudite persons. Given the considerable weight of Christianities and Religion in American public life and in higher education, the debates represent wholly central political and scientific engagement. They involve no more and no less than the power and authority recognized in those who, in the public forum, are entitled to express themselves in matters religious. The question underlying this is: who retains a legitimate and acknowledged authority to express himself or herself on these subjects?

If we follow McCutcheon[13] and Donald Wiebe,[14] from its origins this conflict set seminaries and faculties of theology (divinity schools) in opposition to the first teaching of the History of Religions, and it continues to structure the major debates taking place at the heart of the field of Religious Studies today. From 1991, Wiebe, after many others, concluded that religion and science as systems of thought are incommensurable and incompatible.[15] At the time, he added two remarks that were more original and that I cite for the record. According to the first remark, these modes of thought, seemingly mutually exclusive, nevertheless succeed in co-existing within the same individual and at the heart of a given community. Wiebe cited Paul Veyne,[16] who had already noted that men adjusted very well to truth-programs that, from a strictly logical point of view, are incompatible or even exclusive. Thus, one can quite well accept equations of scientific astronomy while believing at the same time in the influence of the stars. As to the second point, which is no more than a generalization, Wiebe posited the existence of a funda-mental contradiction (or duplicity?) at the heart of Western civiliza-tion. Has this been a driving mechanism? If so, that would mean that progress is capable of taking completely unexpected paths. But what do we know, definitively, of the engineering behind how cul-tures function?

In the much more polemical work published by Wiebe in 1999, the contents of which are collected writings of earlier years, one idea imposes itself from the beginning, expressed as it is with such strength and conviction.[17] He hammers forth that Religious Studies must break away from revisionist tendencies that are by nature religio-theological (or crypto-theological)[18] and which run contrary to secularization. He fears that religious forces will re-appropriate these studies, which would be the equivalent to reintroducing an openly religious agenda at the heart of university curricula and which would bring about the disappearance of any authentically scientific approach (that is, one that is *a priori* free from all religious or theological preoccupation). He states, moreover, that there has been an aggravation of confessionalism in studies published over the ten years preceding his book. To sum up, the statement he made in 1999 is fundamentally pessimistic. Not only has the scientific ori-entation of Religious Studies failed to impose itself over the course of the fifty years since World War Two,[19] but in addition, despite the constitutionally dictated rules of 1963, the teaching of religion and theology within American public universities seems to have become a *de facto* reality,[20] allowing this teaching—a delicious paradox—to clothe itself in a sort of scientific legitimacy that it in fact does not possess, as it is sequestered in seminaries and faculties of theology. If the confusion between theology and science has been so frequent and so easy, it is simply because this confusion was conceived and presented while following too rigidly the broad orientations of a liberal and humanist Protestantism—indeed, of a transcultural ecu-menism. This is also the conclusion one could draw from examining programs of instruction, as well as textbooks and readers intended for students, which we will see below.

It must be repeated quite firmly that this is not about a quarrel between specialists, taking place within the confines of the university world, in a sub-specialty whose existence is unknown to the vast majority. When one considers the rather lively controversies today between the partisans of Darwinism and those touting creationism, it is clear that this is a debate that involves contemporary American society and culture, as well as its political life and major internal conflicts, and is one of the cross-cutting orientations of its system of higher education. If it is difficult not to think, by analogy, of the debates that took place in France a little over a century ago concerning the law relative to the separation of Church and State, ought we not to admit that the stakes in the United States are greater? Once more, and this is not for the last time, the History of Religions is found at the center of debates that extend beyond its destiny as erudite university discipline.

I nevertheless differ from Wiebe on one specific point. One can agree with his setting of science in opposition to religion, as I myself do here, as it is rather easy to dissociate scientific inquiry from religious apologetics (that always end up invoking divine or supernatural powers). On the other hand, his formulated wish to see the imposition of a science of religions devoid of any political and especially ideological preoccupation seems to me more utopian.[21] For, as I have tried to show above, our culture over the course of its long development has been so interlaced with religious themes (anthropological, ethical, cosmological, political, etc.) that we will have to wait a long time yet before we can engineer analyses free from any presupposition of this sort. This kind of presupposition works its way in everywhere and does not always appear to be religious. It is this way, for example, with certain cosmological or anthropological frameworks that have long since been rendered banal and laicized by Western culture.

Nonetheless, Wiebe's statement of the mid- and late nineties, placing theology in opposition to science, is indisputable. It coincides with the opposition between two major institutions, the American Academy of Religion (henceforth AAR) and the North American Association for the Study of Religion (henceforth NAASR), whose members, specialists in their field, divvy up on the one side or the other and still oppose each other today. First created in 1909 as the Association of Biblical Instructors in American Colleges and Secondary Schools (which then, in 1933, became the National Association of Biblical Instructors, or NABI), the AAR did not receive its current appellation until 1963.[22] This evolution was in response to two major concerns, themselves in conformity with the evolution of the world and of ideas but also with that of the number of students, practically tripling over the course of the sixties: first, to open the institution up to religions other than the Christianities (which was easy); and second, to try to dissociate better the domains emanating from theology from those dependent on the academic study of religions (which proved to be much more difficult). It was necessary to dispel, in a way, the confusion that had prevailed for so long. These two intellectual orientations, scientific and theological, appeared increasingly divergent and thus increasingly incompatible. The first gave priority to history and other human sciences, whereas the second recognized interventions by supernatural revelation. Up to that point, departments of theology and of the history of religions were able to cohabit within the same university structures, and indeed still do, at times, in a functional way that in France is only found in Protestant and Catholic faculties of theology at the University of Strasbourg.[23] It must not be forgotten that numerous American universities are affiliated with the different Protestant Churches (Yale, Cornell, Vanderbilt, Harvard, Chicago, etc.), and that the influence of wealthy founders (Henry Sage at Cornell or John D. Rockefeller at Chicago) and trustees has been a determining factor.[24]

The AAR is a powerful institution. It has more than 9000 members, and organizes an Annual Meeting that is attended by several thousands of listeners and several hundreds of speakers. The extremely large number of teachers and researchers that make up the American universities and colleges allows the AAR to offer at its Meeting a program the breadth of which is unimaginable for an observer used only to the size of the French gatherings devoted to studies in the History of Religions. The 2018 AAR program included over 150 program units.[25] It would be tedious to name them all, but it needs to be highlighted that no fewer than four are on Buddhism and seven on African religions (of which four are on the history of Afro-American religions). Sessions were also devoted to "Critical Theory and Discourse on Religion," "Indigenous Religious Traditions," and also to "New Religious Movements," without forgetting sessions concerning feminism, "Queer Studies in Religions" (which figure on the alphabetical list after "Quaker Studies"), and relations between religions and the gay and lesbian rights movements.

In spite of appearances and titles that would seem subversive or even misplaced to some, this unique vista onto the rainbow-colored world of religions should not be taken at face value as proof of transgression in favor of science. For it did not prevent an internal break that prompted the birth of NAASR in 1985 at the initiative of E. Thomas Lawson, Luther H. Martin, and Donald Wiebe.

Wiebe and Martin have traced the history of this creation and explained the reasons for its establishment.[26] After recalling that the new institution wanted to promote "the historical, comparative and structural study of religion" within the North American academic community, to publish the latter's works, and to represent it in international contexts specializing in the same domain, the two authors present decisive arguments. And these arguments quite clearly target the AAR. To all of those in the field of Religious Studies, they say, who defend what they claim is a comparative and scientific approach alongside a parallel development of theoretical tools, the AAR looks like a refuge dominated by conflicts of interest. Moreover, and this reproach is much more serious, the AAR has remained an institution that has been unable to break from the hegemonic frame of Liberal Protestantism that had dominated NABI, and in which religious interests are still in the majority. Now, to put this even more directly, what we see is a conservative institution that has not succeeded in developing a new and scientific approach, since religious facts are still so very much a part of its Protestant ethos and *Weltanschauung*.[27]

This is the polemical context under and into which NAASR was born. In 1990 it became affiliated with the IAHR (International Association for the History of Religions), and, more particularly, in 1993 *Method and Theory in the Study of Religion*[28] became the official journal of NAASR. NAASR was admitted in 2001 among numerous related scholarly organizations affiliated with the AAR.[29] The originality of NAASR and, by association, of *Method and Theory in the Study of Religion*, has consisted, as Martin and Wiebe remind us, in bringing about innovation within the framework of the panels proposed for specialized congresses, but especially in choosing these panels in such a way that right up front are placed those theoretical and methodological questions that have always been treated as the "poor cousins" — indeed, very poor — of Religious Studies. Hitherto, the concept of religion had functioned as a skeleton key, efficiently opening all doors. Relying more or less implicitly on the idea of divine revelation, it provides the inestimable advantage of offering a solution even before all the questions that would indeed be entirely legitimate have been raised.

Now, the *critical* orientation is situated in opposition to the act of blind faith, whatever the latter might be. Thus:

> Criticism is a form of rational thought that consists in examining another product of thought in order to judge it and determine its true value, by the weighing of pros and cons. True or false, just or unjust, beautiful or ugly. The term 'criticism,' even though not appearing until late in the history of thought, in its current application designates an intellectual activity that is quite old and, for certain authors, essential to philosophy. The term 'criticism' finds its origin in the Greek verb '*krinô*' and its substantive '*krisis*': to distinguish, judge, dissect, sift.[30]

In the same way, the stress placed on method had as its goal the liberation of Religious Studies from all arguments and implicit notions that the discipline has been driving since the time of its origins.

In spite of its successes, its incontestable dynamism, the important number of Meetings organized by NAASR, and its articles published in *Method and Theory in the Study of Religion*, the issue for the twenty-fifth anniversary (published in 2014) was the occasion for conducting an "examination of conscience," formulating some severe (self-)criticism and expressing some wishes for the near future.

Thus, Hughes,[31] opposed to the concern with looking for an ever broader public and an ever larger number of panels for the big Meetings of the AAR, declares himself on the one hand to be in favor of a "more exclusive group" that would adopt an increasingly specialized and scientific orientation; and on the other hand he states the wish to break with the AAR. In his view, NAASR must not be content simply to be what the AAR is not, for it is the latter that then would be defining the contours of debate. By leaving it, NAASR would recover an independence and a space that would allow it, for Hughes, to take up its development once again and better affirm its scientific personality (which is on the way to disappearing).

Just as radical, Arnal, for his part, also thinks that NAASR has become more and more an organism subaltern to the AAR over the last few years, in which "AAR-like papers and AAR-like discussions" are presented. Thus, he pronounces in favor of a quite precise clarification of the ambitions of NAASR: either it abandons its pretensions to being scientific from the outset and intellectually distinct, or it behaves in conformity to that ambition "as clearly and emphatically as possible."[32]

As for McCutcheon, who is one of the linchpins of NAASR and of *Method and Theory in the Study of Religion,* he echoes the opinions of Hughes and Arnal. Citing a panel presented in 2010 under the aegis of NAASR and having as its title "The Untranslatability of Religion, The Untranslatability of Life," he deplores the fact that NAASR was succumbing to the type of mysticism characteristic of the AAR, and he asks with disdain: "how did we — whatever this *we* may be — end up doing much the same?"[33]

In the light of these polemics, it is difficult — indeed, impossible — to escape the impression that the major paradigm that has guided us here is still just as present and just as current. It is situated at the center of the controversies that divide the American university community linked to the numerous departments of religious studies. We now need to look much more closely at the history of this critical movement that, as is admitted even by those responsible, finds itself now at a crossroads, waiting for a second wind.

4.3 The Influence of French Theory

No task is as formidable nor as ungrateful as that of finding and tracing the intellectual genealogy of the influences that preceded and favored the appearance of a new scientific current. How can one establish a hierarchy of the different influences capable of playing a role from one moment to the next? And how should one ponder each of them in order to avoid obvious disequilibrium? Such clear influence today will in twenty years appear secondary; and inversely, what we ignore right now may prove determining in the eyes of our successors. And how far back in time should we go, knowing that the very long trajectory of Western culture, particularly in the areas of theology and philosophy, does not prohibit anyone from finding a source of inspiration in, say, Sextus Empiricus or in the writings of Jean-Paul Sartre? In addition, authors are not always careful to reveal which persons have been of greatest influence, and for this reason, they have a tendency to downplay their influence. Inversely, there are negative influences in the face of which authors have felt an aversion and therefore do not mention, but who have influenced the evolution of their thought nevertheless.

McCutcheon himself proposes this in *The Discipline of Religion.*[34] I was compelled to find the pieces of this puzzle by disengaging those that seemed indisputable. But we are, of course, dealing with a puzzle that cannot be completed. We will never know either the number of pieces or the final image that we would like to reconstruct. Thus, in the very same way, Religious Studies has been unable to avoid the spirit or fashion of its time. It is not without use to remember that the researchers who animated this critical trend were in many ways the heirs of intellectual movements that flourished noisily in the 1960s and 1970s.[35] And they were influenced in an indisputable manner, which one can see by looking at an index of their works.

This *critical* period, itself supporting radical *critical theory* (particularly in the fields of *social critical theory* and *literary critical theory*), was marked by a certain number of orientations that shared the ambition of bringing back to the fore the majority of the principles and values that had dominated up to then. This explains why, in spite of their sometimes-profound theoretical disagreements, these different influences in some ways converged; they sustained each other, doubling their strength and their influence in many fields of human and social sciences. Each, to a certain extent, was a beneficiary of the subversive support of the others.

It would be tempting to put at the head of these orientations a historical vision of the socio-cultural entities and the material procedures involved in their production. As such, they ceased to be eternal and immutable categories (Art, Literature, Religion, etc.), and were transformed into products of history. This movement, which first affected religious values felt to be immutable, was inspired by a consequent materialism and led to a more or less generalized relativism. In parallel, the profound influence (although diffuse and often indirect) of Marxism was found, among other places, in the recognition of the determining role attributed to ideologies. The latter are recognized as a preponderant activity in the production of collective representations, such as mythologies, which are themselves destined to conceal and disguise the true relationships of domination and power within societies. This point of view introduced into the debate questions and analyses of a political order that had never been encountered in the United States in the field of the History of Religions. The latter had always remained at a good distance from this sort of debate, which had previously been considered far too trivial.

Added to this social background, and politically quite pronounced, were the great waves of post-Saussurean linguistics (Jakobson, Chomsky, Searle) and contemporary literary critical theory, with their contributions of new objects to the debate (such as myth) and new ways to apprehend and analyze texts *objectively* (such as structural analysis, which claimed to substitute for personal preferences and aesthetic judgment), all the while focusing on traditional hierarchies such as the perpetuation of the opposition between "great" and minor works. From this point on, ordinary or trivial objects also became worthy of scientific regard. In spite of insufficiency and internal contradictions that did not fail to be raised, this synergy has contributed to a renewed, enduring and profound concentration on all established certainties. I would be tempted to say that this rather brief period exploited in the heart of human sciences all of the resources inherited from the ère du soupçon (era of suspicion), often giving it its most radical expression.

It is also easy to find very clear influences in the work left by authors of contemporary Critical Studies—twenty at the most—who determined this period. Among these, one may count several French thinkers in prominent places: Pierre Bourdieu, Roland Barthes, Claude Lévi-Strauss, Michel Foucault, Michel de Certeau, Jacques Derrida, Jacques Lacan, Louis Althusser, and Jean Baudrillard.[36] However, it must be noted that no specialist in religions is to be found among them. The work of this cohort, actually rather heteroclite, has been called collectively, on the other side of the Atlantic, "French Theory".[37] Despite the presence of certain names, particularly that of Derrida, the postmodern touch has not affected Religious Studies profoundly; in particular, it did not engender the excesses of jargon or unreadability[38] that marked the fabric of Cultural and Visual Studies at about that time.[39] It is true that Religious Studies was never situated at the center of, or even close to, the most virulent polemics that provoked debates around French Theory in American universities. Nor did they inspire comparable narcissistic flights.

Despite the prestige associated with certain names individually (Marx, Durkheim, Foucault, Lacan, and Derrida), I will be citing them and speaking here of a rather casual synthesis or at least eclecticism, associating them in the same movement and in a sort of unanimity (when what separates them and distinguishes them is actually enormous). And here I must insert a brief aside: the fact of citing an idea borrowed from such and such an author and then, ten lines later, something from another thinker, does not mean that one accepts all the major theses of these authors, nor that a synthesis of the ideas is possible:

> The work of quotation is at the centre of these procedures. It acts as a microcosm, suffices to transmit a complex argument, an entire oeuvre, and is able literally to *present* them: not to summarize them or re-present them, but to make them present — or at least to call forth their phantoms. Quotation provides, in the end, the primary material of this intellectual composite called French Theory, which is itself contained entirely in a handful of these quotations.[40]

What do these major concepts utilized by Lacan, Lévi-Strauss, and Barthes have in common, presented freely, as they were in France in the 1970s, as living symbols of the most extreme intellectual modernity? And I am not even speaking of the misunderstanding that allowed Lévi-Strauss to figure on this list, when he rejected the Freudian idea of the unconscious and, more generally, that of progress — he who was glad to take refuge in the great classics of the past. This arbitrary dimension — indeed, this imbalance — is still accentuated by the fact that authors in Critical Studies cite only foreign works (especially French) that have been translated into English. Now, these are relatively few in number and concern only very few authors. The numerous American bibliographies that I have perused include almost no original works in French, and scarcely more in German. The great reader, Jonathan Z. Smith, is a double exception. The influential French Theory has thus been in essence "French Theory in English Translation".

These reservations aside, it remains that what impresses at first glance in Critical Studies is precisely, with apologies for the tautology, its critical dimension. It is omnipresent and spreads itself out with a sort of contagious *joie de vivre* and exuberance. It is true that this wave succeeded decades of stuffiness and conformity in submission to a religious approach to religious facts. This other tautology, often dissimulated under the name of "phenomenology of religion," may seem as naive as it is hollow. We will see later, however, that it represents the major equation upon which generations of religionist-inspired research has been based.

This critical wave, then, was at first contemporary with the great radical views at the beginning of the 1960s, and under different names — deconstruction, decomposition, criticism, analysis — that shook up the grand institutions upon which humanism and a large part of European idealism had been built: The Subject, Conscience, Art, Literature, The Novel, and, of course, The Sacred, Myth, and Religion. The capital letters here are used to underline the ideal dimension that, being timeless, is still often ascribed to them today. The most determined partisans of the movement were aiming at a radical desacralization of the religious fetishes of the tribe (as represented by the terms evoked here). Note, in this regard, that with the exception of what happened in the seventeenth and eighteenth centuries, it was not the existence of God that was placed at the center of critical work (did he exist or not?), but rather the existence of religion itself.

This work was at first made possible, and favored, by the iconoclastic spirit and the new tools brought at the same era by modern literary criticism and linguistics. To understand better this absolutely crucial point, let us go back for a moment. We have noted above that the power of the Church had been indissociable with the role played by its clerics in the composition and diffusion of innumerable texts, both orally and written. And, even more efficaciously, this diffusion was itself accompanied by numerous modes of censure. The Church was at the beginning, and for centuries, a formidable discursive machine and incomparable producer of texts whose form was perfected in function of needs and aims (education, cults, conversion, edification, controversies, etc.). The Christian culture was a culture of text(s). This *poièsis*, or poetic creation, was all the more important in that it possessed a political finality, piggy-backing upon an absolute power that never abandoned its hegemonic domination. From the time of the New Testament up to today, it has composed thousands of texts reiterating the same certainties over centuries. With this goal it has succeeded in skillfully interlacing childish tales for the young, a small number of mythological tales centered on the person of Jesus, lives of exemplary saints, scholarly treatises as voluminous as they are austere, lyric poems, collections of exegeses, and commentaries without number — commentaries whose initial vocation was to defend ecclesial orthodoxy on all fronts where it was under attack (heresies, materialistic or atheistic theories, etc.).

Under these conditions, the work of the historians of Christianity, and in a more general way of the other great religions (Buddhism and Hinduism foremost), was ever the work of philologists. Historians of religion are all, from the get-go, specialists in languages (Greek, Latin, Hebrew, Old Irish, Sanskrit, Avestan, Pali, Tibetan, Chinese, and so on) in which the major works of these cultures were written. And they are at the same time specialists in the reading, translating, and interpreting of these texts. As a consequence, when new methods of analysis appeared, these same historians of religions (some of them, at least) succeeded rather easily in recycling them into their own field of research. In conformity with another methodological principle developed in the same era, these new tools served not only for the interpretation of original sources, but also, reflectively, for the analysis of theoretical works that had accompanied the constitution of the discipline itself.[41] To take just one example: to be complete, the study of Vedic myths should not stop at the knowledge of Sanskrit texts, but should further integrate knowledge of the theories that followed from the time of Max Müller. This last development was completely unprecedented. The discipline that up to then had often been content to borrow its foundations from traditional approaches to Religion needed from then on to adopt itself as object of study, just as it would any other body of text(s).[42] This led inevitably to an interrogation of the principles at the base of the discipline.

It is difficult not to see in retrospect that the new forms of analysis making themselves known from the beginning of the 1960s were equally supported by the structural analysis vogue, in particular the vogue of myths. The latter transdisciplinary object, malleable and in the end rather poorly defined, offered an excellent pretext for testing new methods and new interpretive theories. In spite of its austere appearance, this type of analysis enjoyed great success at the time. Lévi-Strauss's *The Savage Mind* and the first volume of his *Mythologiques* (*The Raw and the Cooked*) were published in 1962 and 1964, respectively. At practically the same time, Marcel Detienne and Jean-Pierre Vernant published their first works also devoted to myths—Greek, in their case. Roland Barthes had slightly preceded them in this with his *Mythologies* (1957). All of these contributions primarily focused not on the individual creator (the genius or the great man), but on production as anonymous and collective.

Ivan Strenski,[43] Bruce Lincoln,[44] Robert A. Segal,[45] and Dean A. Miller,[46] in particular, brought to the Anglo-Saxon world this new interest in myth that Dumézil[47] had renewed in his way vis-à-vis the Indo-European world prior to World War Two.

What these new theories of language, story, and discourse brought with them can be summarized in a few points. They corresponded to the profound upheavals that struck at the heart of humanist tradition and culture dominant up to then. And they prompted brutal awakenings of conscience that dispelled many an illusion.

The first point to make is that words are neither the equivalent nor the faithful translation of what they designate. Far from replacing them or melting together, a gap exists between them that is sometimes considerable due to the fact that words always benefit from the ideological impetus that accompanied their poetic, mythical, or novelistic context. One has only to pronounce the words *cross*, *bread*, and *wine* to confirm this immediately. And it is this considerably enriched simulacrum that we take as our object. This law is equally valid (and perhaps more so) for terms such as *Religion*, or *Sacred*, found at the heart of our culture, and upon which this culture was in part constructed. It offers a semantic density and consistency that are quite exceptional. And it is precisely this consistency, arising from culture, that has ceased to be considered supernatural and has been handed over to history.

A second point is that Foucault played an essential role in this phase, as McCutcheon recognized.[48] The dizzying nominalism that he inspired went much farther still. He dissolved objects, substituting for them a game of discursive practices and formulations that, according to him, had engendered and had not ceased to transform them. Nor did these practices cease to change along with the theories that were capable of explaining them. Thus "objects," as religions, that up to then had been considered indestructible, had no existence before these unpredictable processes. At the opposite extreme of the traditional concept of an immutable and eternal object, it was necessary, says McCutcheon, quoting Foucault, to ask "whether the unity of a discourse is based not so much on the permanence and uniqueness of an object as on the space in which various objects emerge and are continuously transformed."[49] Breaking sharply with all forms of idealism, the provocative title of his first work, *Manufacturing Religion* – somewhat like "The Religion Factory," or, even better, "The Religious Factory" — is revealing in this regard. Not only do objects *not* exist from eternity (their "non-identity throughout time," as Foucault specifies on the same page), not only have they been fabricated, but this had happened at the core of moving, discursive strategies which themselves were subjected to power games. The only ontology of any value, and which would subsist in this context, would be comparable to Stéphane Mallarmé's *bibelot d'inanité sonore*.[50]

The third point is that the sophisticated rhetorical and poetical processes allow, at a level superior to the isolated linguistic sign, the construction of stories and tales, at the forefront of which are myths capable of being substituted for reality in the conscience of the individual. Strenski, as cited by McCutcheon,[51] speaks of this not as a "real thing," but as a "thriving industry" "manufacturing and marketing" mythic material. Myth, *a fortiori* in its idealized and timeless form, is thus an illusion, a simulacrum constructed retrospectively by the artists and intellectuals in the workshops of the myth industry, which supposes that the finality of myth obeys interests of the same sort—that is, interests that are just as material. Here again, especially if we take as reference the idealist and Platonic point of view dominant in the West for centuries, we are witnessing a complete reversal of perspective. The most prestigious ideal objects, about which a good part of Western culture had instructed itself for centuries, are methodically stripped of their prestige, reduced to the state of simulacra that are themselves the result of unforeseeable and unstable discursive procedures. Not only is all form of transcendence and teleology excluded from this process, but a certain historical materialism acting as primary source is itself re-interrogated, since the material causes themselves (the famous Marxist superstructures) that were thought to have been identified disappeared in discursive formations. Here again, by means of the Foucauldian, ultra-nominalist path, we reach Degree Zero of any form of ontology.

Fourthly, we have seen that the 1960s in France were marked by a rather large number of theories regarding myth(s).[52] Among them is the work of Barthes, translated into English at the beginning of the 1970s,[53] which McCutcheon cites in both *Manufacturing Religion* and *The Discipline of Religion*.[54] Barthes's study stands out in the sense that it describes a double process that reveals a subversive hypothesis according to which myths, beneath their inoffensive appearance, are in fact powerful ideological tools. In masking, layering over, and transfiguring the relations of power and domination, these myths in fact look to naturalize them – that is, to give them the most indisputable security; what is natural is by definition immutable. Thus, the mythic tales that illustrate the inferiority of women, workers, or African servants serve as justification or legitimation in real society. In this way, the social origin of these prejudices is hidden: it is not the white man who subordinates the African servant, for, as the myth lets on, the latter is inferior by nature. As Barthes said in summarizing his main conclusion, myth effects supreme metamorphosis by *apparently* transforming cultural products into natural givens:

> The world enters language as a dialectical relation between activities, between human actions; it comes out of myth as a harmonious display of essences. A conjuring trick has taken place; it has turned reality inside out, it has emptied it of history and has filled it with nature, it has removed from things their human meaning so as to make them signify a human insignificance.[55]

This reference to Barthes is important from another, equally decisive point of view. It recalls that the main representatives of this critical movement do not separate discursive analysis from the sociopolitical context in which these texts, contemporary or earlier, were produced, be they actual sources or current theoretical texts. This development now concerns the texts of the New Testament that until then had remained the well-guarded pursuit of theologians. The latter had piously placed them out of context, in order to reduce them to the status of intrinsically *religious* texts that it was inappropriate to approach in the same manner. Anything else would be a sacrilege, especially if the approach introduced – and as a priority – political, social, and material causes. These new analyses, allowing for a dissection of the myths as different functions of collective representations, revealed at the same time the role of these myths in the social engineering that brings with it the relations of power and domination. The History of Religions thus becomes a social and political critic, which it had not often had occasion to be in the past – even the recent past. The vertigo provoked by the dissolving nominalism of Foucault found its antidote in this return to social realities. This can be verified by turning to the debated notion of ideology[56] that we have just encountered.

For McCutcheon, ideology is characterized by the political functions that Barthes, for his part, ascribes to contemporary myths.

The two orders of things are very close, since myth expresses the ideology of a class or an era. In a human world, where all aspects are socially and historically conditioned, this ideology seeks, as does myth, to hide and make over this reality and these contexts in order to justify them. To do this, it transfigures them, rendering them unrecognizable. Summarizing and developing what we have acquired, and which is generally assigned to Marx, Althusser,[57] and Barthes, McCutcheon maintains the use of the notion of ideology[58] (in contrast to Foucault, who reduced it to a powder and thus made it unusable) in order to transfer it into the register of Religious Studies. In the same work, he details the various functions that ideology is able to fulfill.[59] They form a fairly coherent ensemble that is possible to subdivide into three complementary categories or stages: decontextualization, dehistoricization, and depoliticization. They summarize a process that always culminates in the creation of local ontologies endowed with immutable essences (The Sacred, Religion, Myth, Royalty, Homeland, Art, etc.)

The first two stages — decontextualization and dehistoricization — have as their consequence essentialization, abstraction, and aestheticization, which themselves lead to generalization, naturalization, and universalization. Over the course of these first two stages, the world is voided, in a way, of anything that can recall its contingent origins, its composition made of heteroclite elements, and the chaotic chapters of its history. Equally suppressed is the play that existed between material causes and shameful motives, as this would tarnish its image. As to the third stage — depoliticization — to which Barthes had already drawn attention,[60] it consists of erasing all reference to real power and domination, and substituting a pacified version. Once again, as Barthes puts it, myth "organizes a world which is without contradictions because it is without depth, a world wide open and wallowing in the evident, it establishes a blissful clarity: things appear to mean something by themselves."[61] These processes have been seen at work in the final version of the life of Jesus — that is, the version canonized by the Church. As a result of these successive polishings, any contradictions, adaptations, and reinventions have been suppressed from the final story, which retains only the archetypal figure of the divine savior at the heart of a heroic gesture. It is in this way that one may speak of Jesus as a fictional character and of his life as a myth.

After this great cleaning-out, there is space free for the reception of purified ideas — ideas that are rid of their historical matrix. Setting himself out as acerbic critic, Marx, in *The German Ideology*, had already dissected this idealizing mechanism found at the center of Hegelian thought. He underlined the fact that, once detached from the real power relations regnant among men, "it is very easy to abstract from these various ideas '*the* idea,' the notion, etc., as the dominant force in history, and thus to understand all these separate ideas and concepts as 'forms of self-determination' on the part of *the* concept developing in history."[62] One of these ideas, par excellence, would of course be, for the Catholic Church, that of Religion. In and of itself, this idea on the one hand summarizes all of its ambitions and, on the other, it justifies all of its choices. At the end of this process of extraction and abstraction, the Platonic idea, freed from all contingency and all historical background, rises up and mixes with the notion of essence. The latter then waits only for the aestheticization-phase which will make of it a work of art for eye and spirit.[63]

Arrived at the level of essence, the purified idea, rid of its uncertain history, of all contingent accretions and all servitude, possesses the evidence and simplicity of the natural things that impose themselves naturally. Moreover, it escapes all of the cultural and historical particularities that would alienate it in a particular *hic et nunc*, then it can aim to apply to each of them equally. How could we talk about Egyptian art, prehistoric art, Greek art, of Dutch art, or French art of the seventeenth century if we did not dispose of a concept — Art — that has also made this long journey, finally transcending all determinations and all particularisms that afflict *the* arts? It comes back to us that we must not forget that, here, we have a concept elaborated in the crucible of modern Western culture, and that it was subsequently exported and imposed all across the world.[64] This remark gives me the chance to recall once more the idea, dear to our authors, that rhetoric, far from being a simple embellishment or structural tool, is the indispensable accomplice of any project of domination, be it social, political, or colonial.

And it is these diverse critical functions that Religious Studies compels itself to introduce into its program. What is more, these functions are recognized and, truly, offer nothing completely new. On the other hand, their brutal introduction into the domain of Religious Studies must have been a surprise to many readers. Nothing in its agenda had prepared Religious Studies for their rendez-vous. In this new context, such an upheaval represented much more than a simple change of lexicon. In the eyes of the religionists, these functions meant the supreme scandal, since religion itself could from then on be assimilated as being one ideological production among others. Any form of transcendence was *ipso facto* eliminated. Furthermore, from a methodological point of view, the accent was from that point on placed on trivial mechanisms, to which were attributed quasi-mechanical functions (such as the "Religious Factory") far removed from the hermeneutical approach that had privileged the question of meaning alone, conforming to the teaching of canonical texts.

Having come thus far, this bundle of new theses in fact found itself in quite close proximity to the three great masters of suspicion (Marx, Nietzsche, and Freud): Nietzsche, who in the Antichrist evoked "this purely fictitious world"[65] of Christianity, which it was, in his eyes; or Marx, who wrote in a celebrated passage of *The German Ideology*:

> Morality, religion, metaphysics, all the rest of ideology and their corresponding forms of consciousness, thus no longer retain the semblance of independence. They have no history, no development; but men, developing their material production and their material intercourse, alter, along with this their real existence, their thinking and the products of their thinking. Life is not determined by consciousness, but consciousness by life.[66]

With this last reference to Marx, a French reader might be surprised to learn that the influence of Marxism was equally determining in the context of Critical Studies. In addition to McCutcheon, favorable citations of Marx are found in Fitzgerald, (Craig) Martin, Arnal, and Asad, among others.[67] On the whole, these authors are in agreement with Fitzgerald in recognizing in religion an "ideological mystification."[68] But here I have to dispel a possible misunderstanding. These authors are not necessarily looking to become great exegetes of Marxist thought in the manner of Althusser or Gramsci—even less of Marxist-Leninism. Their Marxist vulgate is, on the whole, that of the programmatic theses contained in *The German Ideology*, cited by McCutcheon, for example, in his *Manufacturing Religion* and *The Discipline of Religion*. It is revealing, incidentally, that in this last book, having referred to Marx he immediately cites Barthes. What we see here is a sort of strategy (scholars also have these...) that consists in conjointly using certain theses of Marx, with or without those of Bourdieu,[69] and of Barthes. This strategy is used especially when these thinkers offer arguments that allow for the unveiling of ideological functionings that, in particular with mythologies of the religious type, cloak the fundamental reality of the authentic power-relations at the heart of society. It is indeed there, at this level, that we find the principal objective. In the end, it involves bringing together and honing arguments that will allow to reproduce, in the domain of Religious Studies, the complete reversal that Marx had proposed with respect to Hegelian idealism, or Barthes regarding social mythologies. At the heart of our initial paradigm (idealism *versus* materialism), this reversal of perspective means that the idealist side must be exposed and treated in order to reveal the influence of the underpinning material powers and power-relations.

One final, perhaps less evident, influence must be mentioned, for it has also prepared the soil for Critical Studies. As all great books, that of Edward Said, *Orientalism*, has been the object of much discussion and thus of criticism, especially from the area of Subaltern and Postcolonial Studies.[70] It nonetheless remains that the originality and general orientation of this book are still quite exemplary today. What indeed did Said say that entered into resonance with the project of American academics? Among their common preoccupations, we must doubtless assign first place to the question of power and dominating relations, be they between individuals, social classes, or indeed between cultures. In second place we assign the recognition given to the power of *poièsis* that we saw at work earlier in the creation of the figure of Jesus. And finally, as faithful heirs of the thinkers of the ère du *soupçon*, all are interested, as we hear in the famous comment of Jacques Prévert, "in the things hidden behind things," in order to uncover them. The Orient that Said talks about is in fact the one invented by the West in its books. This *literary* Orient is a sort of textual fantasm that obeys a precise *topos* where we find, systematized, the prejudices of the West, especially those concerning the inferiority of Islam. Western European Orientalism, which must include the scholarly studies devoted to the Orient, has served as matrix for this fantasmic Orient. Said remarks quite correctly in this regard that there is no "Occidentalism" that could have been created by specialists of Western studies in Oriental countries. The asymmetry here is indisputable. But this cultural domination prepares and justifies colonial and imperialist domination. The current history of the Near and Middle East recalls to us daily that the story of this domination is not over.

Summing up, Said offered an exemplary and novel study whose lessons one could generalize and then transpose with necessary adjustments into the field of Religious Studies — with *religion* replacing the Orient. It showed the way in demonstrating that it was possible to reverse the usual point of view. Contrary to the advice of common sense, one ought not to start with the object as if it were a given, but rather show how, by whom, and under what conditions this object has been constituted. Furthermore, as we will soon show, the many questions raised by the existence of Oriental religions were themselves indissociable from the role played in the nineteenth century by colonial powers, as much in Africa as in the immense Indian sub-continent, "an Italy of Asiatic dimensions," as Marx called it.[71] Here, as well, historians of religions could benefit from the lessons of Said.

Chapter Five

The Targets

With the use of the critical tools, analyses, and concepts elaborated in the field of human sciences as a consequence of the 1960s, scholars of Religious Studies were armed and ready to re-question the methods and results of the studies conducted from the beginning of the 1920s. This long stretch of time can be characterized by what we are tempted to call, doubly, a "return *of* the religious" and a "return *to* the religious". By this, one must understand that the History of Religions, in a way turning its back on the support that the human sciences could have given, was often transformed into an advocate of religious facts, looking by various ways to rehabilitate them in giving them an entirely singular status. And in this, one can naturally see a vivid reaction to the materialistic, atheistic, and/or scientific theories that had flourished since the end of the nineteenth century.

5.1 The Phenomenology of Religion

From this vast reactionary movement, works that stand out in particular are those of Rudolf Otto, *The Idea of the Holy*[1] (*Das Heilige: Über das Irrationale in der Idee des Göttlichen und sein Verhältnis zum Rationalen*, 1917); of Gerardus van der Leeuw, *Religion in Essence and Manifestation* (*Phänomenologie der Religion*, 1933), published in English in 1938 and in French in 1948; and of many works of Mircea Eliade published after World War Two. One could complete this list of major works with those of Max Scheler, *Probleme der Religion* (1921);[2] Jean Hering, *Phénoménologie et philosophie religieuse: Étude sur la théorie de la connaissance religieuse* (1926); and Joachim Wach, *Sociology of Religion* (1947).[3]

Most of these works are normally attached to the phenomenological current and for this reason receive most of the concentrated attacks of Critical Studies. In beginning with the phenomenology of religion,[4] we will also have the opportunity to unravel a tough question that has accrued misunderstanding. This chapter is in fact one of the most difficult to treat, due as much to its intrinsic complexity as to the confusion that reigns about it. This confusion has to do, in large measure, with the polysemy of the word "phenomenology," encompassing at the same time the prosaic empiricism (study of phenomenality) and the idealistic points of view of philosophic phenomenology springing from Edmund Husserl. Moreover, it also refers to the *mixture* of *genres* between philosophy, metaphysics, and the History of Religions. Last, it connotes the frequent use of a philosophical jargon that sometimes tries the patience of the reader.

The confusion also stems from the fact that certain authors (Otto and Eliade in particular) are often connected to the phenomenological wave, whereas, strictly speaking, one must admit that their respective intellectual orientations are fundamentally different. As for van der Leeuw, he represents quite a softened version of phenomenology, influenced by Otto, and his work has little to do with the theoretical and rather technical developments found in Husserl. In fact, it would be simpler to say (out of laziness? Or worry of over simplification? Or neglect?) that all of these authors have been included in the phenomenological movement for the wrong reasons. It is not the novel insights of the Husserlian project that carried them, but rather what have to be called its religious detours and generalizations. All of these authors agree, in fact, in underlining the irreducible and universal specificity of religious phenomena, which does not mean, however, that they approach them all in the same manner. It remains that the simple acceptance of this principle or, on the contrary, its condemnation, suffice for drawing an unbreachable line between the religionists, with their mixed tendencies and their adversaries.

Yet everything seemed simple, at least at the beginning and for a very brief period. Does not the word "phenomenology" seem to designate *a priori*, as many think, the study of phenomena — that is, of things and events that present themselves or occur before our eyes? Phenomenology would then be a sort of empirical study of the external world as we perceive it. Many of those who still use the word today do so with this confined acceptation. But Kant had introduced a primary distinction that would open the debate. Contrary to what common sense dictates, "phenomenon," he says, is not to be mixed up with "object"; although the latter appears as something "really given; [...] in so far as this or that property depends upon the mode of intuition of the subject, in the relation of the given object to the subject, the object as *phenomenon* is to be distinguished from the object as a thing *in itself*."[5] Nothing assures us that the phenomenon that we perceive is identical with the object in itself and which always remains unknown to us. Kant adds this precision, in a famous passage, showing clearly that he is not calling on any supernatural cause, nor invoking any kind of ideal essence in the cognitive processes:

> Our nature is so constituted that intuition with us never can be other than sensuous, that is, it contains only the mode in which we are affected by objects. On the other hand, the faculty of thinking the object of sensuous intuition is the understanding. Neither of these faculties has a preference over the other. Without the sensuous faculty no object would be given to us, and without the understanding no object would be thought. Thoughts without content are void; intuitions without conceptions, blind. Hence it is as necessary for the mind to make its conceptions sensuous (that is, to join to them the object in intuition), as to make its intuitions intelligible (that is, to bring them under conceptions). Neither of these faculties can exchange its proper function. Understanding cannot intuite [*sic*], and the sensuous faculty cannot think. In no other way than from the united operation of both, can knowledge arise.[6]

If we take this Kantian point of view as a convenient reference, one may say that Georg W. F. Hegel, often forgotten or neglected by historians of religions, would add two crucial modifications that Kant would certainly have challenged and that we will encounter below. On the one hand, Hegel reintroduced, with the notion of essence, a fundamentally idealistic philosophical point of view:

> Indeed, appearance is essential to being. Truth would not be, if it did not "appear" for someone—in itself as well as for the spirit overall.[7]

And he made of the conscience that perceives these appearances not a passive observer, but "the 'singular' expression of the total process by which the Spirit, over history, has appeared and been affirmed in its veracity: the experience of the conscience is thus indeed the articulation, in the singular, of a *Phenomenology of Spirit*."[8] The roots of this conscience are therefore not found in individual psychic life, but instead in the (divine) Spirit, whose realization in history it accompanies. Thus, with Hegel we find the two concepts, essence and conscience, that, associated with Spirit—which is only one of the expressions of the Absolute (that is, of God, definitively)—constitute the fundamental elements of any phenomenological construction of religion:

> Human reason—the consciousness of one's being—is indeed reason; it is the divine in man, and Spirit, in so far as it is the Spirit of God, is not a spirit beyond the stars, beyond the world. On the contrary, God is present, omnipresent, and exists as Spirit in all spirits. God is a living God, who is acting and working. [...] According to the philosophical conception, God is Spirit, is concrete; and if we inquire more closely what Spirit is, we find that the whole of religious doctrine consists in the development of the fundamental conception of Spirit.[9]

Among the historians of religions, Dutch scholar Chantepie de la Saussaye (also a professor of Protestant Theology), whom we have already encountered, would be the first to take up again the term "phenomenology" in his *Manual of the Science of Religions* (original German version, 1887; English translation, 1891). But for him "phenomenon" stays close to its ordinary meaning: "The collecting and grouping of various religious phenomena forms the transition from the history to the philosophy of religion. The latter treats religion according to its subjective and objective sides, and therefore consists of a psychological and a metaphysical part."[10]

Thus, for de la Saussaye, phenomenology occupies only a marginal position and is tinged with Hegelianism. It is situated somewhere between the classification of "givens" and their philosophical treatment. That would not be the case with certain later promoters and disciples of Edmund Husserl (1859–1938), who is considered the founder of modern phenomenology. It is important to specify that Husserl (and also his illustrious student, Martin Heidegger) was himself no historian of religions, nor even a specialist in the Philosophy of Religion. The phenomenology that he constructed was not destined *a priori* to serve religion, nor to be utilized in the framework of religious studies. This would not be the case with some of his close disciples. Two, in particular, distinguished themselves and capture the attention: Max Scheler (1874–1928) and Jean Hering[11] (1890–1966), the latter of whom cited the former in the work that I will refer to here as guide and reference. In the case of those two men, it is possible to speak of the phenomenology of *religion*, for they brought *religion* directly into the vast company of those occupied with understanding so-called religious facts—that is, historians, anthropologists, metaphysicians, theologians, and philosophers. And in a certain sense, via this new perspective they also re-interpreted some of the principal metaphysical elements of the Hegelian apparatus.

Although virtually forgotten today, and consequently rarely cited, the work of Hering is nonetheless closest to the philosophical teaching of Husserl, therefore allowing one best to understand the transposition of Husserl's thought into the domain of studies devoted to *religion* (and it will be clear later, although one could already guess in the light of what has already been said, why the expression "studies devoted to *religion*" is more fitting than "... to religions"). Hering's book also presents the greatest number of didactic aspects, which is no small compliment in this area. Hering, who also taught Protestant Theology, and who knew Husserl personally, published his work in 1926, a mere thirteen years after Husserl's major work, *Ideas: General Introduction to Pure Phenomenology* (*Ideen zu einer reinen Phänomenologie und phänomenologischen Philosophie*, I), and five years before the *Méditations cartésiennes* (later translated into German as *Cartesianische Meditationen*, 1950; and into English as *Cartesian Meditations* in 1960). Hering thus witnessed the appearance of the first (French) edition.

As we have just said, Husserl's phenomenology was *a priori* unconcerned with religion in particular, and even less with religions. But at the same time, it was almost entirely organized around a central notion—that of *essence*—which is as old as Western idealist philosophy (especially Platonic). Indeed, Hering frequently uses the corresponding Greek word *eidos*, εἶδος (from which we get the adjective "eidetic"), to recall and connect with this distant filiation. It is also the reason this notion has arisen so often in the preceding pages, for it represents the kernel around which all Western idealist thought has developed since antiquity, whether of religious inspiration or not. From this, the notion of *essence* displays a kind of evident predisposition to slide from one idealist domain to another, be it from Plato to Christianity or, as is the case this time, from Husserlian philosophy to *religion*. Now, although not fundamentally religious or turned toward Religion, phenomenology incontestably remains a philosophical school among the idealisms. In other words, despite its high degree of technicality, the transposition of the principles of phenomenology to Religious Studies was a far from insurmountable challenge. Inevitable evolution? One might think so when one considers the parallel evolution of contemporary French phenomenology toward theology.[12] And especially since, with phenomenology being a reaction against the "-isms" (historicism, positivism, sociologism, pragmatism, Kantian criticism and particularly psychologism), which were considered from its point of view as reductionist, it could not avoid the major claims by religionists and theologians who, in the face of science, also defended the irreducible specificity of religious facts.

Let us now follow Hering's demonstration in order to understand how this sliding toward the philosophy of religion was effected. We will see later how the adaptation of this philosophy was made — a philosophy whose methodology and conceptual framework still remain rather close to their model of reference — to the History of Religions properly speaking. Having arrived at this stage, phenomenology, all the while keeping the name, would be considerably distanced from its philosophical model from which followed innumerable possibilities for confusion and misunderstanding.

I would also add that Hering relies on a simplified version of Husserlian phenomenology; although faithful in spirit, with Hering it appears simultaneously to be a lot less technical and much more readable. Manifestly, his book was written with a pedagogical concern for popular use. Nevertheless, with the notions of *essence*, *intentional consciousness*, and *intuition*, we still see the three pillars of the Husserlian system. How does this philosophical construction function, whose principal terms, it is still important to specify, are devoid of their usual acceptance?

As with Husserl, Hering's consciousness is "intentional," for, as consciousness extended toward an *object*, it is susceptible to intuitions — that is, it is capable of seizing essences "as our world grants us access to them."[13] However, this type of intuition is in no way the expression of a subjectivity or particular psychic state, referred to disdainfully by Hering as "states of the soul," the internal and affective life of a concrete individual belonging to a particular era and society. Psychologism is indeed the mortal enemy of phenomenology since, reverting endlessly to the internal, subjective, and personal *Ego*, it forbids the attainment of "original and ultimate realities."[14]

It will have been understood then that, as with Hegel, Hering's conscience is neither empirical nor worldly. Hering is talking about a pure conscience,[15] or, in other words, a *transcendental* conscience. And its intuitions conform to this exceptional status. In effect, it has "in itself an autonomous existence (*"die Einsicht, daß Bewusstsein in sich selbst ein Eigensein hat"*) that, in its absolute sovereignty (*"in seinem absoluten Eigenwesen"*), is not obtained by the exclusions of phenomenology. This conscience remains as 'phenomenological residue' and an absolutely original area that can become the field of a new science—Phenomenology."[16] This is of course a crucial affirmation, but one that cannot be refuted, just as the Platonic thesis of Ideas, for it is impossible to test it by experiment. The same goes for this other statement: "Every act of conscience reveals itself, by its very essence, as extended toward an 'object' that transcends it."[17] In this quite restricted sense, one can say that evidence "is an inherent characteristic of the object, or, better put, of the manner in which it presents itself to the conscience."[18] In other words, this *evidence* has nothing to do with the banal acceptance that we give the term daily. This *transcendence* refers, then, back to the original relation that unites the *pure* conscience to the phenomenon as manifested and as first intuited by the conscience, not as the empirical individual perceives it in his or her deep interior with its biased mental representations.

As to essences, "they are ideal entities devoid of all empirical contingency, and not some sort of mysterious astral copies of material objects," as is seen in the example of the color red, "considered not just as part of the empirical world but in its 'constitutive essence.'"[19] This latter involves a crucial point, itself affirmed in an *a priori* manner and thus just as indemonstrable, and from which the recourse to the argument of authority: "From the very beginning the extra-mental existence of *essences* [...] has always been considered by all phenomenologists as a fact that reveals itself indubitably to phenomenological analysis."[20] If one is not convinced *a priori* by the existence of essences, as apparently "all phenomenologists" are, it seems difficult to become thus persuaded in the light of these rhetorical arguments.

How is religious phenomenology going to recuperate this philosophical heritage in order to enrich it and, especially, to orientate it into its domain and make of it a phenomenology of religion? In fact, it is simply going to cheat. It would reintroduce, as contraband, "givens" that are in fact taken from the most orthodox Christian theology, and then simply cover them in rhetorical garb borrowed from philosophy, all the while multiplying the arguments of authority (using, for example, as in the previous paragraph, expressions such as "all phenomenologists").

What are these most evident *a prioris*? Those in which Christian borrowings seem the least disputable. First of all, and at the most general level, there is the constant use of the words *religion* and *religious*, as if they designated not particular cultural and historical constructions, but rather the bearers of transhistoric essences. Let us take up again Hering's *Phénoménologie et philosophie religieuse* from pages 105 to 107. It concerns examining the following affirmation: the rebirth of a sinner, he says, is impossible without the necessary repentance. Now, in Hering's phenomenologist eyes, this has to do with "a synthetic *a priori* law (using Kant's terms) whose truth or falsity can only be demonstrated by an intuitive study of the essences and phenomena involved in the terms 'rebirth,' 'sin,' and 'to repent'." But how can one avoid seeing that the three decisive terms of this assertion are borrowed solely from Christian culture? In other words, it is only within that context that they possess their full meaning, and this meaning is the result of a singular history. How could a Hindu or a person from China grasp the essence of "sinner's repentance" when this cultural notion is unknown to them? It does not even figure in their vocabulary, and thus would be untranslatable into their language. As a result, the notion "religious experience" is just as incongruous. Only a historical conscience (that is, historically constituted, and not a *pure* or *transcendental* conscience) would be able to grasp it, but such a conscience is *de facto* foreign to the hypothesis relative to the existence of a ghostly world peopled with essences.

To convince us of this, let us turn now to the example evoked on pages 144 and 115. Here, we read of the "essence of Christianity," although reduced to its Lutheran version. Hering begins by studying the "different types of piety, theologies, moral or intellectual institutions, each constituting a phase of the movement," in order to disengage the empirical essence of each type. Let us acknowledge that for every beginning phase of this study there is already an extant, mammoth corpus of work susceptible of occupying a historian's entire life, and capable of giving birth, along the way, to problems, questions, and controversies without number. How can they be resolved? That is a mystery. But let us nevertheless note, importantly, that they are not even mentioned. Hering, however, hardly discouraged by this first, exhausting stage, then asks whether "some intimate affinity between the different traits of their character allows one to catch a glimpse of the eternal essences manifest in their complex unity." The inquiry then must extend to every era and every domain capable of "shedding light on the material." It is then necessary, in the final chapter, to ask whether or not these essence-types are apparent to each other. "This can only be told by an 'eidetic' study, going back into the context of the philosophy of religion or eidetic psychology. In the case of an affirmative answer, one will try to determine the essence that unites (by absorption) the secondary essences that are only partial aspects."

If the first chapter corresponds in broad strokes to a doubling of the research into sources conducted in a comparative context, the second chapter, which begins once Hering starts to "glimpse the eternal essences," is itself dominated by the teleology that has inspired it from the start. It is clear, in fact, that only those philosophers who believe in the existence of eternal essences — and Christian ones to boot — are able to glimpse them. The others, whose feet are firmly planted on the ground, look only for those causes and conditions that can explain historical situations, evolutions, and transformations for which comparative study will eventually provide homologies. Once again, a divorce is effected between idealist affirmation and historical explanation.

Here, again, Hering is careful not to raise all of the difficulties and objections. We have seen earlier, from the beginning of Part One of the present book, the extent to which the notion of religion was marked by confused origins and a turbulent intellectual history. Under such conditions, how could "intuiting" religion grasp its essence? Is its history not constituted of thousands and thousands of successive pieces of information over the centuries? At what level could one locate its proper, indisputable evidence? In what place and at what moment should one try to grasp it? As to the supposition of a unique essence hidden behind all expressions of Western Religion, it seems clear that it would have to decide from dozens of concurrent and incompatible acceptations (Lucretius's *Religio*, Bossuet's Religion, or that of Schleiermacher, to name only three). And things would get even more complicated for the person aiming at a universal essence situated behind or below all the so-called religions of humanity. And one may entirely exclude the hypothesis that an exotic phenomenologist would find this essence among

Buddhists or Hindus, since that would invalidate *ipso facto* the pretentions of a Christian theology adept in phenomenology. The same
goes for all historico-cultural creations. If, strictly speaking, one
can evoke the constitutive essence of the simple color red (even if
the exercise is of limited interest), these more complex objects that
have taken centuries to be constituted, through many an accidental
and unforeseeable adventure, cannot possess an *essence*, unless one
looked for it in historicity itself. But would not the essence of fundamental instability mean the end or the death of all other essences,
transcendent in principle, because they claim to evade history?

At the very end of his book, Hering delivers his three most disputable theses, which are also those upon which his phenomenology of
(Christian) religion is definitively based. The first thesis, which we
have already encountered and will do again, involves the affirmation relative to the absolute autonomy of religion. This is the essential claim, for without it, religion, which like any human creation
is subject to the play of contexts, diverse causes, and unforeseeable
transformations, loses all supernatural and immutable character:

> [P]henomenology places itself, without hesitation, alongside the
> theologians who proclaim the autonomy of religion relative to sci-
> entific thought. And as it is known that ultimately the concern to
> assure this independence dominated the theology stemming from
> Schleiermacher, one can say on this point that the phenomenological
> movement is at once its defender and heir.[21]

The second thesis concerns the absolute transcendence and singularity of God:

> This involves knowing whether or not the *quaestio Dei* occupies a com-
> pletely unique place in epistemological considerations. For as God is
> neither essence nor empirical fact, everything leads to the belief that
> the way in which He is present to the conscience makes His existence
> something beyond the division of truths into those of fact and those of
> reason—that is, it is a truth unique in its genre, requiring an entirely
> special kind of research.[22]

Where does Hering get these certitudes, if not from the theological
catechism on whose side he deliberately sets himself? But if God is
neither essence nor empirical fact, how does he manifest himself
in the conscience of the believer? By what channel? Even though a
major contradiction, the hint here consists in removing the "God"
piece from the construction in order to guarantee his absolute

transcendence. But how, in such novel conditions, would the conscience still recognize him? Would the conscience possess a supplementary and quite specialized innate predisposition, a sort of innate religious instinct allowing for certain grasp?

The last thesis, which can be considered the most banal Christian-centric point of view, consists of proclaiming the indisputable superiority of the Christian religion over all others. Now, in so doing, Hering is not conducting phenomenology, even superficially. Instead, he is content here to reaffirm an ancient bias:

> From this point of view, a good number of religions and cults would reveal themselves as sterile—not for studying the idea of God, but for proving the existence of a living and contemporary God. It would thus be absolutely erroneous to want to teach, in the name of phenomenology, the cognitive equivalence of all acts of faith.[23]

This is a rather intellectually refined way to remind phenomenology of its duties and to reaffirm that there exists a superior religion— and one alone—in the face of the sterile rank and file of heresies and inferior religions. But as these subaltern religions (voodoo, shamanism) are also phenomena that "manifest themselves," one can and even should ask: how are their essences alike? And, while we're at it, what about the essences of all superstitions, magics, and sorceries? One will then ask, with a good deal of perplexity and curiosity: inside the world of essences, do we find the hierarchies and classifications that the Christian West had introduced on Earth among all religions? And, if so, where is the border separating the good essences from the inferior? This comes back to saying—the supreme paradox—that this world of essences in reality reflects the world around us rather than transcending it, unless we are to assume that inferior religions have no essences. This is a simple hypothesis, one might say, but one that needs to be formulated with care, since it has never been demonstrated by phenomenologists that the only essences that exist conform to the major truths of Christian Revelation. Essences, moreover, that require explanation as to how they adapted themselves to the evolutions and transformations known to that Revelation, beginning with those concerning the person of Jesus.[24] It is indisputable that, as victims of their presuppositions, the phenomenological theses relative to the essences run into insoluble contradictions as soon as they are required to integrate the turbulent history of Christian truths. For the latter were clearly not conceived for those theses. Is it not simpler to admit, under these conditions, that this phenomenology of religion is just a new garb intended to rejuvenate old prejudices and commonplaces?

How does phenomenology claim to demonstrate the complete autonomy of religion, the absolute transcendence of one god, and, finally, the indisputable superiority of the Christian religion? Hering does not respond to these questions. Indeed, he does not raise them. What is a stumbling block in his case, but which is quite far from unique in the contemporary annals of the History of Religions, is the incessant mixture of scientific or philosophical protocols encased in a strong logical frame on the one hand, and on the other hand direct borrowings of indemonstrable arguments straight from theological tradition.[25]

With the work of van der Leeuw, phenomenology of religion undergoes a supplementary transformation—or, rather, degradation. In an irreversible manner it provokes a profound alteration of the fundamental theses of its distant model. It is useless to take up these demonstrations point by point (since there really aren't any as such) on essential issues; what the Dutch scholar frequently hammers home are categorical affirmations that are never demonstrated. It is rare to find anyone who went so far along the path of a sort of pan-religiosity that infiltrated all intellectual aspects of human life. On this point, van der Leeuw is situated on the same level as the most radical theologians. And, like them, he sees no solution of continuity between the phenomenology he defends, the History of Religions, and theology.

Mirroring Otto and Eliade, van der Leeuw insists on the lived religious experience. The word "lived" must be given the fullness of its existential acceptation here. It has to do with an experience that engages the person in totality. At the same time, what is understood is the idea that such experiences are universal, and that they are sufficiently alike to belong to the category, whatever their different historical or cultural contexts. It would remain to show that the lived experiences of the Buryat shaman, the Indian yogi, the Cistercian monk, the Brazilian mambo, the Celtic druid, or the Roman *pontifex maximus*, to name but a few, effectively reveal an identical source and structure. Now, van der Leeuw has no anthropologist's head whatsoever, nor a historian's, for that matter. His preference is always to fall back on traditional Christian givens, whose significance he generalizes over collective humanity. As we see in the following passage, he never envisages religion—appropriately named, once again—except in reference to the Christian model. This model is always found in the background: "But in any case, religion is always directed towards salvation, never towards life itself as it is given: and in this respect all religion, with no exception, is the religion of deliverance."[26] His *homo religious*, a notion which is also found in Eliade, therefore has a very weak anthropological value despite its apparent immediate acceptance: "[E]xperience is a phenomenon. Revelation is not; but man's reply to revelation, his assertion about what has been revealed, is also a phenomenon from which, indirectly, conclusions concerning the revelation itself can be derived (*per viam negationis*)."[27]

This conclusion rests on rather twisted reasoning, the key to which van der Leeuw delivers to us a few pages later: "[A]ll understanding that extends 'to the ground' ceases to be understanding before it reaches the ground, and recognizes itself as a 'becoming understood.' In other terms: all understanding, irrespective of whatever object it refers to, is ultimately religious: all significance sooner or later leads to ultimate significance."[28]

I am reminded of pastiche: if I speak, it is because someone is listening to me. Now this someone can only be, ultimately, the someone who spoke to me first, all communication being "ultimately religious." This curious reasoning applies first of all to the phenomenon. The latter always remains what is manifest, but van der Leeuw modifies its Husserlian acceptance. It more or less inverts the function. On the one hand, the phenomenon inserts itself "into our own lives"; it penetrates our psychic and affectively concrete life. On the other hand, if it does not "submit itself to us directly and immediately," it is because it is acting "as a symbol of some meaning to be interpreted by us, as something which offers itself to us for interpretation."[29] This comes back to saying that it is no longer the conscience that is characterized by its intentionality, but rather the phenomenon, as if it only manifested itself in the life of the individual in order to tell him or her something essential, all the while preserving its mysterious side. We are no longer very far from another mystery: that of the Incarnation. As a critic of Eliade quite correctly remarked, with not a little humor, "a science of religion based upon a mystery remains a mysterious science."[30]

Interpretation becomes, in the same stroke, a central piece in this new framework. The hermeneutic, inherited from Schleiermacher, attaches itself from this point on to all religious "objects" (texts, images, myths, symbols, etc.), not just to the books of the Bible, in order to elucidate the meaning that will clearly be religious. The hermeneutic circle here is so perfectly closed that it is impossible to emerge from it: only a religious meaning can be attributed to an object considered *a priori* to be religious. This hermeneutic will flourish with Eliade, to the point of constituting one of the major references in his own conception of religious universes: his *homo religiosus* will first be a hermeneut. This meaning to be discovered is also the mysterious, absolute, and ultimate meaning of things, since it is by nature religious. In fact:

> The religious significance of things, therefore, is that on which no wider nor deeper meaning whatever can follow. It is the meaning of the whole: it is the last word. But this meaning is never understood, this last word is never spoken; they always remain superior, the ultimate concealed. It implies an advance to the farthest boundary, where only one sole fact is understood: that all comprehension is 'beyond'; and thus the ultimate meaning is at the same moment the limit of meaning.[31]

Whereas the Husserlian épochè[32] (or the phenomenological reduction) consisted of provisionally bracketing the "natural world," it will henceforth signify — also radically changing meaning, unafraid of ridicule — "the loving gaze of the lover on the beloved object. For all understanding rests upon self-surrendering love. [...] [S]ince to him who does not love, nothing whatever is manifested."[33] The phenomenology of religion at that point has accomplished a complete mutation, sacrificing its foundational principles and putting itself at the service of the interests of *its* religion alone.

But let us go back twenty years or so, in order better to situate the contribution of Rudolf Otto in this phenomenological context.

5.2 *"The Holy" according to Rudolf Otto*

When faithful to the inspiration of its creator, the phenomenology of religion, such as with Hering, presents rather an arid and speculative character. In this form it would be difficult to arouse enthusiasm in believers, and even more so to motivate vocation. Its influence on religious practices and feelings had little chance to develop, as its intellectual vocation was far from the real life of the faithful. Unless they were animated by a living faith, these faithful could not see themselves in the phenomenological context or find spiritual nourishment there that matched their aspirations.

Another Protestant German theologian, Rudolf Otto (1869–1937), and his most famous work, *The Idea of the Holy*,[34] would be left the task of defending a concept of religious universes in which feeling, affectivity, emotions, and even mystic exaltation would hold an entirely central place. This re-balancing, so to speak, followed a pivotal era. In the face of atheistic and materialist philosophers of the eighteenth and nineteenth centuries (D'Holbach, Marx, Nietzsche, Freud, etc.), and of Kantian criticism, positivist historicism, nascent sociologism (Durkheim, Mauss), natural sciences (Darwin), and even the aesthetic revolutions from the beginning of the twentieth century, the intellectual positions of religious partisans seemed increasingly under threat. If these partisans wanted to reconquer hearts and minds, they needed to rethink their arguments.

Although Otto is not *stricto sensu*, or even *lato sensu*, a phenomenologist (that is, a philosopher, disciple, interpreter, or successor of Husserl), he is frequently linked to the phenomenological stream. So too is Eliade, moreover. From this fact, as it has been said, the misinterpretations, overlappings, and misunderstandings regarding the two of them are frequent to the point that, without looking to refine and distinguish the opinions of both sides, we often find the word "phenomenologist" applied to all those who, at the heart of the contemporary field of the History of Religions, have defended or defend points of view favorable to the irreducible specificity of religions. In this particular sense it is not far from what is designated (and without adding a note of irony) by the word *religionist*.

That being specified, we may judge that the contribution of Otto was entirely decisive, even more so for its great originality. But Otto remains nonetheless a professional theologian, an intellectual who tries with theological resources (even if rethought) to demonstrate certain truths that, in his view, are essential. These truths sometimes run across questions raised by the History of Religions; *a fortiori* when the latter adopts a religionist orientation. And this is the case when it touts as its own the theses originating with Otto. The major difficulty that arises in the work of Otto appears, in fact, in the light of this intellectual promiscuity (exposed several times already). Certain specialists therefore consider this promiscuity to be unacceptable, for it needs to be repeated that, in the work, the theological responses provided to theological questions are *a priori* only of interest to theology. Any profit for science, for this reason, is non-existent: the History of Religions is no academic, non-sectarian, or liberal version of theology, nor is theology an auxiliary discipline of the History of Religions. In order to clarify the terms of this debate, one should even add that, despite appearances, the areas just mentioned do not have the same object; the religions (in the plural) of anthropologists and historians are incommensurate (and should never be otherwise) with the *religion* of theologians. They belong to radically different epistemic regimes and universes. Would one dare say that the constellations of astrologists are the same (onto-logically speaking) as those of astrophysicists because they have the same names and because both groups situate their interests in the sky? In spite of the confusion between science and theology enter-tained by religionists, neither side raises the same questions, tar-gets the same results, or uses the same conceptual tools. For the first named, religions are, as with all human products, historical, transi-tory creations; and for the others, religions possess an indisputable, supernatural dimension that places them beyond human time.

The great originality of Otto consisted in his developing a new concept of religion in which the traditional positions of the various Christian theologies appeared (at least at the beginning of his book) stuck and surpassed. This includes the ecclesial institution, the sac-raments, rational dogmas, conventional morality, canonical theol-ogy, sacred texts, the defense of orthodoxy and original Revelation. In a word, Christian religion as it conforms most to its own identity no longer appears *a priori* as a necessary element, although we will see how these traditional positions resurface *a posteriori*. They are never invoked at the outset by Otto in order to build from them a fundamental truth. Otto, who advises "to escape as far as possible from the mental atmosphere of our dogmatic interpretations and judiciously toned-down catechisms,"[35] will propose early on that it be discovered elsewhere.

To take the measure of this transgression, it is enough to note the following. In the title of his famous book, *The Idea of the Holy*, the word "holy" is a substantive, preceded by the definite article ("*das Heilige*"); it is not a simple adjective. This seemingly slight distinc-tion has, in fact, a great effect. Otto is not saying something like "in this or that culture men considered this object, this personage or this myth as sacred"; he is affirming the existence of a singular substance that cannot be confused with any other and that exists absolutely.[36] To underline its exceptional character, Otto calls it the "Wholly Other" ("*das ganz Andere*") or the "numinous," a neologism constructed from the Latin word "*numen*," which itself goes back to the will, the power, and the majesty of the divine.

From that point on, the chain of propositions will unfold, culminating in a *pro domo* argument with which we are by now entirely familiar, for it constitutes one of the constant claims of Christianity since its origins: that is, that it is above all second-order religions, being the one true religion of the one true God. As any theological demonstration is also (indeed, from the outset) a question of rhetoric, Otto will *a priori* attribute his vision of the Holy to a certain number of characteristics that are doubtless deemed to distance it and harbor it from all criticism. What Otto chose allows him in effect to circumscribe a theoretically homogenous space that seems *de facto* closed to investigation by analytical reasoning, among which its old enemy, Kantian criticism,[37] holds pride of place.

Otto considers the Holy first and foremost as a *sui generis* category—a notion that we have already encountered with Durkheim and that we will find again, particularly in Eliade. This qualification is quite useful, since it consists of affirming that the object mentioned (religion, the Holy, myth, etc.) disposes of absolute autonomy and thus has no other cause or origin than itself. As with Plotinus's One, in a way it exists as itself, from its own energy, its own dynamism. Thus, adroitly it is removed from the tumult of history, and, in a more general manner still, from all known forms (biological, sociological, psychological, etc.) of categorization. As an original, it is considered by Otto as the unique essence of the religious and can therefore be assigned the task of serving as the ontological foundation for all religions. All religions emerged from it, but as we will see in a moment, all did not make the same use of their heritage. Some were more astute than others…

Now, as Otto specifies *a priori* and somewhat redundantly, rational concepts (even if theological in origin) cannot exhaust, by definition or analysis, this universal and mysterious essence of *religion*. It escapes any systematic investigation that would claim to drain it of meaning. For the purposes of thought, the Holy is indeed the Wholly Other, as unknowable as it is inconceivable and ineffable. Radically different, but also mysterious, Otto's Holy possesses all the characteristics that allow for evoking states of the soul or feelings fed by religiosity. It "set the numinous object in contrast not only to everything wonted and familiar (i.e., in the end, to nature in general), thereby turning it into the 'supernatural,' but finally to the world itself, and thereby exalt[ed] it to the 'supramundane' (*'das Übernatürliche'*), that which is above the whole world-order (*'das Überweltliche'*)."[38] Therefore, any approach that would grasp its profound nature in this world is *a priori* disqualified.

This profound nature is in fact only revealed at the heart of personal experience, as specific as it is incommunicable, where the Holy, bearer of fear, shows itself, endowed with its power, energy, and all of its majesty.[39] This foundational experience is still no "given" whose genesis can be found in history or culture. It, too, is *sui generis*; in the final analysis "it cannot be expressed by means of anything else, just because it is so primary and elementary a datum in our psychical life, and therefore only definable through itself."[40] In a way, the soul possesses an innate pre-knowledge of this. Otto specifies a few lines later: "Desiring to give it a name of its own, I propose to call it 'creature-consciousness' (*'Kreaturgefühl'*) or 'creature-feeling.' It is the emotion of a creature, submerged and overwhelmed by its own nothingness in contrast to that which is supreme above all creatures" (*"die in ihrem eigenen Nichts versinkt und vergeht gegenüber dem, was über dem, was über aller Kreatur ist"*).[41] All doors by which one might be tempted to introduce rational inquiry are double-bolted. Neither the Holy, nor the experience of the individual, nor the soul, all as defined by Otto, has an opening allowing access to the outside. Together they constitute a closed, hermetic universe, sealed unto itself.

Having arrived at this point, which at first glance is quite far from traditional conceptions, a problem appears that is in no way slight. What paths will it be necessary to travel in order to recover the prestige of the Christianity that has seemingly receded into the background? How can one imagine, in fact, that a theologian would not see this background as the endpoint of his long efforts? As Hering had done at around the same time, and as van der Leeuw would also do a few years later, Otto introduced into his system some useful Christian crutches. They would allow him to rediscover the path of a certain orthodoxy. The least disputable are two in number. The first was in fact introduced surreptitiously, and always *a priori*, from the beginning of his work, without a scrap of proof:

> It will be our endeavour to suggest this unnamed Something [the
> Holy] to the reader as far as we may, so that he may himself feel it.
> There is no religion in which it does not live as the real innermost core,
> and without it no religion would be worthy of the name. It is pre-
> eminently a living force in the Semitic religions, and of these again in
> none has it such vigour as in that of the Bible.[42]

Is it necessary to specify that this new affirmation relies on no demonstration? From the point of view of science, it is just one more
fiction.

On this basis, the second crutch introduces a subtle distinction: if
the Holy is a *sui generis* category and, as we have seen, evades history in terms of a force capable of engendering or even simply con-
ditioning it, the Holy has nevertheless evolved over the course of
history. How does Otto succeed in justifying this difference, which
at first glance seems rather surprising, if not incomprehensible?
How can the Holy, which does not belong to history, evolve? In
fact, the line followed by Otto from this point becomes once again
quite orthodox, as if placing its feet into the footprints of tradition.
This evolution is, in effect, dictated by the very classical theory of
the economy of salvation, according to which things occur according to the plan devised and accomplished by God. In this way, the
evolution obeys an irrepressible movement of which the future
Christianity is the motor and goal:

> This permeation of the rational with the non-rational is to lead, then,
> to the deepening of our rational conception of God; it must not be the
> means of blurring or diminishing it. For if (as suggested at the close
> of the last chapter), the disregard of the numinous elements tends
> to impoverish religion, it is no less true that 'holiness,' 'sanctity,' as
> Christianity intends the words, cannot dispense with the rational, and
> especially the clear ethical elements of meaning which Protestantism
> more particularly emphasizes in the idea of God. To get the full mean-
> ing of the word 'holy' as we find it used in the New Testament (and
> religious usage has established it in the New Testament sense to the
> exclusion of others), we must no longer understand by 'the holy' or
> 'sacred' the merely numinous in general, nor even the numinous at
> its own highest development; we must always understand by it the
> numinous completely permeated and saturated with elements signi-
> fying rationality, purpose, personality, morality.[43]

Let us translate this passage so that it can become clearer: the
numinous only existed in order to become Christian, as if the latter

had disciplined and civilized it. It gave the numinous its telos. How, one may ask, are produced "almost at the same time of this evolution, and all together, the internal rationalization and moralization of the numinous"? Otto continues: "Almost everywhere we find the numinous attracting and appropriating meanings derived from social and individual ideals of obligation, justice, and goodness. These become the 'will' of the numen, and the numen their guardian, ordainer, and author. More and more these ideas come to enter into the very essence of the numen and charge the term with ethical content."[44]

Even if it is difficult to understand how an essence can change over time, especially by enriching itself with the fruits of culture (here, that would be "conceptions formed by the social as well as the individual ideal"), it has to be recognized that Otto's *numinous*, in becoming moralized and rationalized, acts and reveals itself as a divinity: "And this process of rationalization and moralization of the numinous, as it grows ever clearer and more potent, is in fact the most essential part of what we call 'the History of Salvation' and prize as the ever-growing self-revelation of the divine."[45]

Contrary to what one might have imagined, the original numinous was not eliminated over the course of this evolution. There "is in no way a suppression of the numinous or its supersession by something else — which would result not in a God, but a God-substitute — but rather the completion and charging of it with a new content. That is to say, the 'moralization' process assumes the numinous and is only completed upon this basis."[46]

At the end of this theodicy of the Holy, which seems to have been conceived from beginning to end in order to finish in apotheosis and the greater glory of Christianity, it can be affirmed simply that the Christian God preserves in the highest degree the original characteristics of the numinous: the Heavenly Father "is not less, but far more 'holy,' 'numinous,' mysterious, [...] than His Kingdom. He is all those in an absolute degree."[47]

As with Hering, so with van der Leeuw: history ends once again by following its theological model. In spite of a long detour, during which certain of the most established dogmas seem to have become quite secondary, all's well that ends well. Christian religion has overcome the *numinous* and finally reclaimed first place among all religions. Who would have doubted it?

5.3 *The Great Eliadean Themes*

Writing after Otto, van de Leeuw, and Wach,[48] and in a time that coincided with the period when critical currents were imposed with force, Eliade became posthumously the favorite target of all those who opposed the fundamentally religionist conceptions of Religious Studies. It must be admitted, in their defense, that Eliade made the task easy, given the frequency with which themes and ideas arose that could appear in the eyes of scientists simultaneously as great weaknesses and as veritable provocations.

When speaking of Eliade's work, one cannot call it a very elaborate conceptual synthesis. Rather, it is an eclectic meeting of general themes and commonplaces borrowed from phenomenology, Otto's theory of the Holy, Jungian psychology of archetypes, hermeneutic tradition, a certain pagan naturalism and pantheism, ancient Gnosticism, theosophy, and modern esotericism, as well as from rural ethnology and the Romanian anti-Semitism of the 1930s. The term *syncretism* without doubt summarizes appropriately the result he obtained.[49] From these heterogeneous "givens" he conceived a personal synthesis that enjoyed very quick success with the wider public but also with numerous academic institutions, of whom France was not the last to celebrate him. The Sorbonne, among others, awarded him with a doctorate *honoris causa*, and the Académie française assigned him a prize. And yet Eliade conceived the most bizarre system that was the farthest possible removed from the fundamental principles of a Protestantism faithful to the inspiration of its founders. One could not for a moment imagine Luther seeing himself in Eliade's work. The latter ignores the notions of faith, love of neighbor, and examination of conscience. They play no role and indeed only appear anecdotally. If one finds there a certain lyricism that must have pleased many readers, one also encounters almost no austere chapters concerning ethical questions. Religion, for Eliade, is not a religion of the conscience and of love. Nor is it a religion of altruism and self-sacrifice. On the contrary, more than once it celebrates liberating orgies and bloody sacrifices in the way that (according to Eliade) they were celebrated in ancient societies. And there is no reason that the energy exerted by these earlier rituals ought to be dried up today. Eliade indeed regrets their disappearance as sealing the morbid destiny of modern man who lives in a desacralized world, forever distanced from the benefits of the great ancient liturgies.[50]

Eliade was no historian, sociologist, or anthropologist. And he always kept himself a good deal apart from the exigencies of these disciplines.[51] Going so far as to refuse even the most elementary examination, which would have had to exclude *ipso facto* the domain of human sciences, he says:

> I must add that I will approach all these phenomena as a historian of religions, which is to say, I will not attempt to discuss their psychological, sociological, or even political contexts, meanings, or functions (leaving that to those who may be better qualified to do so).[52]

> But [this little book] is not a study in the history of religions in the strict sense, for the writer, in citing examples, has not undertaken to indicate their historico-cultural contexts.[53]

This refusal of any deeply probing or methodical inquiry allows him to favor a superficial and thus deceptive treatment of the facts. So many things are similar when one remains on the surface and neglects their historical dimension. No objects exist outside of history, beginning with the work of Eliade itself.

His initial education in philosophy did not leave deep traces in his work. One hardly finds there any form of elaborated or original conceptualization. In fact, his major contributions consisted in adopting a rather theatrical posture of prophet or inspired guru, and in inventing a new way of writing in this reputedly austere field by adopting a lyrical, impressionist, and optimistic style much closer to an essay than to an argued thesis.[54] All the while, he led the most credulous readers to believe that he would reveal the secrets of the cosmos, whose mysterious existence he indeed did not cease to celebrate. It is true that his books, often short and easy to read, avoid any arduous demonstration and any form of erudition that could rebuff the reader. Repeating themselves from one title to another, they often give the impression of being the work of an autodidact who cursorily scanned the material, sticking with the most general and most seductive ideas.

Four quite distinct and quite different periods occupied the life of Eliade. The Romanian period extends from his birth in 1907 up to the beginning of World War Two. It is marked by a long sojourn in India (1928–1931), by his first literary success, his first contact with the works of the great esotericists of that era[55] (René Guénon, Julius

Evola, and Ananda Coomaraswamy), and, in the second half of the 1930s, by his ever-closer relations with the ultranationalist and anti-Semitic movement, the Iron Guard. After a brief period in London (October 1940–January 1941), a long period spent in Portugal follows until the end of the War, which he spent as a cultural attaché in the service of the dictatorial and anti-Semitic regime of Marshal Ion Antonescu, allied with Nazi Germany up until August of 1944. Recently, from the translation and publication of his long unknown *Portugal Journal*,[56] we have learned that Eliade retained his earlier political loyalties. For example, he considered the defeat of the Germans at Stalingrad to be a catastrophe.[57]

After the war, in September of 1945, Eliade, justly fearful of the occupation of his native country by Soviet troops, reached France, where he remained for around ten years until his departure in 1956 for the University of Chicago, where he succeeded Wach.[58] It is during his time in France that he begins to write the long series of works that will subsequently establish his international reputation. He spent thirty years (1956–1986) at this great American university. Many of his contemporaries considered him at this time to be the world's greatest specialist in the discipline of the History of Religions. His works were translated then into a great number of languages and underwent reprintings such as no one would dream of today. The revelations regarding his dark Romanian past did not begin to appear until the end of the 1980s.[59]

Some simple themes dominate his work, forming an ensemble relating to a picture — so easy does it seem to imagine and visualize numerous picturesque scenes, even if fed by metaphysical fictions and implausible scenarios. Eliade clearly took from Otto the universal idea of the Holy that manifests itself in the form of hierophanies that people experience immediately, without need of intermediaries (clergy, church, education, ethics, etc.). But the Eliadean Holy distinguishes itself from Otto's model in the sense that, far from becoming rationalized and moralized during the course of its own internal evolution, it remains, in its primitive and vitalist acceptance, a synonym of life (as "a disguise worn by Being"),[60] fertility, and strength:

> For religious man, nature is never only 'natural'; it is always fraught with a religious value. This is easy to understand, for the cosmos is a divine creation; coming from the hands of the gods, the world is impregnated with sacredness. [...] [These gods] *manifested the different*

modalities of the sacred in the very structure of the world and of cosmic phenomena. [...] The cosmos as a whole is an organism at once *real, living,* and *sacred*; it simultaneously reveals the modalities of being and of sacrality. Ontophany [or: manifestation of Being] and hierophany [or: manifestation of the Holy] meet.[61]

Under these conditions, and since the ontological destiny of the cosmos depends on it, is it necessary to specify that the list of religions — archaic, especially — seems positive in Eliade's eyes? Of course, at the stratospheric level where he situates himself, their negative aspects, despite being well known to the victims of their intolerance and their excessive power, are seen as negligible.

Since the Eliadean Holy, as "reality *par excellence,*" is mixed up with nature and its rhythms, these latter find the energy capable of periodical regeneration in the sexual and/or bloody rituals celebrated in its honor. This involves quite a banal idea taken from nineteenth- and twentieth-century theoreticians of naturalist and agrarian myths (Mannhardt and Frazer, for example). Nevertheless, the archaic *homo religiosus* of Eliade displays none of the peaceful and sympathetic traits of the noble savage:

> The myths of the 'primitives' and the rituals that stem from them show us no archaic Arcadia. By assuming the responsibility for making the vegetable world prosper, the paleo-cultivators also accepted torturing victims for the benefit of crops, sexual orgies, cannibalism, headhunting. [...] To be sure, cruelty, torture, and murder are not forms of conduct peculiar only to 'primitives.' They are found throughout the course of History, sometimes to a paroxysmic degree never reached in the archaic societies. The difference lies primarily in the fact that, for primitives, this violent behaviour has a religious value and is imitated from transhuman models. This conception survived quite late into History; Genghis Khan's mass extermination, for example, still claimed to have a religious justification.[62]

This form of paganism, which is primitive, pantheistic, and stripped of all moral preoccupation, and which Eliade is not afraid of calling "cosmic Christianity," is found at the utmost extreme of any Christian ethic, which, quite curiously, has not impeded numerous Christian thinkers and theologians to lay claim to Eliade, as if the simple lyrical evocation of the Holy were enough to extinguish all critical thought: "On the other hand, the peasants, because of their own mode of existing in the Cosmos, were not attracted by a 'historical' and moral Christianity. The religious experience peculiar to the rural populations was nourished by what could be called a 'cosmic Christianity.' In other words, the peasants of Europe understood Christianity as a cosmic liturgy."[63]

Despite their perfect inadequacy, the most ordinary natural elements and phenomena (the moon, the sun, waters, trees, rocks) are promoted by Eliade to the dignity of manifestations of the Holy. And, as thus indisputable signs of a transcendent reality, they possess symbolic significance.[64] The process of decoding these symbols is the responsibility of a "creative hermeneutic," so-called by Eliade because it modifies the conscience of the person who devotes himself to it. Leaving the field of science for good, Eliade goes so far as to assign to the contemporary historian of religions the task of "transmuting his materials into spiritual messages." Thus, he will fulfill his "role in contemporary culture."[65] One must not doubt for an instant that, in this apology for the quasi-prophetic role attributed to the historian of religions, Eliade was singing the praises of his own person and his work — he who gladly compared his genius to that of Goethe,[66] but also, and in fact favorably, to that of Marx, Freud, Nietzsche, and Teilhard de Chardin.[67]

Where nineteenth-century science recognized primitive and savage men in our far-off ancestors, Eliade, with another spectacular reversal, would see in them, and in contemporary Romanian peasants, the privileged intermediaries of the Holy and the servants of what he calls Cosmic Religion. Eliade, faithful to his aversion to modernity, inverts the habitual codes and attributes to archaic and traditional societies those aptitudes that, under the influence of the Jews and Judaism, modern man, and Western man in particular, has lost forever. In fact, at the cost of an implausible scenario, Eliade affirms that the Jews invented linear history, the history that has a beginning point and will inevitably have an end. From this they have annihilated archaic metaphysics based, according to him, on the myth of the Eternal Return in the framework of a temporality that is subject to cosmic cycles recurring indefinitely.[68]

One will have understood by now that Eliade's *homo religiosus* is no Cistercian monk devoting his life to prayer, no benefactor of suffering humanity such as Abbé Pierre, no spiritual director in the way of Francis of Sales, but much more certainly either a peasant in permanent contact with the Holy of nature, or, on the contrary, a specialist in archaic techniques in ecstasy (yogi, shaman, bard). These two opposite figures of the Eliadean *homo religiosus* illustrate the elitist, antidemocratic sociopolitical convictions that Eliade expressed even before the War.[69] On the one hand, the aristocracy of "the specialists in ecstasy, the familiars of fantastic universes, who nourish, increase, and elaborate the traditional mythological motifs";[70] on the other, the organic, collective life of the masses who are subject to them. Democracy being at any rate in Eliade's view nothing but "a desperate attempt to find in the mass of ordinary people the qualities of a small number."[71]

In the same way, Eliade took from his predecessors the most precious idea of all, according to which the Holy, just as with religious phenomena in general, had no other reason or source than itself. In this sense, the expression *sui generis* applies to them ideally. Cardinal Julien Ries, who died in 2013, gave this synthetic commentary, or, rather, plea:

> In fact, if the religious phenomenon cannot be understood outside its cultural and socio-economic context, we must nevertheless know that religious experiences are not reducible to non-religious forms of behaviour. All religious phenomena must be grasped within its own modality. It will not be understood in its totality unless one goes beyond historical aspects with their different conditionings. Any religious fact constitutes a *sui generis* experience brought about by man's encounter with the sacred. From this we must focus on the symbolic side, the spiritual side, and the internal coherence of religious phenomena. Phenomenological steps try to understand the essence and structures of religious phenomena perceived both in their historical conditioning and in the optic of the behaviour of *homo religiosus*. What is at stake is the deepening of the articulations and meanings of this behaviour, by decoding religious facts in terms of man's experience in his attempt to transcend the temporal and make contact with ultimate Reality.[72]

Hering, Otto, van der Leeuw, and Eliade, restricting ourselves to this small representative group alone, definitively imagined different solutions to the same problem. In the face of the ten or so World Religions officially recognized by science at the turn of the twentieth century, how could one from that point on think in terms of a sole *religion*? That is — and here is the crux of the problem — how could one still justify the superiority of Christianity, and thus of the West, without returning to orthodox theological arguments that in this new context had hardly any veritable authority beyond their circle of the faithful? Hering, Otto, and van der Leeuw, as we have seen, revitalized the old Platonic notion of *eidos* or essence; they insisted on the specificity of irrational religious experiences and they reintroduced Christian notions into their scenarios in order to preserve *in fine* the essential difference: religion *versus* religions. And all of these men took great intellectual pains to elaborate, to this end, a new type of argumentation, breaking with traditional rhetoric. Eliade stands out at the heart of this group of Protestant thinkers. If he granted the same prestige as they do to religions and to the Holy, and if, like them, he defended their *sui generis* nature, it is evident that in his eyes, as in those of his pagan, pantheistic peasants, this religion could not be represented by the "historic and moral" Christianity of Mother Church.

Chapter Six

Major Criticisms

6.1 The End of the Essences

The phenomenologists of religion (Hering, Otto, van der Leeuw, and Eliade), as we have adopted the bad habit of calling them, nonetheless represent a coherent series of thinkers who, in spite of what distinguishes them, are in fact unanimous in affirming the absolute singularity and autonomy of religious facts. From the postwar years through the 1980s their theses dominated the North American field of Religious Studies.

The central place accorded by philosophical phenomenology to the essences — "religious" essences, among them — could not avoid giving ideas to certain historians of religions. Refusing to recognize the heterogeneity, impermanence, and lack of consistency of the phenomena referred to as "religious,"[1] they were tempted to substitute "essences," that is, transcendent, immutable entities that, following the image of Parmenides, were entirely self-referential (the Holy, Myth, the Orient, Hinduism, mysticism). This is the content of numerous essays whose theses were called into question by Critical Studies.[2] In effect, similar to recalling the *sui generis* argument, invoking essences is a way of transfiguring cultural objects by shielding them from the reign of history. This strategy has long been used to idealize several products of our European culture (Religion, Art, Literature, Myth, the Holy, for example). It is the reason we find identical rhetorical turns of phrase in texts speaking of religion, poetry, or art. In fact, idealization implies the employment of certain recurrent procedures, characterized by their emphasis, their chosen lexicon (not at all trivial), and, quite clearly, the hostility of their topic to any materialistic argument.

Just as with the criticisms aimed at the essences, those addressed to the works of (to be brief) *phenomenologists* were definitive, and most of the time without appeal. If one had to summarize in a word the reasons for this condemnation, it would be enough to say that they reproached the phenomenology of religion for being, in effect, a crypto-theology. It is indisputable that the positions adopted by these sycophants of religion always end (or start) by distorting their judgments in its favor. They are thus rendered incapable of adopting the impartial, detached point of view required by science.[3] According to the authors of these critiques, the latter are not so much targeting individual errors; rather, they are taking aim at serious *a prioris* that are contrary to the methods and principles of the human sciences, or, in other words, the proper deployment of scientific principles when studying the role and functioning of beliefs and superstitions of such and such a human group. By contrast, they cast that role aside by disclosing that they possess competences allowing them to affirm, in the way of theologians, that the objects corresponding to these beliefs (God, the Holy, the essence of redemption, etc.) in fact exist. Paraphrasing Gregory Alles ("How does he know?"),[4] one is tempted to ask, "How do they know?", for describing the functions, personality, and rituals attached to a certain divinity in a certain culture is an intellectual activity that does not, and will never, allow the affirmation that the divinity exists. In his major work, *The Ideology of Religious Studies*,[5] Fitzgerald remarks with great perspicacity that the phenomenology elaborated around the Holy definitively proposes a sort of "ecumenical theology". Although a typically Western product, it presents itself in effect as the converging point of all religions (and not just of Christian Churches), since all of them, even if they are unaware of it, which is frequently the case, are considered to be expressions of what is in fact *our* indigenous Holiness, a notion that is born with this new aura and, as we have seen, in the workshop of Protestant theologians. At the outside, and even better than the Holy, it is the simple idea of religion that claims to unite all religions under its name, in a non-sectarian manner. The disturbing dimension of religious pluralism is minimized, in the sense that it has been replaced by a universal and eternal essence conceived from the model of *religion*. Once again, we cannot for a moment imagine that these Western thinkers, (crypto-) theologians in fact, could have attributed this essence to a notion borrowed from Indian—or, worse, African—cultures. This particularly twisted mechanism is summarized by Fitzgerald in the aptly devised expression "The Modern Myth of Religion". But who cannot see that, even under this apparently tolerant form, this ecumenism is another way for the West, with its conception of transcendence, to impose a model — in fact, *its* model — for all religions? In the hands of the West, ecumenism (which is in any case another Western invention) is giving up none of the earlier pretentions of the Christian religion. The universal, as with ecumenism and pluralism, is accepted on the condition that it be conceived under *its*, that is to say *our*, indigenous norms.

Let us remain for a moment in this political register and look to Ivan Strenski, who allows us to find Eliade again, summarizing all the opinions rejected by Critical Studies. Strenski was no doubt the first, in 1987, to propose a "decoding" (employing the religious prose of Eliade) of the euphemized transposition of political themes that would have been imprudent for the Romanian scholar to defend after the War.[6] This was a subversive act and a break with the recent epistemological past. Up to then, a political explanation of the Eliadean religious, *a fortiori* polemic was difficult to conceive and contrary to academic usage; the religious had to be explained by the religious alone, and this virtuous circle could not be broken by any means. According to Strenski, the condemnations of the modern world — democratic, secular, and materialist, uttered in the name of a "cosmic Christianity" — took up, transposed, and transfigured elements of the program of the pre-war traditionalist Romanian Right, the rural and anti-Semitic Right whose prejudices Eliade had shared. In addition, the mythico-religious orientation of Orthodox Romanian Christianity, as well as the *völkisch* feelings of this same Right, served as a foundation for his vision of the archaic religious worlds. In his eyes, they were distinguished by their elitist, cosmic, and telluric nature.

From 1976, John A. Saliba,[7] with an anthropologist's point of view, had launched a certain number of severe criticisms toward Eliade's work, confirming the presence of inexcusable methodological weaknesses and errors. But that was the price Eliade had to pay to isolate his timeless essences from any historical influence. The point of view of *homo religiosus* defended by Eliade was one that should have kindled the interest of anthropologists. How could a theory of religious man contradict to such a point the least contestable givens of the academic discipline that is *par excellence* the science of man, other than to say that this *homo religiosus* is but a poetic fiction?

As with many, Saliba reproached Eliade less for his indifference to contexts (political, social, institutional, etc.) than for his hostile approach to any contextualization of religious phenomena, as if the latter did not belong to the world of men. In doing this, Eliade offers himself the possibility of saying practically anything, since the facts that could contradict him are *a priori* disqualified. In effect, the contexts only bear any intelligibility if they are taken into account and analyzed. Eliade refuses to accord the least attention to these contexts, which for him cannot furnish any valuable explanation for religious phenomena.

Saliba then reproaches him for his dangerous, imprecise or erroneous generalizations. He raises, among the most significant, the point that the sacred-profane opposition is not universal; that myths that (as all things) change over time are polysemic and multifunctional; that symbols do not exist only in religions (and, inversely, that there is more in religions than the symbolic); and that the universal conception of cyclical time in the primitives, as well as their supposed terror of history, have difficulty finding confirmation in ethnographic literature. In this respect, Saliba, contrary to Eliade, emphasizes that Christian time is cyclical (indefinite, recommended repetition of the events marking the liturgical year) and that, if Judeo-Christianity has invented a historical time, it is possible to say as much for China.

Saliba also notes that the treatment to which Eliade submits his sources often reveals itself as approximate or arbitrary. In the same way, his taste for hermeneutics makes him forget that interpretation (of an image, a symbol, etc.) is not the same as explanation. And to finish, Saliba remarks that most cultures seek, often courageously, to accommodate to this world, to live in it whatever the cost, and not to escape it.

We must still add to this negative list, whose conclusions are shared by all serious specialists, those criticisms that have been aimed at principal themes that are specifically "religious" — those upon which Eliade built his work as polygraph and visionary.

The most important of these, and without doubt the most precious for his framework, is his *sui generis* conception of religious phenomena, to which he returned dozens and dozens of times. He is not the author of this, no more than he was of the notion of the Holy. But he often neglected to cite his sources, especially when they concerned "borrowings" related to central points of his theory. To stick with specialists of religion, the expression *sui generis* had already been found in Otto,[8] Scheler[9] and Hering.[10] In the last of these three, the expression had given rise to a very elaborate theory that would in fact be taken up later by Eliadean religionists, but often with less sophistication.

It was McCutcheon who developed the more systematic critique of this notion that became entirely central, both for Eliade and for the field of Religious Studies, by recalling first of all that its use represented quite a useful strategy, both discursive and political. In fact, it brackets the facts as well as the researcher, and thus looks to shelter them from all minute critical examination, since phenomenologists and religionists have decreed *a priori* that religion alone could explain the religious.[11] In *The Discipline of Religion*,[12] McCutcheon returned to this subject and profits from it to denounce as antiscientific what one must call the inestimable advantages of this thesis. It first of all accords an absolute autonomy to "religious" facts, which comes back to the *a priori* exclusion of all questions relative to social and political contexts. It also demands that, in their place, specific interpretive methods should be employed, since their task is to decode "deep" meanings.[13] It is here that hermeneutics enters. This scholarly term signifies the sacrifice of austere research into rational and often sociopolitical explanations that would give no credulous person pause. Moreover, considering their importance, such studies require dedicated space and independent, specialized institutions. And the specialists who teach there, given their importance and the great value of their studies, deserve no less than freedom of expression and opinion concerning social states of affairs. Here, we find the ambition Eliade dreamed of for himself and his disciples in the History of Religions as he conceived it: to become mentors of the contemporary world, since only they knew how to reveal its ontic destiny.

Nevertheless, a disturbing question persists: how could this heavy metaphysical fable, which is built on unverifiable *a prioris* and nourished on cavalier generalizations and crude approximations, which is so defective, and which is dedicated to the Holy but to such an extent devoid of moral reference, seduce not only a wide public but also important and responsible academics and "religious persons" the world over? The answers to this question doubtless depend to a large extent on the form that Critical Studies would take in the future—and not just in the United States. The example of Eliade confirms, in its way, that the work of analysis and criticism must be as complete as possible. It must take into account the ensemble of factors — be they rhetorical, historical, or ideological — that are found at the base of a work. And one must especially avoid being misled by a certain ideological influence that would like to forbid certain inquiry or directions of research, considering them sacrilegious or too prosaic. It is thus that, among the number of the above factors, we find all of the political questions relative to games of power. This dimension has fortunately been taken into account by several recent critics (Strenski, King, Fitzgerald, Chidester, McCutcheon, Wiebe, and myself), whereas the History of Religions often appears to wish to ignore it. It is true that to situate power in the center of its preoccupations is probably the best way to show that power is also present at the heart of religions, and that, in this regard, whatever the thurifers (literal and figurative) say, religions are no different from so many other human creations whose destiny belongs well and truly to the world around us.

6.2 Readers and Textbooks

The general impression that emerges from the preceding chapters is confirmed by recent analyses of the "World Religions Textbooks"[14] used by students in the United States. Given the considerable number of these students, it was inevitable that people would produce editions for them — the famous readers, textbooks, companions, introductions, and guides that characterize the system of American higher education. But in avoiding making students aware of the works *in extenso,* in reducing the said works to their conceptual skeleton and to a few chosen pieces, does this not contribute to a false and lazy image of the intellectual endeavor? By exhibiting these skeletons, they are offering for criticism a denuded version of the dominant discourse, reduced to its essentials. In this way, we see valuable witnesses to the concepts that reign on campus.

In 2005, the *Religious Studies Review* published a voluminous double issue, to which twelve authors contributed.[15] Its aim was to assess the scientific value of several textbooks. The question asked of the contributors was the following: do current textbooks offer a useful introduction to the study of World Religions, respecting their richness, identity, and diversity? The expression "World Religions" is not devoid of ambiguity for it does not designate universal religions, since those eligible would be only Christianity, Islam, and Buddhism, as they alone address themselves to all people. Nor does it designate all of the world's religions (many unknown or ignored), nor only the "great" religions, since Jainism, Sikhism, and Zoroastrianism, today only involving small human communities, still belong. Here, too, a certain historical arbitrariness has presided over these choices, which is impossible to justify from a scientific point of view. We will come back to this shortly. It is nevertheless important to specify that we are speaking of textbooks primarily intended for undergraduate students, which have to respond to the insane challenge of presenting these World Religions over fifteen course sessions.[16] Under these conditions, it is very difficult to give anything other than general introductions and to spout stereotypes maintained in the dominant discourse. It is no doubt more difficult still to enter into delicate theoretical debate. But that takes nothing away from their ideological influence, especially if this influence carries with it the regnant *a prioris* in the surrounding society and culture. The analyses that followed displayed a certain number of general traits common to most of these textbooks. Globally, we find there the theoretical prejudices and weaknesses associated with the notion of religion when one wants to give it the role of universal anthropological reference. The word "ethnocentrism" summarizes most of these prejudices very well.

The most unjust no doubt consists in using the Christian model as a unique reference for all cultures, implicitly or not, and immediately to add that these cultures do not respect the model (often implied, either because the cultures are located in a far removed past or because they are incapable of raising themselves up to the Christian level). As Deborah Sommer notes with humor,[17] Chinese religions always lack something essential to being a religion worthy of the (Christian) name. To remark, for example, that a religion has neither an eschatology nor a concept of the Last Judgment is always an indirect way of saying that it is situated in the lowest zone of human religiosity, which is immediately understood by the interlocutor who indeed shares this prejudice, since it is embedded since childhood in the Christian education he or she has received.

The inequalities of treatment in these textbooks are numerous, and there is never any attempt to justify them. Kay Read,[18] taking the figures from a 2001 survey by the AAR, thus notes that, among the American and Canadian programs devoted to religions, 95.9% offer

Christianity; 30% Judaism; 25.8% Islam; 21.1% Hinduism, Jainism, and Sikhism; 16.6% Confucianism and Taoism; and, finally, 14% indigenous religions. Read adds that one must remember that these worlds considered "indigenous" represent about two-thirds of the globe (the Americas, Africa, the South Pacific, and the sub-polar regions). More curiously, this ensemble is artificial, for it groups cultures that have not the slightest characteristic in common except for being as exotic and primitive as possible in Western eyes. Or, making a quick tour of the world, from the Baruya of New Guinea to the Buryat shamans, by way of the Aztec descendants in Mexico and the Nuba peoples of Sudan. Nothing allows us now to refer to such heterogeneity by the vague term "indigenous religions," despite the claims of those who present religion as a fundamental human characteristic. Furthermore, the problem is disposed of by creating a marginal grab-bag category which, from a scientific point of view, is devoid of all convincing justification.

The model of (Christian) religion shows up again, if implicitly, when confronted with traditions that distance themselves indisputably. Not being able to account for them satisfactorily, the simplest solution seems to have consisted, in this case, of ignoring them. That is what Selva J. Raj notes in her essay devoted to religions of the Indian subcontinent.[19] It is quite clear that Buddhism and Hinduism are always privileged. Jainism and Sikhism, if still retained, occupy a secondary place, but it is true (if the demographic argument has any meaning here) that they only represent 0.4% and 1.9%, respectively, of the Indian population. But the Hinduism that has held out is not at all the entirety of Hinduism — far from it. The Hinduism that is recognized is that of the cultivated elites and the great Sanskrit texts, at the expense of the Hinduism of the masses (the influence exercised by the nineteenth-century British would be seen later, in the invention and installation of this scholarly, refined, and Westernized Hinduism). The syncretisms (synonymous with impurity), popular cults, bloody and noisy rituals, minority or marginal traditions, and possessions are all sacrificed. The same can be said for Indian Islam and Christianity: although they alone represent tens of millions of faithful, they are forgotten (from this last case, one can see that the demographic argument is not always determinant). Doubtless, the exotic Indian Christianity does not conform to the image Westerners can make of Christian religion, especially when, as good disciples of Max Weber, they have been influenced by the Protestant ethic and way of life. In a general way, when it comes to accounting for foreign practices, contemplation, examination of conscience, and silent prayer are quiet clearly preferred (yet, once again, tacitly) to public demonstrations, spectacular manifestations, and magic-type superstitions. At the same time, the dogmas defined and affirmed in the scholarly texts are favorably retained, and one gladly forgets that these dogmas in the far past have quite often been the object of compromise, synthesis, and negotiation without end. In a word, the underlying axiological point of view is never very far off, whereas these textbooks should at least take account of human reality in all its diversity and complexity. That is the reason Raj had introduced her contribution by remarking that she has never found, to this day, a single textbook that presents the ensemble of traditions of the Indian subcontinent in a balanced way. It is possible to add that the traditions from the vast ensemble formed by Indonesia and Malaysia (in which aboriginal traditions, the influence of Hinduism and of Islam, without forgetting the weight of Western acculturation, are telescoped) represent another challenge that no textbook has dared to take on. Thus, we see the sketching of a map with great blank areas not covered in these textbooks.

No doubt sharing these same preoccupations, Sommer notes that, in spite of their great antiquity and the fairly large populations involved with them, the part within these textbooks accorded to Chinese traditions represents but a small fraction of what reverted to the "upstart Mediterranean cult"—that is, Christianity.[20] And she adds, quite correctly, that these works are much more robust when dealing with the "centre of the world"—that is, with the Abrahamic traditions that spread throughout the perimeters of the Mediterranean—and that, on the contrary, they are less and less eloquent as they move away from there, to the point of becoming practically dumb once they arrive at the shores of the Pacific. Once again, we see here how studies on religion(s) reinforce, in their way, the representations of the world that are centered on the (Christian) West; what is familiar and similar is much more favorably studied than what is far off and foreign. And, with not a little irony, Sommer adds that it is no shock that the AAR Congress of 2003 was held at Disneyland, since once leaving that Magic Kingdom, one landed in yet another enchanted world: the Magic Kingdom of religions. Distinct from Chinese religions, Buddhism receives more equitable and also more favorable treatment.[21] Since the end of the nineteenth century, it is true that, in the West, Buddhism, albeit a scholarly and erudite Buddhism of the cultivated elite, has enjoyed rather benevolent treatment.

Beyond the inevitable factual errors, faults in translation, incomplete information, poorly chosen sources, and badly justified editorial preferences, one finds in these textbooks some unacceptable omissions, which happens with this sort of synthesizing text designed for broad readership. The theoretical questions (for example, arising in Critical Studies) and the debates they could provoke are consistently absent. In addition, the comparative perspectives to which this kind of work could easily lend itself, dealing as it does with a great number of traditions concurrently, are neither explored nor exploited.

If the treatment of the "great" Oriental religions is often unjust or inexact, that of minor religions—outside the Big Six (Christianity, Judaism, Islam, Hinduism, Buddhism and the "East Asian traditions" of China and Japan)—accumulates in addition a large number of prejudices, especially concerning Africa.[22] Robert Baum distinguishes three separate treatments that applied to African religions in the 32 textbooks he analyzed. Of these, 20% simply and completely neglect the continent; 40% give it a special entry; and 40% include it in a chapter devoted to indigenous religions, which, following an old prejudice of the nineteenth century, are seen together with … prehistoric religions. Contemporary indigenous peoples, according to this prejudice, are their closest relatives, as both groups in particular have no knowledge of writing. The presentation of the African religions also reappropriates the other great prejudice of the nineteenth century, the one relative to the evolutionist concept of religions, which, as we have already noted, always amounts to placing Christian religions at the top and as the endpoint of this evolution. The religions of illiterate peoples are located exactly at the polar opposite of this summit, since the lack of writing means the absence of sacred texts. The presence of a corpus of sacred texts is, in the eyes of Westerners, one of the indisputable criteria for recognizing superior religions. In this regard, one must not forget that, if Western culture, particularly that of the Church, possesses proven methods to interpret texts from antiquity onwards, it is, in contrast, rather poorly stocked when confronted with loud rituals that bring in music, dance, and possession. Under these conditions, the condemnation of these rituals was inevitable.

Baum underlines another misleading failing of these textbooks: that of essentializing African cultures, which in this case does not at all mean idealizing them. The example cited by Baum offers a new illustration of how this functions. When an author speaks of African religion and not of African religions, he invites this reproach. In fact, he allows one to think that there is a simple prototype unique to all African religions, whereas this abstract religion is usually just a synthesis of the prejudices that have accompanied African religions in the Western (con)science, sometimes for a long time.

From the analysis of simple school texts, we see it is possible to find and extract some of the deep structures of ideology that underlie the study of religions in the United States. Identical thought processes found in these simple textbooks are also found in the greater theoretical works produced by the most renowned scholars. It is such dominant structures that constitute the fundamental paradigms of a culture. This is the reason they can seem so familiar, for in addition to this they are mutually translatable and the objects of inexhaustible paraphrase. But perhaps this is the price that must be paid, repetition after repetition, so that individuals arrive at recognizing each other within their culture.

The presentation of Christianities and, to a lesser extent, of Judaism, obey conditions that are noticeably different: the texts and the corresponding courses are intended for students who have received a religious education in the family setting. In this case, texts, professors, and students speak the same language, as they belong to the same culture. The proximity and familiarity are immediate, and everyone understands each other. And problems of translation, which are always a hindrance, do not manifest themselves. But this peaceful image must not make one forget that this transparency is frequently an illusion: if the fact of speaking the same language facilitates communication, it also frequently keeps all speakers in the same error and illusion.

The situation is less comfortable with Islam. This third Abrahamic monotheism does not enjoy the same status or consideration, as we have already noted.[23] It is not placed on the same footing as the two others, according to Khaled Keshk.[24] For him, three characteristics again take up negative stereotypes: the name of Allah; the prophetic role played by Mahomet, which seems so little to conform to its biblical models; and the inferior status of women in Islam. The first point is completely revealing. In these textbooks, the god of the Muslims is not called God but Allah. This is enough, according to Keshk, to break the original unity of the three monotheisms and make of Islam a religion that is more ethnic than universal.

On the Christian use of the convention that for Christians consists of calling their divinity God, one would naturally refer to Thomas Aquinas (*Summa theologiae*, section 1, question 3, article 1).[25] On this sensitive point, approaches remain for the majority under the influence of theological discourse and have not manifestly been secularized. The progression does not at all follow the same path when one is interested in a Hindu or Aztec divinity, concerning whom the question of their existence (and thus the respect they are due) is not even asked. For his part, McCutcheon asks about the frequent use of the word "God" to designate, despite their differences, the god of Christians, that of Jews, and (much less frequently) that of Muslims.[26] He sees there another manifestation of the imperialist attitude that consists in erasing the differences in order to let it be understood that the Christian, thus Western, usage reflects a universal tendency. He asks quite correctly what the reaction of Catholics would be if they were told their god would be called, indifferently, Brahma or Vishnu.

Beyond these questions, raised by unequal treatment, approximate or incorrect translation, ethnocentric prejudice, stereotypes,[27] and errors of perspective, other much more disturbing weaknesses have been discovered. The most insidious, because it is the least explicit, consisted in the construction of all presentations on the same level and using the same categories (founders, sacred text, beliefs, major dogmas, ritual, and solemn practices).[28] Now, if they are suitable for the Christianities that inspired them, they are not adaptable to most other cases. But in acting as if each of these "religions," as with Christianity, tends toward fundamental unity and homogeneity, the authors of these presentations are not just ascribing more to Christianities than they deserve; for all other cases they are making a travesty of reality. In this, they are relying on a homogenous model of religion elaborated by theologians who have always looked to minimize or silence the turbulent beginnings of Christianity, confirmed by the continued favorable citations, by some people, of Tillich, Otto, or Eliade.[29] One can only say of these citations that they do not represent an innovative form of critical and theoretical modernity. But it is true that this theoretical and reflective dimension, which constitutes the value of contemporary Critical Studies, is missing from these monographs. Students cannot imagine, based on these latter monographs, the extent to which this field of study provides the framework for lively controversy that is capable of reconsidering several principles of the History of Religions found themselves at the base of the very textbooks they have in front of them.

The lack of historical depth is another major fault in these monographs. For example, how can one present Buddhism without first recalling the scholarly history of Buddhist studies in the West that contributed towards making it what it is today? And, even more generally, how can one present religions (such as Hinduism or Shintoism) without mentioning the fact that they are recent historical constructions, and that their study has a history itself?

In suppressing the multiple historical dimensions, the critical studies, the lively contemporary controversies, and the problems emanating from different colonial situations,[30] and instead adopting a uniform plan of Christian inspiration applied uniformly to all cultures, one arrives more or less happily at the creation of a reassuring image, "objective and neutral," says Mark MacWilliams, of World Religions. But one may ask oneself, with MacWilliams, if under these conditions this image is still of great interest today as a descriptive and comparative category,[31] especially if, as McCutcheon says at the end of the review's issue,[32] religion is nothing but a "historical accident" that we have become accustomed to.

Chapter Seven

Major Contributions

7.1 Colonialism and Cultural Imperialism

At the end of Chapter Three, we left the nineteenth century before addressing a theme that is fundamental for that era and for the history of the History of Religions in general. The treatment of this theme is relatively recent, and has seen several Anglo-Saxon representatives of Critical Studies (King, Fitzgerald, Chidester, McCutcheon, etc.). The present section, Colonialism and Cultural Imperialism, quite logically precedes section two, which is devoted to The Invention of Religions.

"The Civilizing Work of the West"

This title is evidently ironic, since it takes up and summarizes the justification, used frequently by Europeans with political authority, for their vast colonial enterprise when, in fact, it gave rise to so much spoliation, servitude, and massacre. "[A] practice of permanent violence" destined "to maintain metropolitan domination over colonial spaces and a non-egalitarian structure between whites and colonists" was indeed the common denominator of their politics of conquest and annexation.[1] The horizon of Catholics and Protestants would doubtless have remained European if, following upon their great discoveries, the European colonial enterprise had not taken off again in the nineteenth century, considerably extending its empire — principally in Africa, the Indian subcontinent, Oceania, and the Far East. The close collaboration linking the policy of conquest and the missionary enterprise is indisputable, both on the Protestant and Evangelical side (300 missionary societies in around 1900)[2] and on the Catholic side. In France, many dozens of societies, for men and for women, came into existence during the course of the nineteenth century. And in these far-off lands, the secularism, which was the object of such cutting debate in the French metropolis, was scarcely transformed into any such subject of polemics.[3]

The same conquering optimism and the same desire for close collaboration reign on the side of the highest authorities of the Catholic Church, since "the missions are the indispensable auxiliary of any fruitful colonial policy."[4] This connivance plunges its roots into the common and immediate interest that brings together the political authorities, anxious to extend their conquests and the frontiers of their new empire, and the Catholic and Protestant Churches, impatient to take up an evangelization of souls that had slowed down considerably over the previous century.[5] In both cases, the rivalry that existed between the great colonial powers (headed up by France and Great Britain) fed this élan.

But beyond these rivalries (political, religious, economic, military), let us not forget that all of these actors (political and religious authorities, entrepreneurs, military, intellectuals) shared the same hierarchical conception of the rapport that should regulate the relations between the "races" considered superior and those considered inferior. What brought them together then was just as strong as the rivalry that kept them apart in far-off, exotic lands. During the Berlin Conference, which took place from November 1884 to February 1885, the great European powers defined the rules that fixed the occupation and sharing of Africa. At this same time, most contemporaries (Victor Hugo, Jules Ferry, and, later, Leon Blum) shared this same sentiment (with some rare exceptions, for example Georges Clemenceau), expressed by one or the other unreservedly. The judgment of Ernest Renan has remained sadly famous, but it has the merit of being devoid of ambiguity:

> The conquest of a country of inferior race by a superior race that has established itself there to govern has nothing shocking about it. [...] As much as conquests between equal races should be frowned upon, just as much is the regeneration of inferior or bastardized races in the providential order of humanity.[6]

And these are not the least of the paradoxes confronting republican France, the Land of Human Rights. Superiority of the white race was so evident and indisputable in the eyes of these men of the nineteenth century that they felt no compulsion to ask themselves about the "universal" rights that colonized people merited as human beings, nor about the use of violence to which the colonized had fallen victim. Unqualified excesses were not rare. Belgians, British, Germans, and French rivaled each other equally in this area, mercilessly following the adage "The end justifies the means."[7] At the beginning of the following century, the German General Lothar von Trotha would apply this sort of program literally by proceeding with the genocidal massacre of the Herero (1904–1911) in the southwest of Africa. Indeed, in *Heart of Darkness* (Joseph Conrad), the colonial shadows of the Congo, the other great massacre of innumerable native victims was perpetrated, under the authority of King Leopold II of Belgium.

And this is where the History of Religions enters, in a way that was no doubt unexpected, since one could truly ask oneself *a priori* what this respectable and peaceful academic discipline, better designed for the dust of libraries than for the fields of battle, is doing coming to this sickening field where one finds, side by side, ceaseless hypocrisy, violence, and the most cynical inhumanity. This working hypothesis, I admit, is a bit surprising, as it contradicts an implicit and sluggish division of labor according to which the erudite study of religions has *a priori* nothing to do with the violence of colonial conquest. But the division of knowledge also has its tacit *a prioris*; thus, it is still too often admitted that the History of Religions only treats subjects that are spiritual and lofty, quite far from, for example, the mercantile and inhuman colonial enterprises. That is the reason that this naive question leads to one of the most astonishing chapters of the history of this discipline—a discipline that has very little innocence about it, and is not all inoffensive, despite appearances.

"Cognitive Imperialism" and "Epistemic Violence"

In the last few years, several Anglo-Saxon historians who belong to the wave of Critical Studies have associated closely (as I have myself done in *The Western Construction of Religion* and in *Religion and Magic*)[8] the policy of conquest (particularly as followed in France and Great Britain), the establishment and administration of vast colonial empires, missionary activity, and the role played by the History of Religions.[9] For my part, I saw more than simple coincidence in the fact that, in the second half of the nineteenth century, the countries of birth of the founding fathers and the first institutions of this discipline (Great Britain, the Netherlands, France, Belgium) were also those that were at the head of this vast colonial enterprise during the same era. For Chidester, specializing in South Africa, the Comparative History of Religions is indissociable from the relations of power that associated the imperial capitals with the colonized periphery. But he deplores, as do many, the fact that a strictly "religious" approach too often contributes to hiding these realities and especially to fundamental collusion. Or, in other words, the explanation furnished by religion does not explain everything it does, nor everything done in its name. In fact, the discourse that it holds, even concerning itself, always minimizes its numerous parallel influences — political and social, among others. And it is at this precise point that the analysis of the ideological functions of religious mythologies enters in. It allows us in a way to proceed to a complete reversal, which re-establishes the truth of its role.

What are we talking about here? What role? To take only one example: what ties did the establishment of the critical edition by Max Müller of the *Rigveda* foster with the British domination in the Indian subcontinent? These links do not seem evident at all, *a priori*, unless one remembers that the erudite enterprise of Max Müller received the financial support of the East India Company, as Chidester recalls.[10] History does not shy away from the most unexpected detours and mediations.

Once again, we have a case where we see the nascent History of Religions definitively in the service of European colonial politics. It concerns no more and no less than a weapon of ideology and propaganda, all the more redoubtable and efficacious since religion still occupied, at that same time, a central, indeed hegemonic, position in European cultures. Mediations were necessary to connect the scholarly workshop to the activity of missionary or military personnel gone astray in the middle of southern Africa or Australia. But when the scholar declares that superior races exist who are made to command the inferior races (demonstrated, in their view, by their primitive culture and the savagery of their cults), and that the former have a duty to civilize the latter, then this constitutes an intellectual and moral warning to those who are politically responsible for deciding on the conquest of this or that territory — territory where their missionaries and military hurry in, who in turn will research the land and inform the scholars.[11] Thus, via these successive mediations, the History of Religions found itself, on the one hand, close to the center — that is, to the metropolitan organs of power — and, on the other hand, in contact with peripheral cultures that were still badly known but preceded by solid, unfavorable prejudices. It comes back to the duty of the History of Religions to reduce the extraordinary diversity of the above, to present it as something uniform by first of all following structures that are very simple and familiar to all Western consciences (superior/inferior; civilized/primitive; cultivated/savage; man/animal; religion/idolatry, etc.). In this way, they are rendered thinkable, which is a necessary condition for their integration into the discourses at the foundation of the Western conception of the world. Knowledge(s) and power(s) are the two complementary and indissociable sides of this process. That is the reason Chidester, for example, does not hesitate to qualify the comparative study of religions of this era as an "imperial science,"[12] for it was the irreplaceable auxiliary of this politics of conquest. On the same page of his work, Chidester evokes the hypothesis of a triple mediation (native, colonial, and imperial). The first of these concerns the negotiations undergone locally between ancestral, indigenous traditions and, for example, Christian missions. In the second case, intermediaries between the center and the periphery — that is, the local experts (missionaries, administrators, travelers, and so on) — supply the reports at the metropolitan decision-center concerning native life. In the third case we have the ideological synthesis of imperial theory. It will later translate itself, on site, via the policy followed with regard to the natives. In a neighboring and contemporary register, the phenomenon of human zoos also supposes, in preparation, the intellectual work that will transform the raw ethnographical givens into "scholarly" discourse meant to justify the inferiority of the other (whatever its name may be: black, savage, primitive, etc.).[13] By the ideas it provides, the study of indigenous religions feeds this hermeneutic circle. In the course of this, the information gathered locally is transformed into ideological arguments that then serve to justify the policy carried out on site.

The need to define more precisely what is (or are) religion(s) has evolved in parallel to these vast monuments of annexation and occupation. During this process, the discipline itself is enriched by "givens" of all nature that oblige it to refine its concepts. The crude categories of analysis of the beginning of the nineteenth century were no longer suitable in the face of realities as rich, for example, as those discovered in the immense Indian subcontinent.[14] Beyond this immediate advantage, the other considerable result, and the least contestable, is clear: imposing overall the notion of religion as unique norm (an ambition that Christianity had no difficulty adopting as its own, since it had for centuries already considered itself the only true *religion* of the only true god), as transhistoric,[15] and as universal, while simultaneously evaluating the others in terms of this norm. This attitude joins and explains the extremely tendentious elaboration of the classification systems of religions that we have come across previously. Next to these classification systems, the absence of religion is concerning people located outside of humanity, and thus close to animals. From the point of view of Westerners this situation authorized them to take hold of their lives and their lands.[16] That means, first and foremost, that religion becomes, if not unique, at any rate the criterion *par excellence* for humanity; and second, that the West appropriates for itself the exorbitant privilege of saying who deserves to be called human. And this it does on the basis of one of its most indigenous notions! Religion thus becomes one of the decisive criteria, allowing for a hierarchy of men (in fact, a confirmation of this hierarchy…) and, in a rather twisted way, for a legitimation of their servitude and their exploitation. Need one recall that no one in the West has ever thought to make use of an originally Chinese or Indian notion to characterize man in terms of what humanity has as its most typical or most admirable? The terms borrowed from foreign cultures, such as "taboo," "totem," "shaman," or "*mana*," have only ever served to designate cultural levels considered primitive by the West. Thus, through the bias of religion, the fundamental asymmetrical[17] relation between superior and inferior races becomes perpetuated and justified in contemporary eyes. If history does not neglect detours, it also unreservedly embraces vicious circles.

I must mention two other benefits of this "cognitive imperialism," this "rhetoric of domination," and this "epistemic violence."[18] Their least questionable outcome is to force others to adopt our norm and finally to think of themselves in terms of this foreign norm. This is the smoothest example of cultural imperialism, since those dominated are led to think of themselves and of their own identities as being in categories (which, for them, are artificial) that have been imposed by their masters. Some of those dominated, nonetheless, would no doubt succeed in this beyond what the Europeans had imagined, as we will see. By an amusing reversal of perspective, and by an entirely unforeseen process of recycling,[19] certain native elites, particularly in India, knew how to make use of the same categories in order to turn them to their own advantage, for with religion, the Europeans equally exported cultural identity, democracy, nationalism (etc.), which became weapons in the hands of the native elite. Indeed, some of them had been formed by the missionaries and their schools! Pushing the process of assimilation to quite an extreme, some of them in fact had no problem replacing their former masters after the independence of their country.[20]

Making religion *de facto* a transversal and transcultural criterion, and not uniquely "religious," *stricto sensu*, allows for the alignment (vertical or hierarchical, that is) of all other cultures according to this criterion. While this is quite familiar for Westerners, for other cultures the criterion is entirely exotic, being *a priori* foreign to their own categories. In this way, a new type of domination is added to the political, military, and economic, which is both cultural and ideological. In imposing on every continent the idea of religion, a valid criterion is defined universally — a *sine qua non* for the West's ability to envisage a domination that is just as universal. It would be abundantly facilitated by the fact that the West alone held the codes and the keys. Was this uniformization (which one might call "globalization" today) inevitable? If the powers of the great imperialisms nourish themselves on dreams of unlimited domination, then one can probably answer in the affirmative.[21]

To arrive at this result, it was first necessary for the Christian West to invent other religions, to a certain degree, for it only recognized four at the beginning of the nineteenth century. This policy of acculturation and assimilation would culminate in the invention of the Oriental religions (of India, China, Japan), an invention that would inscribe itself in the even wider picture of World Religions. Having attained this ultimate point, it is the idea of religion itself that would become *catholicus*. And we are talking about a non-negligible gain, for beneath or with the idea of religion, all political, economic, imperialist, or other strategies will be able to engulf themselves, demanding for their unlimited development an extended space the size of a homogeneous world, uniformly subject to the same rules and the same laws. It is thus not forbidden to think that, from the nineteenth century, the History of Religions has played a non-negligible role in the installation of today's globalization.

7.2 *The Invention of Religions*

The complex movement that responds to the above title can be summarized in three stages. The first stage corresponds to the invention of *religio(n)* in the Christian West and the indisputable hegemony that, thanks to the latter, the Church exerted on minds and their collective intellectual production for many centuries. This corresponds to Chapter One of this book (Christian Culture and the History of Religions). The next two stages that we will now discover (the Invention of Oriental Religions and the Invention of World Religions) are much better known to us today, thanks to the decisive and pioneering contributions of King, Fitzgerald, Balagangadhara, Chidester, Oddie, and Masuzawa. King and Fitzgerald teach in the United Kingdom, Balagangadhara in Belgium, Chidester in South Africa, Oddie in Australia, and Masuzawa in the United States.

The invention of Oriental religions in the nineteenth century is more than contemporary with the colonial politics of the great Western powers that we have just examined. In fact, these religions, five in number (Hinduism, Buddhism, Jainism, Sikhism, and Zoroastrianism, although the latter was originally from Iran) were issued from the Indian subcontinent that, at the time, was part of the British Empire. The three others (Shinto on the one hand and Taoism and Confucianism on the other) represent Japan and China, respectively.[22] We will see in a moment that Japan represents an entirely original case, since to some extent it deliberately invented a religion for itself conceived on the Western model. This second stage itself led to the third, the invention of World Religions, at the end of the nineteenth century. The eight that we have just enumerated were then added to the three Abrahamic monotheisms (Christianity, Judaism, and Islam). Ten of them (Hinduism, Buddhism, Jainism, Zoroastrianism, Taoism, Confucianism, Shinto, Judaism, Islam, and Christianity) were recognized at the World's Parliament of Religions[23] held in Chicago in 1893. The only religion missing, to make the list current, is Sikhism. Let us note as well, to take the measure of the evolutions that occurred in the course of the nineteenth century, as rapid as they were profound, that the meeting of such a "parliament" would have been quite simply inconceivable — indeed, unimaginable — a century earlier. The gap that then separated the three monotheisms and the collection of idolatrous cults was not measured in terms of degree but instead by their ontological differences. Without external intervention, or, better, supernatural intervention, an idolatrous cult does not itself evolve toward Religion. It is more frequently presented as its degenerated version. Some general remarks will allow us to obtain a balanced view of the ensemble of this vast historic movement.

The ten or eleven World Religions just mentioned only concern part of humankind. Three continents (America, Africa, and Oceania) out of five have no representation. Of these eleven "religions," five today are Indian and three belong to the Abrahamic tradition. This is the conclusion reached, as we have seen, in virtually all of the criticisms launched against the textbook readers used by American students.

Inversely, one could say that minor religions are present, at least if one sticks to the actual number of their followers (Zoroastrianism, Sikhism, and Jainism). From this remark and from the preceding one, it is possible to conclude that, in this list, the only religions that figure are those that came into existence deep within the great past civilizations (Rome, Persia, India, China, and Japan) and that rely on the possession of so-called sacred texts. The latter imply the existence of writing and of specialized colleges and clerks. This criterion seems entirely determining and was indeed at the origin of the famous collection of the *Sacred Books of the East*.[24] And it is, of course, because we are dealing with an essential criterion in the eyes of biblical Christianity (which could only benefit it) that it was placed at this strategic juncture.

The word "religion," in all of its contexts, acts as a common thread or mark of recognition throughout the centuries and continents. It has the great advantage of permitting comparison, but — and what is said less often — on the basis of exclusive criteria chosen and imposed by the West. And, at the price of this small rhetorical artifice, it does more than suggest that man is by nature a *homo religioso*, which Christian theologians for their part proclaim.

Among the Oriental religions, Hinduism and especially Buddhism stirred great interest in the nineteenth century. The first of these did so because it concerned the administrators of the British Empire in the Indian subcontinent; the second because its fundamental originality and intellectual virtuosity quickly fascinated the West.[25] Masuzawa recalls that Buddhism at that time resulted from an intellectual construction effected upon ancient texts (and not on "living" Buddhisms studied on the ground) by Western scholars of the nineteenth century. With Buddhism, the West discovered at any rate an original alternative to Christianity and made a religion of it, even though it was atheistic, denied the existence of a human soul, and taught no form of immortality at all.

On the other hand, as has already been noted, the two monotheistic cousins (but remaining Semitic in Western eyes) of Islam[26] and Judaism were the object of negative judgment, being "ethnic religions."[27] In the eyes of science at the time, these two characteristics, Semite and ethnic, condemned them to remaining prisoners of their origins. Christianity, on the other hand, fertilized by Aryan genius, was able to go beyond its initial limits to become universal. On this level, Buddhism could be its only rival.

It remains for me to formulate what is doubtless the most problematic comment, as it concerns the use of the word "invention" in the three cases.[28] If one remembers that the scholarly West admitted the existence of only three religions (next to the idolatrous cults) at the beginning of the nineteenth century,[29] but that, without having its hand forced, it recognized around ten a century later, one must admit that we are dealing with a series of inventions. One can even add that these inventions were rather well coordinated, as if responding to a collective movement or at least a common preoccupation. The birth dates of the names for these religions invented by the West are in fact known today: 1821 (Buddhism), 1829 (Hinduism),[30] 1839 (Taoism), and 1862 (Confucianism).[31] Seeing this, good sense still cannot prevent one asking and wondering, out of curiosity, but what existed before then? For we cannot be talking about *ex nihilo* creations; one must admit that something existed earlier. But what? And what did these inventions consist of, as a consequence? I would be tempted to add for the moment that this involved arbitrary selection and the selective reorganization of pre-existing givens, in order to come as close as possible to the canonic model provided by Christianity. But I must add immediately that the indigenous elites, particularly in India and Japan, often play an important role in the creation of these sham religions. Indian nationalists and supporters of independence find in them a precious ally.[32]

In order to understand this process a bit better, it is preferable to concentrate on Hinduism and Shinto, for their histories are the best known today. The two Chinese representatives have not sparked the same curiosity by any means.[33] Two factors have no doubt played a role in this lack of interest. In addition to the language obstacle (although Japanese is no less inaccessible), the interest of the Sinologist specialists in questions raised by historians of religions in the nineteenth century and at the beginning of the twentieth century were not comparable to the interest in India, where prehistoric, Indo-European origins had been discovered. And symmetrically, the specific questions asked in China did not attract the theoreticians of Religious Studies. The country has therefore remained apart from the debates that have animated research for the last 150 years.

The Invention of Oriental Religions: Hinduism and Shinto

India will no doubt have occupied a primary place in the birth and development of the History of Religions. We have just recalled that the Indo-European hypothesis came to life in India, a hypothesis which over the course of the nineteenth century would overturn progressively the traditional chronology inherited from the Bible. And it is also among this Himalayan buttress in India that Buddhism was born.

But Hinduism has not been outdone in this area. In what has appropriately been called the invention, construction, or even creation of Hinduism, some expressions are commonly accepted today, to the point where King has been able to write that the term "Hinduism" exists today with a much stronger meaning than it had in the eighteenth century.[34] And no doubt one could say as much for Hinduism itself.

But this invention introduces one of the most passionate problems obsessing specialists in the History of Religions field, as it is also one of the most controversial. The "Hindu Question" in itself summarizes all of the theoretical difficulties that arise when one sets the Christian idea of *religion* up against one of its supposed Oriental hypostases. Thus, inspired by healthy prudence, I am not going to try to bring definitive answers to all of the questions raised by the invention of Hinduism, which are still hotly debated today. On a more modest level, I would like to try to disengage and expose the major problems that the invention has brought forth.[35] And it will be seen that behind the word "invention," we see, once again, the great drama playing out of relations opposing the West to the East, as well as that of the East being subordinated to the norms imposed by its secular rival.

Once again, as King recalls,[36] the Hindu question first crystallized around the use of the word "religion". Whatever its origins, is Hinduism a religion or not? The unsolvable problems[37] that the definition of this term raises makes it delicate – indeed, impossible – to apply it to non-Christian cultures. Moreover, these discussions must not allow us to forget another indisputable given, also mentioned earlier:[38] at the heart of Christianity alone, we encounter very different personalities, currents, and attitudes. And this without mentioning the dozens of heresies that have flourished over the centuries following its creation. What would Roman Catholicism resemble today if, after 2000 years, it had not been cast permanently into a frame by the Church? How many schools, practices, beliefs, cults, heterodox trends, sects, occultist or magic deviations, and rival leaders would have opposed it and would continue to do so, in greatest confusion? What would the churches and sects agree on in matters of dogma and ritual? Even within Buddhism there has never been anything in India comparable to this centralised Church with its hierarchy of clergy under papal authority. Rival schools and controversies proliferated among them, as much in India as elsewhere. Outside of Buddhism, which nevertheless has a rather large doctrinal coherence and subject emanating from the teaching of the Buddha, the situation is even more confused. As a consequence, and in every specific case, the notion of religion in India needs above all else to take account of this banal historical given. In a way, one has to give it *a priori* a more open acceptation and a suppler structure.[39]

However, being polynuclear, fragmented (Hinduisms?), and malleable, would it still appear to be a religion in Western eyes? And would the West be ready to relinquish the Christian model for it? Besides which, how and by what principles could one imagine "a different kind of religion,"[40] when we have been content up to now to reify and, in the best cases, to relax the Christian example which has constantly served simultaneously as unique prototype and reference? This is where, despite everything, we get these almost inevitable questions, to be filed for the moment under "epistemological enigmas": up to what point can we call "religion" a cultural and social configuration that is fundamentally different from the Christian example? And what would it have to possess to pass this "religion entrance-test"? In other words, what is the tolerance-co-efficient of this "material"? And who would be handed the measuring-stick? Between the most conservative strict Catholic orthodoxy and the most liberal Protestant points of view, the choices are many and, needless to say, often incompatible. Thus, it is not certain that, if posed to theologians, these questions would receive an unambiguous reply. Or else the reply would be so abstract and disembodied that it would lose all explanatory power.

Having admitted that, it nonetheless seems difficult to imagine that Hinduism could have been "invented" out of nothing. Here, indeed, two attitudes stand in opposition. The smaller in number[41] think that the phenomenon, if not the word, already existed before the arrival of the Britons. The multi-century contact with the Muslim invader—thus doubly foreign—could in a way have favorized an awareness and the crystallization of a Hindu identity. Inversely, from the constructionist point of view, it was the Westerners who selected and rethought the earlier Indian traditions in order to create a "presentable" religion—Hinduism as we so designate it today.

For those who hold these two theses, something, then, must have existed beforehand. But what? Here, quite logically, the responses diverge. For some, a sort of proto-Hinduism would have existed before the British colonization, confirming, in their eyes, the existence and use of the word "Hindu". But we have noted that this word did not initially imply the religious meaning that it subsequently took on. It would be just as prudent to admit that, in the face of foreign and Muslim invaders, *a fortiori* when they demonstrated a rigid sectarianism, it allowed a part of the indigenous population, characterized by its ethnic and social differences, to acknowledge its unity as well as its singularity.[42] But if one holds that the word "Hindu" already possessed this religious connotation, as the Westerners would come to reinforce later, what was its nature and its breadth? Here, another difficulty arises and immediately forms itself into an objection. One cannot say that a group of heteroclite facts are religious if no religion exists to encircle it, coordinate it, and give it, so to speak, a kind of religious quality and unity. It is precisely this superstructure, and the consciousness it supposes, that seems to be missing. Only the British influence would be able to introduce it, because that influence, aided by the action of its missionaries, was inspired by the canonical model furnished by Christianity. A marriage ceremony or a funeral are not by nature religious. They are only so in the West because the Church has taken charge of them. Without the latter, they would rather be comparable to the *samskâra* described in India in the many treatises (*Dharmasastra*) relative to *dharma*.[43]

Raising these questions is also a courteous way to introduce into the debate an awkward factor — that is, the immensity, antiquity, and incomparable prestige of the Indian culture that has developed in a territory as large as Europe and over more than 3000 years. When the ancestors of the current Britons were still chasing boars to feed themselves, Pânini was analyzing with admirable care all the nuances of the Sanskrit language, including phonology, and Kautilîya was composing his great treatise of political theory, the *Arthashastra*. The extreme diversity of languages, cults, traditions, schools, sects, and native practices makes it impossible, in fact, to disengage a coherent figure from this pre-colonial Hinduism, if such a thing ever even existed.[44] And the exercise would remain just as impossible today, for it is certain that this architectonic unity has never existed, at least outside of the official texts and readers; that is to say, in an entirely rhetorical way. Taking once again the example imagined above, I would gladly ask in order to better grasp the scope of this *aporia* whether one would speak of Christian religion (in the singular) if the latter were only known by dozens and dozens of oral traditions, cults, and beliefs scattered over an immense territory and that differed from one another, never having communicated among themselves in the concern to establish unity.

Alongside this school-hypothesis designed to underline, once more, the singularity of the Catholic example, it is possible, from some examples chosen among dozens just as pertinent, to dispel some stubborn misunderstandings. Thanks to them, one may understand that to encompass the entire "religious" culture of ancient India in the three successive categories invented by Westerners ("Vedic religion," "Brahmanism," and "Hinduism") is very much disputable, as if the three corresponded to a uniform and homogeneous movement crowned by the formation of Westerners. In reality, the history between the Vedic period and contemporary Hinduism is particularly obscure and rather complicated, as we hear from Halbfass,[45] among others. The great royal rituals of Vedic India (*ashvamedha* and *râjasûya*), for example, do not deserve to be called "religious," except by an abuse of the language. Why would they be when they primarily concern the solemn celebration of royal power? The words "priests," "rituals," and "sacrifices," that are used in corresponding presentations in French, must not mislead us. These words in fact translate the poverty of the French lexicon and the strong attraction of the religious galaxy. Specialists can celebrate extremely complicated rituals without being counterparts of Catholic priests. A ritual is not in principle religious. In our Western societies there are numerous civil rituals—military and patriotic—that are observed scrupulously. And that possess their own servants. Ethnographic literature also knows of innumerable magic rituals the world over that are public and solemn. I would gladly say the same for the word "brahman".[46] The members of the superior castes in India are not professional priests, and those so called are not obliged to be brahman (and in fact rarely are). Their privileged relation with things of the spirit, like the Platonic philosophers, have the consequence that brahmans today are jurists, professors, journalists. In other words, and without serious anachronism, a brahman who in ancient days participated in the celebration of an *ashvamedha* was accomplishing nothing that today would merit being called "religious".

In the same way, the teaching of the *Upanishads,* or that of the *yoga*, are sometimes considered as archaic religious elements. Now, if the *Upanishads* are this, then so are all Western metaphysical texts, beginning with the poem of Parmenides. A metaphysical meditation on death and the impermanence of things is not a *religious* activity. And one looks in vain in the *yogasûtra* of Patañjali for a single notion that recalls the words of Jesus (sin, community of believers, individual faith, personal and immortal soul, love of neighbor, retribution in the next world for good or evil acts, and so on).

What common traditions, one may still ask, would be represented by Shankara's *vedânta* (monist quintessence of the Upanishad teaching) and the Krishna *bhakti* within a (quite hypothetical) unified Hinduism? In fact, what distinguishes them would also place them—and more appropriately so—under the names of two different religions.

On the other hand, if there is indeed a pan-Indian notion, it is without question that of *dharma*.[47] This Sanskrit word that designates, as we recall, the cosmic, social, ritual, and moral order, applies in fact to all aspects of human life—individual and collective. The fastidious rules with respect to social hierarchies appear well placed. There we also see the *samskâra*, a word abusively translated as "sacraments," no doubt to give them a more religious tone. In fact, they designate the social ceremonies that punctuate the significant stages of human life, from conception to funeral. Similar terms are found in all societies. Despite an evolution that was hoped for at the end of the nineteenth century,[48] one cannot consider the original notion of *dharma* as a synonym, even approximate, of the word "religion". It is, shall we say, a lot more encompassing than the word "religion," since in fact nothing that is human escapes its empire. Royal power and social order indeed occupy a central place.

According to constructionist points of view, in the Indian culture there were many elements (texts, myths, rituals, moral rules) that, astutely assembled, could evoke the idea of religion, even if, taken in isolation, they were incapable of it. Among these elements, and in order to resemble Christianity the most closely, the presence of ancient and sacred (i.e., metaphysical) texts was privileged, along with an averred tendency toward monotheism, an ecclesiastical organization (for which brahmans were recruited), the recognized capacity of the divine to take human shape, and a universal vocation.[49] All of the rest, such as astrology, had to be rejected as popular superstition. Here, the choice effected by Western scholars reveals their *a prioris*. Still in the image of Christianity, they were looking for a Hindu religion that was homogeneous, uniform, pan-Indian, and offering the picture of a coherent system dominated by morality and spirituality[50] (i.e., not by magic or astrology), even if the result was artificial[51] and did not at all reflect the reality lived by the Indians, particularly the reality known to the lower classes (to say nothing of the untouchable castes). The spirit of this formatting recalls the recipes seen at work in textbook readers. Thus, it is not surprising that the same textbooks would reflect this uniform, elitist, bookish Hinduism.

In this process of creation, the principal source was the old Sanskrit culture of superior castes that enjoyed extremely high prestige, as well as the most famous philosophical texts (such as Shankara's *vedânta*), comparable by their intellectual sophistication and their metaphysical ambition to those found in the West. Moreover, the *vedânta*, centered on the notion of the absolute—the Brahman—could appear as an Indian version of monotheism, even if the gender-neutral word designated an inactive and impersonal absolute principle. All of these were and are unknown to the immense majority of the population who, of course, did not know Sanskrit, which had been a dead language since antiquity. On a more prosaic level, but which cannot be neglected for all that, we should not forget that the brahmans were the privileged interlocutors and translators of the English in all questions of administration, religion, law, literature, etc. In this regard, to summarize the process, one could speak of the brahmanization and sanskritization of Hinduism.[52] The popular oral traditions are absent, and they incarnate without a doubt what are the most vibrant and contemporary traditions in Hinduism. It is thus not the populous, noisy, and multicolored India that inspired this new Hinduism; it is the disembodied Hinduism of superior castes, whose *dharma* held pre-eminence in society for all eternity.

The latter trait introduces a new set of alternatives: was this invention led with the support of, or in spite of, the natives? Was it imposed from above or is it the result of what one might be tempted to call a collaboration? These last lines have brought with them the beginnings of a reply that is entirely clear. Hinduism, invented by Western science, has benefited on site from the intervention of numerous members of the superior caste — the brahmans. If psychology has its place in such a historical procedure, one can add that the brahmans, strengthened by their immemorial privileges, the consciousness of the insurmountable difference separating them from the inferior castes, the prodigious wealth of their intellectual culture, their fortune (in some cases), and the refined nature of their civilization (music, theatre, poetry, literature, architecture, sculpture), would have difficulty recognizing an indisputable superiority in the British occupiers (lovers of alcohol and meat).

It seems unanimously admitted today that, if not the Indians as a group, then at least the representatives of the upper castes and the Sanskrit sources that only they knew played an entirely decisive role in the creation of modern Hinduism.[53] It must be admitted that they had everything to gain. It was their Sanskrit culture and its major works, held by them alone, that were placed at the heart and origin of Hinduism. This culture and these works obtained supplementary prestige and a sort of rehabilitation unhoped for at a time when they must have been for a large part forgotten. As to their social claims and the system of values on which they rested, the brahmans could only rejoice to see them recognized, in conformity with the most traditional teachings of the old dharmic treatises.

In parallel, the Britons, imposing the political, administrative, and religious unity of India (the last of these being artificial), introduced the seeds of a consciousness and a nationalist reprisal that up to then were unknown. These would lead to the independence of the country in the mid-twentieth century.[54] India, we must remember, had been fragmented up to that point and had never possessed a sense of unity, be it political or religious. Furthermore, and even though it was not initially destined for it, the invention of Hinduism allowed India to enter into the collective of the great "civilized" nations.

In the guise of a provisional conclusion, I am tempted to turn to King, who has provided probably the most measured and most nuanced synthetic response.[55] Here, I will summarize his opinion in a few lines. The presence of Muslim invaders in the subcontinent no doubt favored a consciousness on the part of the natives, who could not avoid feeling different from them. This does not mean that the word "Hindu" had already been universally understood as a sign of these differences, nor that the latter had already been thought of and encoded in religious terms. Nevertheless, the impact of Islam and the influence of monotheistic Vishnuite currents that spread from the thirteenth to the eighteenth century during the pre-colonial period must have contributed to preparing favorable conditions for a better reception of the idea of a "national" Hinduism. But for King, what catalyzed and finished this movement remains the encounter with the British Empire and the fact that European colonists favored the ideas of a unique Indian society and religion. King also adds this last and important point: the modern notion of Hinduism, he writes, was initially conceived by foreign observers, but it emerged from the colonial encounter between Indians and Europeans, especially the British.[56] The expression "colonial encounter" is there to forcefully underline the fact that Hinduism is not a unilateral European invention that was plastered onto a passive Indian reality, but rather a result of the dynamic encounter of, on the one hand, urbanized and cultivated social groups belonging to the Indian elite and, on the other hand, the influences brought by Western missionaries, administrators, and scholars.

In spite of this measured conclusion, some more theoretical questions remain hanging. And they are not negligible. Bloch and her co-writers have reviewed and enumerated the most pertinent and, let us say it, the most embarrassing of these.[57] And they will no doubt feed the debates that will continue to arise due to the encounter between exotic cultures and the Western idea of religion. I shall summarize them below.

What has been definitively constructed under the name of Hinduism? A new religion? A concept? A simple "pattern"? An administrative abstraction useful for census-taking? A novel entity in the Western imagination? One thing is certain: these solutions are incompatible and mutually exclusive. The question is not resolved if one opts for the first choice. For if Hinduism is to be considered as a religion or as several religions, what constitutes a religion, or a group of them? In other words, by what justification is it or are they to be so called? The same question arises concerning how to know what made (or did not make) of the Hindu identity a religious identity during pre-colonial India. But, in every case, in order to respond, it is indispensable to agree on what constitutes the empirical essence of (a) religion. On this point, the controversies and debates are livelier today than ever before.

If it is true that Hinduism had never been or was not yet a religion at the end of the eighteenth century, how is it that the Britons, fortified with their Protestant conception of religion, recognized one in India, when the demonstrations they had before them had little chance of bringing to mind the teachings of their home parishes? This question neglects the fact that, since the era of the great discoveries, the Westerners recognized (idolatrous) religions everywhere, even if, as we have seen,[58] they had to exaggerate or suppress reality. For them, to acknowledge a world without religion signified the imperfection of original revelation and the powerlessness of God. All people possessed religion; only animals (and certain primitive tribes) did not. The fact that certain peoples subsequently forgot or cast aside this original heritage begs another question: was Brahmanism the kernel of pre-colonial Hinduism? The authors themselves reply to this question by recalling that the existence of Brahmanism, as a body of unified and homogeneous doctrines, has never been demonstrated. Furthermore, if such a kernel had existed, it would have been discovered long ago at the heart of Hinduism. And the latter would itself have recognized and identified it simultaneously. Which did not happen.

In addition, in order for Brahmanism to set itself at the base of a "pan-Indian religion," it would have needed a unified clergy and center of power devoted to defining the orthodoxy and orthopraxis of the religion's faithful. In India, such a nationwide clerical authority has never existed. Indians have been able to call themselves Hindus without that implying, in their view, some sort of religious identity. Inversely, even today many Indians prefer to follow their ancestral and local traditions rather than those of an official, far-off Hinduism defended by upper castes. But in this case, what remains to be explained is the reasons that recent generations of Indians have behaved as though they had a religion — Hinduism — and why an indigenous movement — *hindutva*[59] ("hinduness") — appeared, demanding that Hinduism be considered one of the World Religions. In summary, then, it is appropriate to wonder about and to understand the reasons (social, political, etc.) for which Indians call themselves Hindus.

Bloch and her co-writers conclude this list of questions with a delicious paradox. Whatever the initial reasons inciting the British to favor the development and recognition of Hinduism, the Indians made use of it to found their unity and emancipation. Curiously, the domination and the resistance to that domination utilized the same arguments.

In 1858, a treaty of friendship and commerce was concluded between Japan and the United States. The English version of the treaty contained the word "religion". At that date, the Japanese did not have a literal or even metaphorical equivalent for the term.[60] Implicitly, this means that the Japanese neither needed nor used it. This is not surprising: how could history have invented twice, in two such different cultures, centuries and great distances apart, two exactly synonymous notions? As Fitzgerald recalls, citing a study by Jun'ichi,[61] several terms were then capable of fulfilling that function, with greater or lesser degrees of appropriateness. Finally, the word "*shûkyô*"[62] came to the fore. What is concerned, then, is an artificial and fairly recent creation. This should suffice to prevent it from being retrospectively projected onto a distant past that was unaware of it, to boot. But what must be noted is that this lexical creation responds to the deliberated will of the Japanese managers of the *Meiji* era (1868–1912) to conform to the Western model. Having understood that possessing a religion represented, in the eyes of Westerners (American and Europeans), the indisputable sign of civilized nations and masters of the world, they invented one for themselves. It was thus not imposed from the outside by a foreign power. It represented in their view a supplementary way, along with the adoption of a constitution, to hoist themselves up to the level of the great Western powers, and with them to enter straight into modernity. Symmetrically, one can doubtless affirm that its admission among the World Religions owes less to its universality (which is inexistent) than to the military and economic power of Japan (Sino-Japanese War, 1895; Russo-Japanese War, 1905).

But what religion? In contrast to Buddhism or Confucianism, it had to be indigenous. And here is where Shinto would come in. Or, more exactly, the reconstruction of ancient Shinto. Its history would no doubt appear quite strange to the eyes of any Westerner with even a rudimentary consciousness of the great Christian dogmas.[63]

Before the Meiji era, Confucianism, Buddhism, and Shinto represented in Japan the three traditional teachings. Among them, this ancient Shinto ("it is difficult to precisely define Shinto" acknowledges Jun'ichi)[64] reflected popular beliefs, superstitions, and practices (magic, divination, funerary customs, etc.). Up until then, Japan had no hope of attaining the rank of World Religion. And it is this indigenous and crude Shinto that the ideologues of the Meiji era transfigured into a sort of State religion, essentially ritualistic, fundamentally nationalistic, organized around the imperial institution, and inculcated by every school. And, ever concerned to come close to its Western model, this official Shinto developed alongside the condemnation of magic-practice and popular superstition.

But, from 1882, modeled on the Western opposition between the public and private spheres, a gap was introduced between the State or National Shinto which concerned morality, public rituals and imperial power, and sect-Shinto, which concerned individual salvation and the *post mortem* destiny of the individual. This latter status was inspired by the Protestant and individualist model imported into Japan. In order to protect State Shinto from potential criticism from the side of freedom of belief recognized from then on in Japan, it was declared non-religious (*bishûkyô*). But at the same time (another paradox), it was admitted to be superior to simply individual beliefs.[65]

In 1945, after the Japanese defeat, U.S. General MacArthur and the occupying Allied Forces published a directive known later as the "Shinto Directive". It stipulated the abolition of State Shinto, and with it would follow the disappearance of the divine status of the Emperor. There would only remain the modernised version of sect-Shinto with its orientation toward the cult of the ancestors and of the spirits (*kami*) who peopled the natural world. Even today, the Japanese ties with "their" religion conform so very little with what is demanded of the faithful by Christian exclusivism, that

it is possible, according to circumstances (New Year, funeral ceremonies, marriage), to be successively or concurrently Protestant,
Shintoist, or even Buddhist. Fujiwara indeed recognized that the
Japanese people are in the majority indifferent to, and have little
interest in, religious matters.[66] Curiously, this does not prevent
Shinto from figuring among the ten or so representatives at the 1893
World's Parliament of Religions. With this we no doubt witness a
phenomenon worthy of interest for any lover of epistemological
paradox. In fact, to be called a "religion," Shinto, in its State-version
as well as its archaic popular version, led the Christian concept to
an expansion of its extreme limits — limits beyond which, we must
note, we have no satisfactory term for what history is revealing. In
fact, if Shinto (in whatever version) is not a religion, then what is it?
This example and this paradox confirm in their way that the stakes
linked to the establishment of religions in the nineteenth century
were of an order other than "religious" (as they are generally summarized to be). Under these conditions, it is appropriate not to try
to resolve these paradoxes but to explain where they came from and
what interests they represent.

World Religions and Universal Religions

As we know, the invention of Hinduism, like that of Shinto, is part
of a much larger context — that of the nineteenth-century invention of the World's Religions, on display among others at the 1893
Chicago Parliament — which offers an excellent reference point for
that *fin-de-siècle*.

In the taxonomy of Tiele, which we encountered earlier,[67] a very
small group of "universal religions" (Christianity, Islam, Buddhism)
is mentioned. These three religions are distinguished from the others in the sense that, just as with the activity of Saint Paul, they have
not remained prisoners of their milieu and their language. On the
contrary, they have deliberately tried to disseminate their teaching. Around this same time, Max Müller enumerated eight World
Religions, all possessing collections of sacred texts[68] (the three preceding, to which were added Hinduism, Judaism, Zoroastrianism,
Confucianism, and Taoism). Three others, also founded on texts,
came to be added later to this group of eight: Sikhism, Jainism, and
State Shinto (which, at that date, would soon be created in Japan), to
form the list officially received in Chicago.

Jonathan Z. Smith considers that the passage of the three Abrahamic monotheisms recognized alongside the paganisms at the beginning of the nineteenth century into the group of eight World Religions a few decades later should be explained in the following way: "If Christianity and Islam count as 'world' religions, it would be rude to exclude Judaism (the original model for the opposite type, 'ethnic' or 'natural' religion). Likewise, if Buddhism, then Hinduism. And again, if Buddhism, then Chinese religions and Japanese religions."[69] I doubt very much whether simple questions of tact and politeness intervened in this evolution that dissimulated games of power and politics that were infinitely more considerable. But the explanation in terms of the key words "colonialism and imperialism" is perhaps not included in the epistemological horizon to which Smith refers. We have seen in an earlier chapter that, as colonial policies became more familiar with the exotic cultures that would become "religions" in the eyes of Westerners, a double movement took place in parallel. The first consisted of distinguishing at the heart of the idolatry and paganism — and thus promoting — a certain number of "religions" that were from then on better known and endowed with their own identity. But it is crucial never to forget that this (shall we say) recognition was made by modeling and formatting these new religions on norms borrowed from the Western — that is, Christian — model. The second movement, complementary to the preceding ones, ended up regrouping the principal religions among them, found at the heart of the category of World Religions. This was the equivalent, no more and no less, of a form of globalization, as efficacious as the globalizations of industry, politics, and economics that were initiated at the same time, thanks to new ways of production (machinery), communication (telegraph), and transportation (ships and steam locomotives).

This evolution was completely essential, for it contributed to the unification of anthropological conceptions, both scholarly and naive, under the aegis of the religious phenomenon. We know from then that World Religions and Universal Religions do not emerge from a primitive hearth and home, a far-off, obscure "religious" prehistory of humanity; they are recent creations that one must ascribe to the Western influence on the rest of the world.

The double movement just evoked thus unfolded at the sole initiative of the West and at a time when the latter was reinforcing its hegemony on the great part of the world, via the installation of its colonial empires. It never had to confront a counter-model arriving, for example, from India or China. To the West alone belonged the nomenclature, the cultural hegemony, the force to impose it, and the rules tied to its *modus operandi*. And, to a large extent, we still live today with that heritage. The defense of ecumenism, in these conditions, becomes easier, since it is the West's own values that it is defending, under the cloak of altruism and freedom. On the whole, the West says to the rest of the world: "Be tolerant, be democratic, be free... but in the way that we ourselves are."

This imperialism has a number of other advantages. The most evident has already been mentioned in these pages. As part of the inheritance of religion, we find, above all, a certain idea of man — *homo religiosus* — defined as a priority by the religious dimensions of his existence. And this "belief system" is tied to historical context only tangentially and contingently, as McCutcheon stresses — that is, the belief system contributes to depoliticizing and dematerial- izing social relations.[70] Moreover, a large number of notions and ideas were exported along with the Western idea of "religion" that are not *stricto sensu* "religious": political institutions, diverse modes and styles of living, male-female relations, work-ethic and profit-motivation, but also the freedoms brought with unionization and democracy (etc.). Numerous elements from the Western view were thus transferred and transported to other cultures and nur- tured the seeds there that "religion" sowed in its wake. In this way, the Western view contributed to the uniformization of the word, facilitating at the same time (as researchers such as Fitzgerald and McCutcheon think) a more fluid type of relations within global capitalism. The influence of this neo-colonialism has lasted to this day; that is to say, it has lasted far beyond the era when colonized nations finally gained independence. In this regard, Masuzawa notes with interest that, in the dialectical and conquering relation that the West was living out with other nations, the discourses held doubtless contributed to reinforcing the consciousness and the form of its own identity, all the while giving more weight and influence to its epistemic imperialism. The discourses permitted the West not just to announce "the others" (to situate, hierarchize, compare, and denigrate them) but, at the same time, to enjoin these "others" to proclaim themselves in the same terms.[71] A single language is spo- ken from then on, and continues to be spoken today: the language of the West.

The above is why I can no longer follow Smith when he writes, with a certain degree of humor, that "a World Religion is a religion like ours; but it is, above all, a tradition which has achieved sufficient power and numbers to enter our history, either to form it, interact with it, or to thwart it."[72] But, in the light of what we have just seen, a "religion like ours" should actually be phrased: "a religion that the West accepted to recognize as such by imposing its form and values." It is the West alone that grants the unction and certification of correct religiosity. Africans, Haitians, Malagasies, and the Paleosiberians know something about this: they were maintained for a long time at the periphery of the civilized world. As to the influence of sufficiently strong traditions coming from the outside to influence the course of our history, there again it would be more correct to say that it is, once again, the West that intervened, often violently, in the history of other peoples. How many have been decimated since the sixteenth century? How many put into servitude? How many converted by force? How many — even more — stripped of their culture?

Whatever the original physiognomy of these peripheral cultures and societies, these prolonged contacts changed them profoundly, as had Islam after the seventh century and Christianity at the beginning of our Common Era. In this respect, the invention of World Religions during the nineteenth century represents the third great "religious" revolution. It also contributed to expanding the disparity between the most powerful civilizations and the local ones devoid of such institutions. Today, the nations that dominate the world (the United States, Europe, India, China, Japan) belong to the same closed club (Christianity, Hinduism, Buddhism, Confucianism, Taoism, Shinto). It is perhaps not secondary to note that these modern reconfigurations and creations (Hinduism, Buddhism, Confucianism, Taoism, Shinto) took place in societies that possessed ancient and solid state political organizations: either royal (India) or imperial (China, Japan). The three "small" religions of Jainism, Sikhism, and Zoroastrianism benefited from their implantation on Indian soil and from the possession of so-called sacred texts. But the position occupied today by Islam and Judaism still seems ambiguous and less prestigious.

Part Three

What to Do with "Religions"?

Chapter Eight

What Future for Critical Studies?

8.1 A Question and Some Options

Over the course of the preceding chapter, a very difficult question has arisen. And beyond its paradoxical nature, it represents a major challenge that addresses itself without exception to all those who in one way or another number in this vast current of Critical Studies. If the religions recognized outside Europe are inventions, creations, and recent outfittings to be credited to the West in its most imperialist phase of the nineteenth and twentieth centuries, ought one not to wonder, as with Hinduism and Shinto, what they were previously? And what they might be today, had they been left untouched by Western influence? Of course, this is purely and simply a moot question, but it has the advantage of raising formidable issues, such as: what should one, or can one, call these pre-colonial, exotic configurations that we have become used to calling "religions"? And this "we" includes simple citizens as well as great scholars; journalists as well as theologians. On this point the consensus of Western opinion seems as complete as possible. Or, to put it another way, and even more directly: what were Hinduism and Buddhism before they acquired these names from Westerners?[1] In other words, did they have a form of doctrinal unity and institution comparable to those of Christianity? In that pre-colonial period, did they belong to this same group of institutions? Could one have thought to place (proto)-Hinduism and (proto)-Buddhism in the same family? But what could this family have been? What were its dominant genetic or structural characteristics? And who could have made this choice? The disarray becomes worse when we become aware, as we have just done, of the poverty of the conceptual and theoretical tools at our disposal for trying to respond with common sense to these questions, proving once more that the subject-ground dominated by "religion" is so deeply ensconced in our *Weltanschauung*, in our ways of thinking, and in the objects and concepts that the latter have conceived, that in a certain way it has practiced a scorched-earth policy around itself by disallowing any access-point for reflection. The hegemony exercised by the Christian model of religion is such, and for so long a time, that it has impoverished our lexicon regarding how to designate anything that it is *not*. It is so diminished in this area that we have to follow the one-way streets that it has itself laid out. Beyond the word "religion," all we have to oppose it is "magic," "superstition," or "sorcery" — that is, its own antitheses. Since it is fairly improbable that we would succeed one day in creating an alternative, specific lexicon that would produce unanimity, one could fear that this confusion and these imprecisions will subsist for a long time yet.

Let us also note that the explanation by the key word "religion" is by opposition simple and fruitful. In fact, for such a minor investment it brings with it quite a complete package: a familiar label universally known today, an anthropological dimension, a topical inventory endowed with its own nomenclature (divinity, belief, individual soul, immortality, dogmas, ritual, clergy, sacred texts), a small number of hypotheses concerning its origin (God and human nature being among the most frequently invoked), and a history co-extensive with that of humanity. In fact, and most serious of all, are we not talking about the religions of pre-historic man?[2]

We should recall again that the term "religion," condemned for two centuries to adapt itself to a great number of different cultural contexts, ended up acquiring an extraordinary plasticity, for it is used equally to designate a voodoo ceremony, a treatise of Franciscan spirituality, a bloody Aztec ritual, and a Vedic hymn, making its definition all the more problematic. But where, then, does its center of gravity lie? In other words, what the term gains in extension, it evidently loses in comprehension. This lack of rigor and precision, which would be scientifically condemned elsewhere, appears here as an indisputable boon. It is no longer just a key; it is a skeleton key. And a very useful skeleton key for those who know how to use it.

By comparison, the way opened up by the partisans of Critical Studies is immediately seen to be quite uncomfortable. Their most significant conclusion consists of saying that the concept of "religion" is incapable of welcoming and explaining all of the historical configurations that, under the pressing influence of the West, have been called "religions". Under these conditions, why not admit that it is the idea itself of religion, as well as its uses, that need to be reconsidered? Faced with this paradoxical question, *a priori* a small number of possible solutions reveal themselves. To be specific, these consist of heuristic hypotheses destined to nourish scientific reflection, for it is entirely improbable that the general public could follow the latter in or into this realm.

The first hypothesis leads to an acute form of relativism and even of solipsism. Each of these "religions" is turned back onto its own singularity and its own solitude. Hinduism, if not a religion, is only ... Hinduism (*sic*). This last sentence shows all of the difficulty of the enterprise that we want to account for here. As has just been said, we have no other term than this to designate that which, under Western influence, would become Hinduism – that is, the Hindu religion or the religion of the Hindus. But in adopting this radical solution, is one not locked into an epistemological impasse? On the one hand, Hinduism would thus be nothing other than itself, but without our being capable of saying what this "itself" is. And it would cease to be one of the members of the great family of World Religions, which itself would disappear. This radical solution presents another major fault that reduces its attractiveness considerably. In fact, it condemns all anthropological reflection concerned with understanding the unity of the human species (at whatever level one postulates its existence). And, this global project abandoned, the edifice of human sciences would also be dispossessed, simultaneously, of one of its indispensable foundations and one of its most legitimate scientific objectives. In fact, in addition to its being an irritation, it is hard to see what improvements would come from a science that limited itself to being a science of innumerable singularities. That science would belong instead to the work of a collector or a chamber of curiosities.

The second way would consist, for lack of anything better, of keeping the word "religion," either by limiting its usage to the Christian civilization alone, which is done with the word "*dharma*" in Hinduism or the word "*tao*" in Taoism; or, on the contrary, by redefining it in such a way that it becomes emptied of all dimensions emanating exclusively from this Christian tradition. It is difficult to imagine that the first option would receive many votes today; the international usage of the term is too anchored in our minds. As for the second, it gives a label to content that does not have much to do with what Western tradition understands by that same term. We have seen above that this sort of lexical or conceptual acrobatics is imposed on those who, wishing to describe "Roman religion" or "Greek religion," rush to add that these "religions" are not really religions in the usual sense of the word.[3] It is certainly possible to go further still in this direction, no longer giving to the word "religion" anything but a deictic function — that is, as a label indicating quite schematically what is meant but without any pronouncement on the nature of what is being discussed. Everyone would continue to use this term, but each person would make his or her own idea of it. Is this solution, which can appear paradoxical, really so far from what sometimes happens now?

In order to avoid the inevitable confusion, misunderstanding, and imprecision that these choices would infinitely multiply, while nevertheless respecting the profound rupture that they advocate, would it not seem more judicious to opt for a third way? If this way is internally coherent, it would open up a new anthropological paradigm — that is, another way to envisage nothing less than man, his history, and his creations. Among other things, it would mean the death — at least epistemological — of *homo religiosus*. The stakes at play are therefore considerable. Fitzgerald, along with the present author, is one of those rare writers to involve himself resolutely in this direction. The wide lines of his argument, developed in *The Ideology of Religious Studies*, thus deserve to be recalled and summarized. Like others before him, and as has been mentioned here as well, Fitzgerald begins his Chapter I by stating that the term "religion" has no satisfying or trustworthy definition when applied to the collection of so-called "religions" of the world and not only to the Christian religion(s) alone.[4] Once it ascribes to itself this universal ambition, its inadequacy and the fluidity of its contours are obvious. In Fitzgerald's view, then, we are dealing with an inefficacious and imprecise category outside its canonical usage in the Christian theological context. The idea of religion, for Fitzgerald, is not an archaic remnant of folklore, or a legacy of the past which is cumbersome and anachronistic. Religion is not an old tool that is no longer useful but that one cannot resign oneself to abandon. On the contrary, for him it is the remainder of an efficacious and powerful weapon, supporting a mystifying ideology itself founded on recourse to a transcendence that is deemed to justify it, while at the same time detaching it from all ties — that is, from all earthly origins.

But what power does it serve? Here, Fitzgerald takes up a subject that we have already encountered, but that he associates with another, eminently political idea. He launches into a reasoning that no doubt will surprise his readers, as it is far from the conventional canons of the History of Religions. In his view, the opposition "religion *versus* profane" today certainly must not be understood as the expression of a conflict between two adversaries, each resolved to eliminate the other. Rather, it represents two sides of the same historical and ideological process: by developing, on the one hand, a sphere that is exclusively religious, the imperialist and (neo-)colonialist West has in parallel favored the emergence of a world that is at the same time just as exclusively secular—the world of objective facts, science, free association of individuals, and parliamentary democracy. The world, in fact, of "liberal capitalism."[5] The invention of this autonomous religious sphere in some way allows for this "liberal capitalism" to be naturalized. From that point it tends to merge with the real world in its simple and "self-evident factuality."[6] One would be tempted to see in this, even if not cited, the influence of the *Mythologies* of Barthes: "Semiology has taught us that myth has the task of giving a historical intention a natural justification, and making contingency appear eternal. [...] A conjuring trick has taken place; it has turned reality inside out, it has emptied it of history and has filled it with nature."[7]

And this model imposed itself in turn on the underdeveloped societies—a *sine qua non* condition for them to gain access to this world of markets and profit, presented as natural and rational when in fact it is also a mere "ideological construction."[8] It is in this specific context that Fitzgerald uses the interesting expression "cognitive imperialism"[9] to designate the mechanism at the end of which the dominated people thinks of itself, and in the end can only think of itself, in terms of the categories imposed by the dominators and exploiters.

As we see, this approach is not one of those habitually found in textbooks and treatises devoted to the study of religions, for it hits at nothing less than the heart of the idea of religion. Fitzgerald leads the process of desacralization to its end, to the refusal of all supernatural and spiritualist fetishes that surround the idea. He repeatedly tells us that, if the latter is human—exclusively human—in this case, the usage of a concept forged by the Fathers of the Church and their theologian successors is not at all satisfactory. From this we come to the radical break that he advocates vis-à-vis everything that may appear to be (of) religious heritage.[10] At the same time, he denounces the ambiguous role played by contemporary Religious Studies of the Eliadean sort. Too often, he says, they contribute to serving as a vehicle for and maintaining the mystifying potential of *religion*.[11]

Chapters II and III of Fitzgerald's *The Ideology of Religious Studies* are devoted to the power grab demonstrated by the transformation of Hinduism and Shinto into "religions" in the nineteenth century. As a consequence, they join the analyses that have been summarized above. Finally, in Chapter IV, Fitzgerald proposes a solution to the difficult problem that he created in suggesting that we abandon the notion of religion. Considering that all of the facts called "religious" can be studied as any other socio-cultural fact, that cultures are human creations aimed at opposing entropy, instability, and chaos, and that cultures are also the protective barriers behind which humans can find shelter, Fitzgerald proposes abandoning the concept of religion and replacing it with that of culture. He supports this with the idea that, once the notion of religion is utilized as a general category, it is no longer separate from the semantic field occupied by the notion of culture.[12] If one follows him, there will no longer be a "Hindu religion" but rather, and more simply, a "Hindu culture."[13]

Considering Christianity alone, it would be difficult to deny that, for centuries, it has played a fundamental role in the construction of European societies, the justification of political powers (Machiavelli,[14] Hobbes, Spinoza, Marx, etc.), and the moral and psychological education of individuals in proposing ideals, ethical rules, and perspectives on salvation. In all of these respects, which are fundamental, it is true that the role and functions of Christianity do not vary from those habitually present in all human cultures. They are even found in numerous societies that are characterized above all by their orthopraxis, or that, like Buddhism, are indifferent and even hostile to the notions of a personal soul, faith, and divinity.

The solution Fitzgerald proposes thus offers an interesting alternative that has as an indisputable advantage the rendering inoperative of all *sui generis* arguments that favor religion. Nevertheless, the objections it faces are not negligible for all that. One may immediately fear that to gain acceptance for a significance that is much richer and much more ambitious than the old anthropological concept of culture celebrated by Tylor[15] would require a great deal of time. And while waiting, there would often be a risk of confusion that could bring with it a number of misunderstandings, for the concept of culture has itself been the object of innumerable controversies and discussions since the time of Tylor.[16]

And this is exactly where we find the first objection that could be made to Fitzgerald's thesis. If the word "religion" does not have a clear and precise definition that would make for unanimity all round, the word "culture" has the same fault. It also has a history during the course of which its acceptation has been modified and has evolved.[17] "Culture" is also a typically occidental creation ascribable to its recent intellectual history. And it, too, is the object of probing questions. For example, of what does the "complex whole" consist that Tylor was talking about a century and a half ago? Patchwork? System? Organic ensemble? Rigid structure or, on the contrary, a simple artificial aggregate of heteroclite elements? Or even a reflection? But of what?[18]

On the other hand, would it not be just as wise to point out what distinguishes the different provinces of this complex whole? What are those discrete elements? Law, morality, art … does each possess real autonomy? Or were they born and did they develop in ceaseless interdependence? And from there, what are the laws and functions that determine the global unity and coherence of every complex whole (if indeed the latter are at the heart of this system — a system that perhaps is not really a system, or that would only be so at the symbolic level of collective representations, which, even if imaginary, are no less constraining)?[19]

As we see, it is difficult for one to do without the notion of culture, but at the same time it is even more difficult to find for it a definition or a satisfactory substitute. It is possible that, in social sciences, scientific reflection also has need of fluid concepts, as in the "dark matter" that astrophysicists research. But such heuristic concepts may only be used for presenting hypotheses that are known to be provisional. They cannot themselves serve as ultimate ends, and even less as substrata for idealist metaphysics.

I have proposed a different solution to this problem, with the notion of a "cosmographic formation,"[20] designed to eliminate the unsatisfactory notion of religion while stressing the irreplaceable role played by the different "world constructions"[21] invented by all human cultures. It means first and foremost, in fact, that people live on the same planet but in different worlds. Each culture, from the most modest to the most complex, conceives of the world in its own way. And by "world" we must consider the ensemble of elements, institutions, discourses, and relations that people have patiently invented and assembled in order to construct an ordered universe — which of course does not mean, for all that, that it is equitable and just. In this ordered world, their persons, activities, expectations, and fears — even their deaths — acquire meaning because they are detached from contingency and they adjust themselves from then on to their fellow creatures. This operation provokes a veritable transubstantiation of the human condition. People are indeed inhabiting the same planet, but they are living in different worlds. The intention underlying this choice had two objectives:

(1) To emancipate the reflection on, and study of, the strait-jackets imposed by the model of Western religion. In other words, not to have to go back to this model in order to explain the diverse "world constructions" imagined by men, but instead to invert in some way our biased way of seeing things. The fundamental principle of these "constructions" does not reside in some religious instinct or other. One could make the same remark apropos the rituals (social, military, political) that are not in essence "religious".[22]

(2) To stress the capital and indisputable anthropological fact that all cultures and all societies have conceived of the world and the universe in their own way. And (almost?) all have imagined its genesis in terms of a cosmogonic myth or series of myths. Each of these conceptions is different from the others, but they are all alike in that each culture lives, if I may dare say it, in its own world. This is true just as much for those who harbor immense empires as for the small tribal societies living in the Amazon forest, which no doubt explains why each one sees itself living in the center of the world. But it is even more fundamental on the more modest level of the individual: a Catholic lives in a Catholic world, a Tibetan Buddhist lives in a Buddhist world, a Russian Communist of the 1930s in a Communist world, etc. And this desired, researched, and constructed harmony between microcosm and macrocosm is probably at the base of all cultures.

Concerning the practical advantages presented by the above notion, I would be tempted to point to the following two:

(1) It allows for the taking account of all World Views (*Weltanschauungen*), of all cosmographies, no matter how diverse. Whether they are Communist, Fascist, atheist, or mystic, whether they believe in the supernatural or in the influences of matter alone, it is possible to understand them based on a single explanatory matrix. What brings them together at the base seems to me much more important than what distinguishes them superficially. They are all in accord over the fact that they are defending a conception of the world and of humanity (Communist, Catholic, materialist, aristocratic, warlike, Fascist, etc.) exactly tailored to the world that welcomes them. This notion therefore seems to me to be capable of furnishing an anthropological foundation that is both solid and universal. The idea of "religion" has failed to do this up to now.

(2) This notion favors and facilitates the comparison between different cultures, since they rest definitively on the same architectonic principles. It is at this deep level that they find a profound human unity beneath their differences.

8.2 Comparativism

The question of comparativism is crucial, and its scope must be generalized. Whatever the option chosen, it is certain that the solutions (still provisional, in any case) to the innumerable questions raised by Critical Studies and, more generally, by the History of Religions, will only appear after extensive comparative work has taken place on the greatest possible number of different human societies and cultures.

Georges Dumézil, who rejuvenated the field of Indo-European comparative mythology, liked to repeat that comparativism is "the form naturally adopted by the experimental method in the humanities."[23] This is also the view of Jonathan Z. Smith, expressed in his own way when he states that "description [must] be framed in light of comparative interests in such a way as to further comparison."[24] Unfortunately, the same author, after having proposed a typology of past approaches (ethnographic, encyclopaedic, morphological, and evolutionist) and more contemporary ones (statistical, structural and systematic description, and comparison), concludes with the frankly pessimistic statement:

> We must conclude this exercise in our own academic history in a most
> unsatisfactory manner. Each of the odes of comparison has been found
> problematic. Each new proposal has been found to be a variant of an
> older mode [...]. We know better how to evaluate comparisons, but
> we have gained little over our predecessors in either the methods for
> making comparisons or the reasons for its practice. [...] It is a problem
> to be solved by theories and reasons, of which we have had too little.[25]

Would we not find the main reason for this negative conclusion
in the arguable concern that the only approaches being used are
mutually exclusive? If I turn to the work of the great Dumézil,[26] I
must state that he extracted the best part of what was concurrently
offered by ethnographic, encyclopaedic, and descriptive methods,
which came to be supplemented by a historicist point of view (a
term preferable to today's "evolutionist") as well as structural analysis. He found the most complete information possible in the critical combination of the sources furnished by the first three methods
just mentioned. The historicist point of view allowed him to remain
attentive to the diachronic dimension of all cultural phenomena; let
us not forget that what we call, in a concise manner, "the Roman
religion" (with the singular form here being deceiving, once again)
is a complex phenomenon that has been perpetuated for almost a
millennium. And what should we say about prehistoric religions?
Finally, as concerns structural analysis, Dumézil never ceased to
state that comparison should not be made with isolated and punctual phenomena, for on this level their similarity is too facile. On the
other hand, if their functions and place in one story are homologous
with those in another, then it is possible to consider that we are in
the presence of not just simple similarity but rather of results that
should encourage us to pursue further research. In this respect, the
results would be susceptible to generalizations endowed with a certain heuristic value. The structural analysis of myths proposed by
Lévi-Strauss rests on theoretical bases and methods that are much
more sophisticated, but it also looks for homologous ensembles — as
comprehensive as possible — that are based on original laws of composition and transformation.[27]

Nevertheless, we can now see in these comparative models, open
without *a priori* to all cultures, the intellectual approaches that stand
in opposition to the Christocentric model. This hegemonic and
imperialist model is unable to detach itself from the fundamental
principles upon which the Christian culture was constructed.

Chapter Nine

Conclusion

The list that one could draw up of studies undertaken in the area of Religious Studies in the name and spirit of Anglo-Saxon Critical Studies is considerable. We may remember, first of all, the radical and probably definitive criticism that they directed toward all earlier idealist and essential theses, which still remains today under the umbrella of phenomenology of religion. In so doing, they showed that these theses contradicted the least contestable principles of all scientific procedures. Next to mention is the discovery and analysis of the "imperialist" mechanisms that, parallel to the great colonial conquests of the nineteenth century, favored the "invention" of Oriental religions, as a prelude to the World Religions at the turn of the twentieth century. And finally, we may add to this list the complete deconstruction of the *sui generis* arguments regarding *religion*, upon which generations of (crypto-) theologians have relied. The critiques replace these circular arguments (what is religious is explained by resources emanating from what is religious alone) with a renewed understanding of the ideological and political resources constructed by the different "inventors" (scholars, missionaries, explorers, theologians, political authorities, etc.) of religions and of their official history. Thus, the most influential scholars of Critical Studies always placed the question of power at the heart of their research. And finally, in every case, they insisted on the central and driving role played by the Western world — a power simultaneously cultural, military, political, economic, and colonial. In fact, we find this Western world at the center of all strategies that have used the "epistemic violence" of religious weaponry to assure its own "cognitive imperialism".

This broad upheaval destroyed the construction that had been erected over centuries to the glory of a myth called *homo religiosus* by Eliade, the flattering reflection of a *homo occidentalis* — that is, of a fantasized anthropology that defines man simultaneously by his innate religious instinct and by his belonging to European culture. While certain philosophers announced the death of God, today we can predict the end of this anthropo-theological fiction. Now, with its disappearance, entire supporting walls of our Western culture will crumble and will need to be rethought upon other bases. This will need to happen even if one may fear a future divorce of ever greater magnitude between wide public prejudices and scientific advances, for the latter will be found at an increased distance from the most common ideas.

Nevertheless, however promising it may be, the above list cannot represent the final and definitive chapter that closes history, and especially the history of Religious Studies, forever. That is, the list also requires (meta-)criticism — a reflective criticism with Critical Studies addressing itself as object.

Several elements of this meta-criticism are found dispersed throughout the pages of this book. I will summarize them rapidly, to permit an easier collected view. I fear that some of the elements are connected to the tropisms of American university systems and editorials. If one regrets the excessive and repetitive formatting of textbooks and courses destined for students, the situation is just as bad for the over-large number of works by individual and collective specialists constituted with the help of articles already published in journals. It may be that this practical process allows for a *rapid* response to editorial demand, but it also leads too frequently to thoughtless repetition, preventing ideas to develop with all their potential and all their amplitude.

The same reproach is incurred by a certain intellectual functioning that grants far too much to isolated citing at the expense of fuller context, corpus of works, or even simply the work itself from which the citation has been taken. This is responsible for the fame of certain words of virtually magic efficacy extracted from the lexicon of Foucault (power! surveillance! genealogy!) as well as certain formulae that (have) become performative. By simplifying and condensing their works, reducing them to Guides or textbook-style Companions for Beginners, it is not at all clear — whether from Barthes to Lacan, from Baudrillard to Derrida, or from Bourdieu to Foucault — if their readers (and among them, their students) are conscious of the gaping theoretical canyons that separate those thinkers,[1] or of the extremely long history preceding them.[2] It is in these disparities and in this heritage that we find the originality of every intellectual step, and thus a great part of its fruitfulness. The "Marxism" of Barthes, the structuralism of Lévi-Strauss, or the sophisms of Foucault would themselves have deserved to be submitted to an analysis as deep (that is, as implacable) as that which phenomenology experienced. But they were not, as if the conceptual tools were lacking that would have permitted the guiding of such reflection. In addition, many cardinal notions (text, story, structure, power, ideology, symbol) were the objects of remarkable analyses in France in the 1980s, but their influence is not distinctly seen in the field of Critical Studies. It is also true that if a French reader may celebrate the considerable influence exerted on this critical wave by a number of authors in French Theory, he or she may regret that the only authors acknowledged have been those translated into English. Rather luckily, French thought did not come to an end with Barthes, Foucault, Bourdieu, Derrida, or Baudrillard.[3] That being said, Francophone readers, who benefited from a clear advantage in this area, have not always made the best use of it. Critical Studies will not be able to occupy their current position indefinitely, as it would condemn them to repeat themselves endlessly and even to the point of favoring the appearance of a type of stereotypical *doxa*. Has it not already found its place in the heart of the textbook readers, these implacable carriers of formatted commonplaces, at the same time cancelling out a part of their subversive and creative potential? Going past the comfort of their initial critical posture, one has to wish that these Critical Studies will henceforth adopt a more constructive attitude in order to propose new theoretical "objects" for specialist reading. This research will no doubt condemn them to defining in parallel new ways to conceive of "The Art of Writing on Religion."[4]

Notes

Introduction

1   Although the author of the present text is French, he has accompanied this critical movement with the publication of his *L'Occident et la religion: Mythe, pensée, idéologie* (Brussels: Éditions Complexe, 1998), translated by William Sayers as *The Western Construction of Religion: Myths, Knowledge, and Ideology* (Baltimore: Johns Hopkins University Press, 2003); *Mythologies du XXe siècle: Dumézil, Lévi-Strauss, Eliade* (Villeneuve d'Ascq: Presses universitaires du Septentrion, 1993), translated by Martha Cunningham as *Twentieth Century Mythologies: Dumézil, Lévi-Strauss, Eliade* (London: Equinox, 2006); *Les Sagesses de l'homme* (Lille: Presses universitaires du Septentrion, 2004), translated by Seth Cherney as *Wisdoms of Humanity: Buddhism, Paganism and Christianity* (Leiden: Brill, 2011); and *Religion and Magic in Western Culture*, trans. Martha Cunningham (Leiden: Brill, 2016).

2   One may also add the recent monumental synthesis, edited under the direction of Richard King, *Religion, Theory, Critique: Classic and Contemporary Approaches and Methodologies* (New York: Columbia University Press, 2017).

3   A very good synthesis may be found in Sébastien Urbanski, *L'enseignement du fait religieux: École, république, laïcité* (Paris: Presses universitaires de France, 2016).

4   Some pertinent information may be gleaned from Michael Stausberg, "Western Europe," in *Religious Studies: A Global View*, ed. Gregory D. Alles (London, Routledge, 2010), 14–49.

5   Reference may be made to the following works by Aaron W. Hughes, *Theorizing Islam: Disciplinary Deconstruction and Reconstruction* (London: Equinox, 2012); "How to Theorize with a Hammer, or On the Destruction and Reconstruction of Islamic Studies," in *Writing Religion: The Case for the Critical Study of Religion*, ed. Steven W. Ramey (Tuscaloosa: University of Alabama Press, 2015), 172–93; "The Study of Islam before and after September 11: A Provocation" in *Method and Theory in the Study of Religion*, 24, nos. 4–5 (2012): 314–36. And what can one say about such a topic as "religion and violence, mainly in relation to Islam," as expressed by Gustavo Benavides in his chapter "North America," in Alles, *Religious Studies*, 254 (referring in particular to Bruce Lincoln, *Holy Terrors: Thinking about Religion after September 11*, 2nd ed. [Chicago: University of Chicago Press, 2006]). On this last point, see also Talal Asad, *Formations of the Secular: Christianity, Islam, Modernity* (Stanford, CA: Stanford University Press, 2003), 9–12.

6   It is revealing that the synthesizing work of Guillaume Cuchet, *Faire de l'histoire religieuse dans une société sortie de la religion* (Paris: Publications de la Sorbonne, 2013), does not mention any study devoted to the Muslims of France who are three times as numerous as the Protestants and ten times as numerous as the Jews.

7   Cf. Timothy Fitzgerald, *The Ideology of Religious Studies* (New York: Oxford University Press, 2000), 253n2. This cardinal notion will come up again in Part Two.

8   These critiques are summarized by Robert Yelle, in "Criticism, and Critique (in, among and of Religions)," in *Vocabulary for the Study of Religion*, ed. Robert A. Segal and Kocku Von Stuckrad. Available at: http://dx.doi.org/10.1163/9789004249707_vsr_COM_00000253

9   Written in italics, the word *"religion"* allows me to designate *"religion par excellence"* — that is, the Christian religion as it defines itself as well as its idealized, essentialized prototype.

Chapter 1

1   Nonetheless, one must not forget (as I stress in *The Western Construction of Religion*, 126–27) that "[i]n reality, for each culture, even one as vast and ancient as ours, there exists only a small number of exemplary theses dealing with the world, mankind, their origin, or their fate."

2   Translations by Frances López-Morillas (Durham: Duke University Press, 2002) and Edward Grimston (vol. 2 [London: The Haklyut Society, 1880]) of *Historia natural y moral de la Indias* (Seville: Juan de Leon, 1590). The traits brought out here are found in the Grimston translation, particularly on pages 330 and 369, and in the López translation throughout Book V (253–328). The exemplary author, Acosta, is also referred to by Philippe Borgeaud in *Aux origines de l'histoire des religions* (Paris: Éditions du Seuil, 2004), 242; and by Jonathan Z. Smith, "Religion, Religions, Religious," in *Critical Terms for Religious Studies*, ed. Mark Taylor (Chicago: University of Chicago Press, 1998), 270.

3   Thus, one cannot consider, as does Gustavo Benavides in "North America" (244), that the presence of the Latin word *"religio"* in pre-Christian sources meant that it already had a "religious" acceptance. If one considers, as a simple schoolroom hypothesis, that certain cultural forms before Christianity were already "religions," it would of course be necessary to admit that they were profoundly rethought and redefined, and that, subsequently, the West utilized this new norm to describe retrospectively the ensemble of cultures. The problem would merely have been displaced and made complicated.

4   Augustine, *City of God*, Vol. III, Book 10:1, trans. David S. Wiesen (Cambridge, MA: Harvard University Press, 1968), 253. Brent Nongbri made use of this extract for the same reasons in *Religion: A History of a Modern Concept* (New Haven: Yale University Press, 2013), 31.

5   John Scheid, *An Introduction to Roman Religion*, trans. Janet Lloyd (Edinburgh: Edinburgh University Press, 2003), 18, from the original French version, *La Religion des Romains* (Paris: Armand Colin, 1998), 20. See also, in the same vein, and regarding the expression *"religio Romana,"* Olivier Bobineau, *L'Empire des papes: Une sociologie du pouvoir dans l'Église* (Paris: CNRS édition, 2013). For his part, Fernand Robert, in his small book devoted to Greek religion (*La Religion grecque* [Paris: Presses Universitaires de France, 1981], 16), wrote: "Total absence of dogma, doctrine, clergy forming a social class; absence of sacred book" (translation by Martha Cunningham). Moses I. Finley shares this opinion in his Foreword to *Greek Religion and Society*, edited by P. E. Easterling and J. V. Muir (Cambridge: Cambridge University Press, 1985). To appreciate better the originality of the polis model that stemmed from the

ancient Greek city, one may consult the subtle and erudite analysis of Julia Kindt, *Rethinking Greek Religion* (Cambridge: Cambridge University Press, 2012).

6   See Georges Dumézil, *Archaic Roman Religion: With an Appendix on the Religion of the Etruscans*, trans. Philip Krapp (Baltimore: Johns Hopkins University Press, 1996), 424–25.

7   Remark made by Arnal and McCutcheon in their *The Sacred Is the Profane: The Political Nature of "Religion"* (New York: Oxford University Press, 2013), 11.

8   Jacques-Bénigne Bossuet, *A Universal History, from the Beginning of the World, to the Empire of Charlemagne*, trans. Mr. Elphinston (London: David Steel, 1767), 1:183–84.

9   See specifically the French translation of the *Praeparatio*, Book XIV, Chapter 3, § 2–5, by Édouard Des Places (Paris, Éditions du Cerf: 1974–1987), 47; and the English translation by E. H. Gifford (Oxford: Clarendon, 1903), 635–37.

10   An echo of this instability is found in Craig Martin's *A Critical Introduction to the Study of Religion* (London: Routledge, 2012), 157–58; and in Malory Nye, *Religion: The Basics*, 2nd ed. (London: Routledge, 2008), 58.

11   Cf. Bart D. Ehrman, *After the New Testament: A Reader in Early Christianity* (Oxford: Oxford University Press, 1999); and Marie-Françoise Baslez, *Comment les chrétiens sont devenus catholiques Ier-Ve siècle* (Paris: Tallandier, 2019). On the different primitive Christianities, see Elaine Pagels, *The Gnostic Gospels* (New York: Random House, 1979).

12   Jennifer Eyl, "Semantic Voids, New Testament Translation, and Anachronism: The Case of Paul's Use of *Ekklêsia*," *Method and Theory in the Study of Religion* 26, nos. 4–5 (2014): 315–39.

13   Paul Robertson, "De-Spiritualizing *Pneuma*: Modernity, Religion, and Anachronism in the Study of Paul," *Method and Theory in the Study of Religion* 26, nos. 4–5 (2014): 365–83.

14   Todd Klutz, "*Christianos*: Defining the Self in the Acts of the Apostles," in *Religion, Language, and Power*, ed. Nile Green and Mary Searle-Chatterjee (New York: Routledge, 2008), 167–85.

15   William E. Arnal, *The Symbolic Jesus: Historical Scholarship, Judaism and the Construction of Contemporary Identity* (London: Equinox, 2005), esp. 76–77. Contemporary political ploys are not absent either in the studies relative to this symbolic Jesus, as we are reminded in the article by Amy-Jill Levine, "De-Judaizing Jesus: Theological Need and Exegetical Execution," in Ramey, *Writing Religion*, 148–71.

16   See note 11, Chapter 4, and note 43, Chapter 7.

17   William E. Arnal, "The Origins of Christianity Within, and Without, 'Religion': A Case Study," in Arnal and McCutcheon, *The Sacred Is the Profane*, 134–70.

18   The words "invention," "construction," "formation," and "creation" have enjoyed new status in recent years at the heart of the Critical Studies movement. Written into a turbulent history that obeys no supernatural teleology or ontology, these words are just as opposed to the question of "origins" that obsessed the nineteenth century as they are to the question of "essences"; cf. Masuzawa, "Regarding Origin: Beginnings, Foundations, and the Bicameral Formations of the Study of Religion," in Ramey, *Writing Religion*, 131–48.

19   Cf. Arnal, "The Origins of Christianity," 147–51.

20   Dubuisson, *Religion and Magic*, 103n114.

21 The current Code of Canon Law can be viewed at: http://www.vatican.va/archive/FRA0037/__P2N.HTM#9P. It should be pondered, perhaps, along with a re-reading of the article by Voltaire, "Droit canonique," part of his *Questions sur l'Encyclopédie*, in *Dictionnaire de la pensée de Voltaire par lui-même*, ed. André Versaille (Brussels: Èditions Complexe: 1994), 361–74.

22 Epistle 13 of Pope Gelasius I, trans. Karl F. Morrison in *Tradition and Authority in the Western Church 300–1140* (Princeton: Princeton University Press, 1969), 99. On this same theme, see the Code of Canon Law, Book 7, Part 2, Title 2, Chapter 3, Canon 1442.

23 M. T. Guyot, *Dictionnaire universel des hérésies, des erreurs et des schismes* (Lyon: Périsse Frères, 1847), 5 and 6.

24 Ibid., 8–9.

25 Bossuet, *A Discourse on the History of the Whole World* (n.t. London: Matthew Turner, 1868), 156–58.

26 *Code of Canon Law*, Book 2, Part 1, Title 3, Chapter 3, Canon 273; Book 2, Part 3, Title 1, Chapter 1, Canon 590, §s 1 and 2, and Canon 601; also Book 2, Part 1, Title 1, Canon 212, §1.

27 Readers who wish to avoid conventional accounts of ecclesiastical history may refer to the rather secular version by David Chidester, *Christianity: A Global History* (New York: Harper Collins, 2000); also to my *Dictionnaire des grands thèmes de l'histoire des religions: De Pythagore à Lévi-Strauss* (Brussels: Éditions Complexe, 2004).

28 See note 5, Chapter 7.

29 Dubuisson, *Religion and Magic*, particularly 56, 108–9, and 112–13. Revisiting Gramsci's notion of "cultural hegemony" would be appropriate here.

30 Fitzgerald, *The Ideology of Religious Studies*, xi. The fact that this spiritual power does not depend upon the possession of territory may doubtless be considered an advantage in many cases.

31 Chidester (*Christianity*, 49–156), in the same vein, opposes the threat ("the prospect") of Hell to the promise of Paradise in his chapter on the power of the Roman Church.

32 See, for example, Bobineau, *L'Empire des Papes*, 211–12.

Chapter 2

1 By an interesting coincidence, Lucretius uses the word "*religio*" from the earliest lines of his poem (I: 62–79). But it would be anachronistic to translate it as "religion," endowed with the Christian acceptation. And the translation offered on the *Université catholique de Louvain* website takes up that of M. Nisard (1857), who quite correctly preferred to speak of "superstition": http://agoraclass.fltr.ucl.ac.be/concordances/lucrece_dnc_I/lecture/3.htm. On the Latin word "*supersititio*," one may consult Émile Benveniste, "Religion and Superstition," in *Indo-European Language and Society*, trans. Jean Lallot (Miami, FL: University of Miami Press, 1973), 516–29.

2 Dubuisson, "A Major Paradigm," in *The Western Construction of Religion*, 129–40. It is revealing, for example, and entirely in conformity with this paradigm, that the exemplary and contemporary definitions of "religion" cited by Smith ("Religion, Religions, Religious," 192–93) are either theologically (see Paul Tillich, *Theology of Culture*, trans. Robert C. Kimball [Oxford: Oxford University Press, 1959], 7–8) or

anthropologically inspired (see Melford E. Spiro's chapter "Religion: Problems of Definition and Explanation," in his *Culture and Human Nature* [London: Transaction, 1994], 187–98).

3   Richard King has ascribed important developments to the history of this notion. See *Orientalism and Religion: Postcolonial Theory, India and 'The Mystic East'* (London: Routledge, 1999), 14–34.

4   For this story, see Stephen Greenblatt, *The Swerve: How the World Became Modern* (New York: Norton, 2011).

5   Augustine, *City of God*, Vol. III, 7.

6   Fitzgerald (*The Ideology of Religious Studies*, 5–6) sees in this re-partition of roles and tasks one of the forces of bourgeois capitalist ideology: on the one side, the interior life and existence in and of the Beyond; and on the other side, the free and rational organization of earthly beings. See also Asad, *Formations of the Secular*, 30–37.

7   Summarized by King in *Orientalism and Religion*, 44–47. Following Peter Hamilton ("The Enlightenment and the Birth of Social Science," in *Formations of Modernity*, ed. Stuart Hall and Braun Gieben [Oxford: Open University, 1992], 21–22), King presents the foremost ten or so factors (the prestige of reason; empiricism; the progress and primacy of science; universalism; the historic vision of societies and their changes; individualism; the progress of tolerance; the importance of freedom of conscience and expression, but also of commerce; the unity of human nature; secularism), while also adding the development of nationalist discourse and natural sciences.

8   Dubuisson, *Religion and Magic*, 97. Here, I join fully in the conclusion of the study made by Mino Bergamo, *L'Anatomie de l'âme* (Grenoble: J. Million, 1994).

9   Asad, *Genealogies of Religion Discipline and Reasons of Power in Christianity and Islam* (Baltimore, MD: Johns Hopkins University Press, 1993), 39; Fitzgerald, "Religions as Private Experience," in *The Ideology of Religious Studies*, 27–28; McCutcheon, *The Discipline of Religion: Structure, Meaning, Rhetoric* (London: Routledge, 2003), 44–45 (citing Smith, "Religion, Religions, Religious," 270–71). King (*Orientalism and Religion*, 21–22), just as McCutcheon, insists in particular on the influence that was exerted by the work of William James at the turn of the twentieth century when he stressed (contrary to institutional and organized religion) the importance of individual religious experiences from deep within.

10   David Chidester, *Savage Systems: Colonialism and Comparative Religion in South Africa* (Charlottesville: University Press of Virginia, 1996), 260.

11   Sam Whimster, ed., *The Essential Max Weber*, 2nd ed. (London: Routledge, 2006), 35. In this passage, "disenchantment" manifestly has a positive meaning. The "disenchanted" world is not opposed to an "enchanted" world—the world of Walt Disney—but to a world dominated by the irrational and frightening forces of magic. And Weber congratulates ascetic Protestantism for having rooted them out.

Chapter 3

1   See Stausberg, "Western Europe," 21.

2   As, for example, the vast fifty-volume collection, *Sacred Books of the East*, published in Oxford between 1879 and 1910. There, one may find translations of the major texts of Hinduism, Buddhism, Taoism, Confucianism, Zoroastrianism,

Jainism, and Islam, called up along with Christianity, Judaism, Sikhism, and Shinto among the dozen or so World Religions.

3   These Lectures are still given today. See: http://www.giffordlectures.org. See also Stausberg, "Western Europe," 20–21.

4   His dates: 1791–1867. Bopp's major work, *Vergleichende Grammatik des Sanskrit, Zend, Griechischen, Lateinischen, Litauischen, Gotischen und Deutschen*, was published between 1833 and 1852. It was translated into English by Edward B. Eastwick from 1845–1850.

5   I will not go into the rather technical discussions and techniques here that concern the original habitat of the Indo-Europeans, nor the state (real? reconstituted? idealized? artificial?) of that primordial language. Rather, I refer to the healthily polemical work of Jean-Paul Demoule, *Mais où sont passés les Indo-Européens?* (Paris: Éditions du Seuil, 2014), 505–92; also to the more orthodox book by Bernard Sergent, *Les Indo-Européens: Histoire, langues, mythes* (Paris: Éditions Payot et Rivages, 1995), 151–65.

6   A summary of this is easily accessible in André Encrevé's article "Histoire," in *Encyclopédie du protestantisme*, 2nd ed., ed. Pierre Gisel (Paris: Presses universitaires de France, 2006), 600–603.

7   See, for example, Bossuet (*Discourse on the Whole History of the World*, 89): "But without any further dispute about the year of our Lord and Savior's Birth, let it be sufficient, that we know it happened about the Year 4000 of the World."

8   This word "Aryan," Sanskrit in origin (*arya*), referred to free men belonging to the upper social classes. It did not acquire its racist connotation until our contemporary era. Max Müller, in the middle of the nineteenth century, would still distinguish between Turanian (or Turco-mongolian), Semitic, and Aryan races, religions and languages.

9   Ernest Renan, *Études d'histoire religieuse* (Paris: Michel Lévy, 1857) and *Nouvelles études d'histoire religieuse* (Paris: Calmann Lévy, 1884). The former work was translated by O. B. Frothingham as *Studies of Religious History and Criticism* (New York: Carleton, 1864).

10   Émile Burnouf, *The Science of Religions*, trans. Julie Liebe (London: Sonnenschein, Lowrey and Co., 1888), 37–38. Both Hellenist and Sanskritist, Émile Bournouf was Director of the École française in Athens from 1867 to 1875.

11   Salomon Reinach, *Manuel de philologie* (Paris: Hachette, 1880), 357. Nevertheless, one cannot implicate these scholars in the mass slaughters that would be carried out some decades later in Germany and Eastern Europe. The latter would, of course, have been completely unimaginable at the time.

12   Originally written in French from 1955 to 1977, it was translated by (respectively) Richard Howard, Natalie Gerardi, Miriam Kochan, and George Klin, from 1966 to 1984. All four volumes were reprinted by the University of Pennsylvania Press in 2003.

13   Written in French and published in the 1835 *Transactions of the Royal Society of Literature of the United Kingdom* (424) and subsequently reproduced in *Essais littéraires et historiques* (Bonn: Édouard Weber, 1842), 475–76.

14   Edward B. Tylor, *Primitive Culture: Researches into the Development of Mythology, Philosophy, Religion, Language, Art and Custom*, 4th ed., rev. ed. (London: John Murray, 1903), 1:27–28. The comparison with classical Greek seems dangerous, to say the least.

15   John A. Lubbock, *The Origin of Civilization and the Primitive Condition of Man: Mental and Social Conditions of Savages*, 2nd ed., with additions (London: Longmans,

Green, and Co., 1870), 133. Lubbock was a friend and close neighbor of Charles Darwin.

16   A collected overview of this history is given in the first three chapters of Gerald Gaillard, *The Routledge Dictionary of Anthropologists*, trans. Peter James Bowman (London: Routledge, 2012).

17   The same observation is made by Talal Asad in *Genealogies of Religion*, 42.

18   Émile Durkheim, *Elementary Forms of the Religious Life*. 2nd ed., trans. Joseph Ward Swain (London: Allen & Unwin, 1976), 1–2.

19   É. Magnin, "Religion," in *Dictionnaire de théologie catholique*, vol. 13, no. 2, ed. Alfred Vacant and Eugène Mangenot (Paris: Letouzey et Ané, 1937), col. 2286. Tertullian had said earlier in his *Apology* (17: 4–6) that the soul is "by nature Christian." I borrow this last quotation from Philippe Borgeaud, *Aux origines de l'histoire des religions* (Paris: Éditions du Seuil, 2004), 226.

20   Durkheim, *Elementary Forms of the Religious Life*, 418.

21   Ibid., 421.

22   Ibid., 423.

23   Ibid., 424.

24   On the anti-materialism of Durkheim, see his 1897 review of Marxist philosopher Antonio Labriola, "Essais sur la conception matérialiste de l'histoire," reprinted and translated by W. D. Halls, in Anthony Giddens, ed., *Durkheim on Politics and the State* (Cambridge: Polity Press, 1986), 128–36. As for Mauss, he denounced from 1924 onward the sociological errors of the Russian communists, in "A Sociological Assessment of Bolshevism (1924–5)," trans. Ben Brewster, *Economy and Society* 13, no. 3 (1984): 331–74.

25   One case in particular is that of the Belgian Goblet d'Alviella, an influential Freemason who married an American woman who had him buried, with his consent, according to the Protestant rite.

26   Published in German in 1799, Schleiermacher's *On Religion: Speeches to Its Cultured Despisers* was translated into English by John Oman and published by Harper & Brothers in New York in 1958.

27   Dubuisson, *The Western Construction of Religion*, 76–78.

28   Smith's article can be found in Taylor, *Critical Terms for Religious Studies*, 269–84, and was reprinted in Jonathan Z. Smith, *Relating Religion: Essays in the Study of Religion* (Chicago: University of Chicago Press, 2004), 169–96 (esp. 189–90). See also, by the same author, the article "Classification," in *Guide to the Study of Religion*, ed. Willi Braun and Russell T. McCutcheon (London: Continuum, 2007), 35–44. Also, see Charles Joseph Adams, "Classification of Religions" in the 2007 edition of the *Encyclopaedia Britannica*.

29   Smith, *Relating Religion*, 189–90; Guy Stroumsa, *A New Science: The Discovery of Religion in the Age of Reason* (Cambridge, MA: Harvard University Press, 2010), 31; Tomoko Masuzawa, *The Invention of World Religions* (Chicago: University of Chicago Press, 2005), 47; David Chidester, *Empire of Religion: Imperialism and Comparative Religion* (Chicago: University of Chicago Press, 2014), 27, amongst others.

30   Edward Said (*Orientalism* [New York: Vintage Books, 1994], 139–43) recalls the wish of Renan to elevate the study of the "neglected inferior languages" to the level of the Indo-European languages.

31   By "ethnic religion", that is, a "race religion": Whitney, cited by Smith, *Relating Religion*, 44. This is another way of saying that, in contrast to Christianity, it is incapable of claiming any sort of universality through which all persons would recognize each other.

32 Said, *Orientalism*, 103–4; Stroumsa, *A New Science*, 125–37; Masuzawa, *The Invention of World Religions*, xiii, 25–26, 145, and Chapter 6 (entitled "Islam: A Semitic Religion"), 179–206, etc. In *Islam and the Tyranny of Authenticity: An Inquiry into Disciplinary Apologetics and Self-Deception* (Sheffield: Equinox, 2016), Hughes has summarized the problems and contradictions raised in the West by Islamic Religious Studies (75–76).

33 See Auguste L. Sabatier, *Religions of Authority and the Religion of the Spirit*, trans. Louise Seymour (New York: McClure, Phillips and Co., 1904).

34 This sometimes conforms to the theory of the three ages — savagery, barbarism, civilization — whose principle likely proceeds from Dicaearchus of Messana (fourth century BCE). On this point, see W. Stoczkowski, "Essai sur la matière première de l'imaginaire anthropologique. Analyse d'un cas," *Revue de synthèse* IV, nos. 3–4 (1992): 439–57.

35 C. P. Tiele, *Outline of the History of Religion to the Spread of Universal Religions* (London: Trübner, 1877). See also the detailed taxonomy in the article "Religions" in the *Encyclopaedia Britannica* (1884); also in Masuzawa, *The Invention of World Religions*, 110. Corresponding discussions are found in Smith, *Relating Religion*, 190–91; see also 183–85 of the latter for several references to works earlier than Tiele.

36 Hans Gerhard Kippenberg, *Discovering Religious History in the Modern Age* (Princeton: Princeton University Press, 2002), 25–83.

37 Stroumsa, *A New Science*.

38 Asad (*Genealogies of Religion*, 40–41) sees in Cherbury the first, in his *De veritate* (1624) and *De religione Gentilium errorumque apud eos causes* (1645), to look for this "common denominator" in all religions (belief in God, cult with God as focus, morality, repentance and retribution in this world and the next). In so doing, and via these five deistic articles, Cherbury defines what subsequently would be considered "natural religion". These two works were placed on the Catholic Church index of forbidden writings.

39 Several references to this are found in my *The Western Construction of Religion*, 55–63.

40 One may recall the protagonist in Rousseau's *Profession of Faith of a Savoyard Vicar*, who initially thought the latter was a "Protestant in disguise" (Rockville, MD: Wildside Press, 2008), 242.

41 Benjamin Constant, *On Religion: Considered in Its Source, Its Forms, and Its Developments*, trans. Peter Paul Seaton Junior (Carmel, IN: Liberty Fund, 2017), 23–24 and 29.

42 This opinion is shared by King (*Orientalism and Religion*, 11–12), to whose analyses I gladly refer. Later on, we will see this idea of an essence at the heart of the phenomenology of religion.

43 Tylor, *Primitive Culture*, 1:25–26.

Chapter 4

1   A very instructive analysis is found in Robert Shepard, *God's People in the Ivory Tower: Religion in the Early American University* (New York: Carlson, 1991), and in McCutcheon, "The Study of Religion's Emergence in the U.S.," in his *The Discipline of Religion*, 38–53. In the latter, McCutcheon underlines (41) that the reception of the new discipline, come over from Europe at the beginning of the twentieth

century, was due to Protestant ministers who abandoned the confined space of their churches in order to benefit from greater intellectual liberty in academic milieus.

2   Emmanuel Kant, *Critique of Pure Reason*, trans. J. M. D. Meiklejohn (London: Henry G. Bohn, 1855), 411.

3   As is announced even in the title of the work of Gerardus van der Leeuw, *Religion in Essence and Manifestation: A Study in Phenomenology*, trans. J. E. Turner (London: Allen & Unwin, 1938), which we will return to in the next chapter.

4   It concerns the famous judicial decision rendered by the Supreme Court in the case of *Abingdon Township School District v Schempp* 374 U.S. 203 (1963). On this, see Jonathan Z. Smith, "Jonathan Z. Smith par lui-même" in *Magie de la comparaison: et autres essais d'histoire des religions*, trans. Daniel Barbu and Nicolas Meylan (Geneva: Labor et Fides, 2014), 177; and "Introduction" in Ramey, *Writing Religion*, 2–3.

5   Here and below I am relying on the figures from the website of the American Academy of Religion, obtained January 5, 2017, which themselves are the product of systematic research: https://www.aarweb.org/programs-services/department-services. McCutcheon warns me, however, that there are different criteria behind the research. Thus, to give only one example, the teaching of theology would be included in one study but not in another.

6   According to Warren Frisina (of the Academic Religion Task Force), in 1999 there were around 1500 programs of religious and theological studies in the United States and Canada: https://www.aarweb.org/node/331#preface.

7   Details of the second Humanities Departmental Survey can be found at: http://www.humanitiesindicators.org/binaries/pdf/HDS2_final.pdf.

8   These correspond to the three European levels of Licence, Master, and Doctorate.

9   This ecumenical version is located above the sectarian groups associated with the different Protestant Churches (Quaker, Baptist, Presbyterian, Congregationalist, etc.). But, following McCutcheon (*The Discipline of Religion*, 50), one must of course add that the so-called "scientific" approach has itself quite frequently been inspired by the liberal Protestant *doxa*. See also the Introduction to Ramey's *Writing Religion* (3), where he emphasizes the role played by Eliade and phenomenology in the establishment of this ecumenical approach devoid of any critical dimension.

10   On this point, see the rather severe analyses and criticisms from McCutcheon in *Manufacturing Religion*, 101 (at the beginning of Chapter 4, entitled "The Poverty of Theory in the Classroom") and 203–5; also those of Jonathan Z. Smith, in "Religious Studies: Whither (Wither) and Why?," *Method and Theory in the Study of Religion* 7 (1995): 407–13. One must add to this the ubiquitous financial considerations and the number of persons—that is, the extremely prosaic strategies and choices tied to the politics and policies behind the offerings available for the students.

11   On this subject, I refer in all humility to the monumental work in five volumes by Pandurang V. Kane, *The History of Dharmaçâstra* (Poona: Bandarkar Oriental Research Institute, 1930–1962). "*Dharma*" designates the impersonal cosmic order to which all creatures are subject, and the norms (social in particular) that devolve from them. This term does not bear any particular religious connotation. The caste system, for example, is one of the best known, as are the duties of the king, the primary duty of which is, quite specifically, the maintenance of this social order. On this particular point I concur with the conclusions of Hans-Michael Haussig in his "Der Religionsbegriff im Hinduismus," in *Der Religionsbegriff in den Religionen: Studien zum Selbst und Religionverständnis in Hinduismus, Buddhismus, Judentum und Islam*

(Berlin: Philo, 1999), 78–102. The word *"nirâtmaka"* means that things and beings, such as they are, are devoid of a substantial "self" — the equivalent of an individual and eternal soul, in Christian anthropology: "Mere suffering exists, but no sufferer is found; / The deeds are, but no doer is found" (Buddhaghosa; extract from the *Visuddhimagga*, quoted in Walpola Rahula, *What the Buddha Taught* [London: Gordon Fraser, 1982], 26). The Arab word *"dîn"* represents the same misleading practice when translated by the word "religion"; cf. McCutcheon, "The Resiliency of Conceptual Anachronism: On Knowing the Limits of 'the West' and 'Religion,'" *Religion* 36, no. 3 (2006): 154–65; and Nongbri, *Before Religion: A History of a Modern Concept* (New Haven: Yale University Press, 2013), 39–45.

12 McCutcheon, *The Discipline of Religion*, 46.

13 Ibid., 45–52.

14 Donald Wiebe, *The Politics of Religious Studies: The Continuing Conflict with Theology in the Academy* (New York: St. Martin's Press, 1999).

15 Donald Wiebe, *The Irony of Theology and the Nature of Religious Thought* (Montreal: McGill-Queen's University Press, 1991), 226–27.

16 Paul Veyne, *Did the Greeks Believe in Their Myths? An Essay on the Constitutive Imagination*, trans. Paula Wissing (Chicago: University of Chicago Press, 1988).

17 The idea is found in Chapters 6 and 8 of Wiebe's *The Politics of Religious Studies* ("Promise and Disappointment: Recent Developments in the Academic Study of Religion in the United States"; and "The Failure of Nerve in the Academic Study of Religion").

18 Wiebe, *The Politics of Religious Studies*, 55.

19 Ibid., 84. On the preceding page, Wiebe remarks that, in contrast to "teaching about religion" and "teaching of religion," one frequently hears now such expressions as "study of religion" and "practice of religion." See page 113 as well, where he voices his disappointment regarding the teaching of the History of Religions in the United States over the preceding fifty years.

20 Ibid., 85.

21 Ibid., xiii.

22 See note 4, Chapter 4.

23 See, for example, the website of the University of Chicago Divinity School: http://divinity.uchicago.edu/about. For Strasbourg, the long-past heir of German occupation from 1870 to 1918, see: https://theopro.unistra.fr and http://theocatho.unistra.fr/la-faculte-de-theologie. The Faculty of Theology of the Université catholique de Lille offers courses in Philosophy and in the Science of Religions. See: http://theologie.icl-lille.fr/enseignement/enseignement-philosophie-sciences-religions.asp.

24 See McCutcheon, *The Discipline of Religion*, 48–49.

25 See https://papers.aarweb.org/program_units. It is worth noting, incidentally, that a certain number of sessions are "co-sponsored."

26 Luther H. Martin and Donald Wiebe, "Establishing a Beachhead: NAASR, Twenty Years Later," in *Theory in a Time of Excess: Beyond Reflection and Explanation in Religious Studies Scholarship*, Aaron Hughes, ed. (London: Equinox, 2017), 13–20. This article, as the title suggests, was written for the twentieth anniversary of the creation of NAASR.

27 See Wiebe, *The Politics of Religious Studies*, 79–85. Also, Chapters 14 and 15 ("Against Science in the Academic Study in Religion: On the Emergence and Development of the AAR"; and "A Religious Agenda Continued: A Review of the Presidential Addresses of the AAR," respectively).

28 A special issue put out for the twenty-fifth anniversary of the journal (*Method and Theory in the Study of Religion* 25, nos. 4–5 [2014]: 309–486) was devoted to "Special Features in the Identity of NAASR and the Character of the Critical Study of Religion." There we find several names of those responsible for the journal's renown (Arnal, Hughes, McCutcheon, Martin, Wiebe). Hughes and Ramey are its current (2018) editors. The journal is published by Brill in the Netherlands.

29 The quite eclectic list of these academic organisms may be found at: www. aarweb.org/about/partnerships. Among these groups, we note the presence of the Adventist Society for Religious Study; European Society for the Study of Western Esotericism; Evangelical Philosophical Society; Hagiography Society; International Association of Shin Buddhist Studies; Karl Barth Society of North America; Society for Hindu-Christian Studies; and the William James Society.

30 G. Achache, "Critique," in *Encyclopédie philosophique universelle II: Les notions philosophiques*, ed. Sylvain Auroux (Paris: Presses universitaires de France, 1990), 1:517.

31 A. W. Hughes, "Sleeping with Elephants," *Method and Theory in the Study of Religion* 25, nos. 4–5 (2013): 319–24.

32 William E. Arnal, "The Identity of NAASR and the Character of the Critical Study of Religion: Introduction," *Method and Theory in the Study of Religion* 25, nos. 4–5 (2013): 317–18.

33 R. T. McCutcheon, "A Modest Proposal on Method," *Method and Theory in the Study of Religion* 25, nos. 4–5 (2013): 339–49. The author gives references (344n9) to a famous debate from 2005 in which the legislator was obliged to clarify the relation between theology and science in the context of a teaching that opposed Darwinian theories to adverse, creationist, theories of "intelligent design". See: https://en.wikipedia.org/wiki/Intelligent_design and https://en.wikipedia.org/wiki/Kitzmiller_v._Dover_Area_School_District. By this polemic, which does not just concern scholarly and university milieus but indeed millions of American citizens, we are transported to the heart of all manner of stakes (societal, pedagogical, political) contained in the paradigm "science *versus* theology." The debates are particularly bitter in the United States because the influence of institutions and religionist lobbying there is much greater than in the majority of the countries of Western Europe.

34 McCutcheon, *The Discipline of Religion*, 5. Quite representative, McCutcheon (originally Canadian, now teaching in the United States) is the first one to be read, for he probably best incarnates the different dimensions of this critical movement in whose birth he actively participated. He is also the one who analyzed this movement the best, in particular with his *Manufacturing Religion*.

35 In order to better situate people and things, I recall here that Jonathan Z. Smith belongs *grosso modo* to the preceding generation, and Eliade, born in 1908, to one generation further back. Eliade died in 1986, after thirty years at the University of Chicago, when McCutcheon was still a student in Canada. Smith and Eliade were colleagues at Chicago for ten or so years, up to the death of the latter. These three researchers summarize rather well the evolution undergone by American Religious Studies over the last sixty years, if not since the mid-1950s.

36 By contrast, with the exception of Marx, the *direct* influence of German thinkers (Weber, Husserl, Heidegger) is not clearly discernible.

37 In his *French Theory: How Foucault, Derrida, Deleuze, & Co. Transformed the Intellectual Life of the United States* (trans. Jeff Fort with Josephine Berganza and Marlon Jones [Minneapolis: University of Minnesota Press, 2008], 76–77), François

Cusset situates this turning point from 1975 to 1980, and first within the field of literary criticism. Paradoxically, its influence was much more profound and longer-lasting in the United States than in France, where it had originated.

38 The chapter "Faith and Knowledge: The Two Sources of 'Religion' at the Limits of Reason Alone," written by Derrida (in Derrida and Gianni Vattimo, eds., *Religion: Cultural Memory in the Present*, trans. Samuel Weber [Stanford, CA: Stanford University Press, 1998], 1–78), does not smack of Historian of Religions. At the most, he writes enigmatic puns. Thus, on page 66 we read, or rather, attempt to decipher: "At the bottom without bottom of this crypt, the One + *n* incalculably engenders all these supplements. *It makes violence of itself, does violence to itself and keeps itself from the other.* The auto-immunity of religion can only indemnify itself without assignable end. On the bottom without bottom of an always virgin impassibility, *chora* of tomorrow in languages we no longer know or do not yet speak. This place is unique, it is the One without name. It *makes way, perhaps,* but without the slightest generosity, neither divine nor human. The dispersion of ashes is not even promised there, nor death given." What will history make of this word salad?

39 See Isabelle Decobecq, "Les *visual studies*: un champ indiscipliné" (doctoral thesis, University of Lille, 2017).

40 This warning by Cusset (*French Theory*, 102) is important, for it underlines the great weaknesses of the intellectual work being done in the United States in the light of theses by authors representing French Theory. His warnings (88–89) concerning editorial conception and the role of textbooks and readers apply equally to those in Religious Studies.

41 See, for example, McCutcheon, *The Discipline of Religion*, xi–xii.

42 One may glean an idea of this sort of work by referring to the thematic volume *Poétique et rhétorique des savoirs dans les sciences humaines* that I directed and coordinated for the Italian journal *Strumenti critici* 85 (September, 1997): 347–545.

43 Ivan Strenski, *Four Theories of Myth in Twentieth-Century History: Cassirer, Eliade, Lévi-Strauss and Malinowski* (Iowa City: University of Iowa Press, 1987).

44 Bruce Lincoln, *Myth, Cosmos, and Society: Indo-European Themes of Creation and Destruction* (Cambridge, MA: Harvard University Press, 1986) and *Theorizing Myth: Narrative, Ideology, and Scholarship* (Chicago: University of Chicago Press, 1999).

45 Robert A. Segal, *Theorizing about Myth* (Amherst: University of Massachusetts Press, 1999).

46 Dean A. Miller, *The Epic Hero* (Baltimore: Johns Hopkins University Press, 2000).

47 Here, we must cite C. Scott Littleton's *The New Comparative Mythology: An Anthropological Assessment of the Theories of Georges Dumézil* (Berkeley, LA: University of California Press, 1966).

48 McCutcheon, *Manufacturing Religion*; and *The Discipline of Religion*. See also, amongst others, Said, *Orientalism*; Asad, *Genealogies of Religion*; King, *Orientalism and Religion*; Chidester, *Savage Systems*; Craig Martin, *A Critical Introduction to the Study of Religion*; Taylor, *Critical Terms for Religious Studies*; Braun and McCutcheon, *Guide to the Study of Religion*. For each of these authors, consult their index, *s.v.* "Foucault." The works of Foucault were translated into English from the beginning of the 1980s (*Archaeology of Knowledge*, 1982). Those of his epigones, Michel de Certeau and Paul Veyne, followed soon after. The first *Foucault Reader* was published in 1984, and a *Foucault for Beginners* in 1994.

49 Michel Foucault, *The Archeology of Knowledge: And the Discourse on Language*, trans. A. M. Sheridan Smith (New York: Pantheon, 1972), 32.

50 This "bauble of sonorous uselessness" (from "*Sonnet allégorique de lui-même*," see https://www.poetryintranslation.com/PITBR/French/Mallarme.php#anchor_Toc223495054) may not speak directly to English readers, but its image is clear enough.

51 McCutcheon, *Manufacturing Religion*, 3. McCutcheon specifies that "the factory" is opposed to the over-peaceful conception of Jonathan Z. Smith, according to which religion would simply be a product of academic imagination (26).

52 For details, see my *Twentieth Century Mythologies*.

53 Roland Barthes, *Mythologies: The Complete Edition, in a New Translation*, 2nd ed., translated by Richard Howard and Annette Lavers (New York: Hill and Wang, 2012).

54 Note the subtitle of the second book: *Structure, Meaning, Rhetoric*. What better way to acknowledge one's debt toward, and perhaps even admiration for, the linguistics and poetics of the sixties?

55 Barthes, *Mythologies*, 142.

56 Cf. McCutcheon, *Manufacturing Religion*, 66.

57 In particular, Louis Althusser, "Idéologies et appareils idéologiques d'État (Notes pour une recherche)," in *Positions (1964–1975)* (Paris: Les éditions sociales, 1976), 67–125. See also his *For Marx*, trans. Ben Brewster (London: Verso, 2005), 231–36.

58 McCutcheon, *Manufacturing Religion*, 66.

59 Ibid., 18, and 245 of the Index, *s.v.* "Ideology" and "Ideological strategies." These are developed throughout the book.

60 Roland Barthes, *Mythologies*, 142–43.

61 Ibid., 143.

62 Karl Marx and Frederick Engels, *The German Ideology. Part One. With Selections from Parts Two and Three and Supplementary Texts*, ed. C. J. Arthur (New York: International Publishers, 2004), 66–67.

63 Cf. Terry Eagleton, *The Ideology of the Aesthetic* (Cambridge, MA: Blackwell, 1990).

64 See Daniel Dubuisson and Sophie Raux, "L'histoire de l'art et les *Visual Studies*: Entre mythe, science et idéologie," *Histoire de l'art* 70 (2012): 13–21.

65 Nietzsche, *The Antichrist*, trans. H. L. Mencken (n.p., 120), §15.

66 Quotation available at: https://www.marxist.org/archive/marx/works/1845/german-ideology/ch01a.htm.

67 A more nuanced point of view can be found in King, *Orientalism and Religion*, 280. See also his Index *s.v.* "Marxism," where he also cites Antonio Gramsci. But King was directly confronted with Marxist readings that were much more sophisticated by Indian specialists in Postcolonial and Subaltern Studies (including G. C. Spivak, P. Chatterjee, A. Ahmen, G. Prakash, and R. Guha).

68 Fitzgerald, *The Ideology of Religious Studies*, 20.

69 Cited copiously by Craig Martin, but in a work published in 2012. For Bourdieu, one could read his "Genèse et structure du champ religieux," *Revue française de sociologie* XII, no. 3 (1971): 295–334, as well as my critique in *Wisdoms of Humanity*, 186–92.

70 A good presentation is found in King, *Orientalism and Religion*, 82–90. Said has also been cited by McCutcheon, Fitzgerald, and Chidester, the last of whom puts his *Savage Systems*, 1–2, under the double patronage of Said and Foucault. Said himself recognizes the influence that Foucault has had upon him.

71   Karl Marx, "The British Rules in India," *New York Daily Tribune* (June 25, 1853).

Chapter 5

1   Rudolf Otto, *The Idea of the Holy*, 2nd ed., trans. John W. Harvey (London: Oxford University Press, 1952).

2   The English version of this work ("Problems in Religion"), translated by Bernard Noble, is contained in Max Scheler, *On the Eternal in Man* (London: Routledge, 2017), 105–356.

3   Originally published as *Einführung in die Religionssoziologie* (1931). On Joachim Wach, who was a professor at Chicago from 1945 to 1955, see Christian K. Wedemeyer and Wendy Doniger, eds., *Hermeneutics, Politics and the History of Religions: The Contested Legacies of Joachim Wach & Mircea Eliade* (Oxford: Oxford University Press, 2010). See also Fitzgerald, *The Ideology of Religious Studies*, 37; and below, note 214.

4   An over-benevolent presentation of the topic is presented by Douglas Allen, "Phenomenology of Religion," in Mircea Eliade (ed.), *The Encyclopedia of Religion*, vol. 11 (New York: Macmillan, 1987), 272–85. Like many, Allen classes Otto, van der Leeuw, and Eliade among the "six influential phenomenologists" (276). The others are W. Brede Kristensen, Friedrich Heiler, and C. Jouco Bleeker, whose work never enjoyed the influence of the first three.

5   Kant, *Critique of Pure Reason*, 53.

6   Ibid., 56.

7   Georg W. Hegel, *Introduction to Lectures on Aesthetics* (quotation translated by M. Cunningham). Originally published in the *Einleitung to Vorlesungen über die Aesthetik*, vol. 1, edited by D. H. G. Hotho, 11–12 (Berlin: Dunker und Humblot, 1835–1838).

8   P. J. Labarrière, "Phénoménologie de l'Esprit," in *Encyclopédie philosophique universelle III: Les Œuvres philosophiques*, ed. Jean-François Mattéi (Paris: Presses universitaires de France, 1992), 1824–25.

9   Georg W. Hegel, *Lectures on the Philosophy of Religion. Together with a Work on the Proofs of the Existence of God*, 2nd ed., trans. E. B. Spiers and J. Burdon Sanderson (London: Routledge, 1962), 1:33 and 46. For Hegel, sharing the prejudices of his time, the other religions cannot claim the title of "true religion," for God "is not as yet known in His true nature, since there is wanting to them the absolute content of Spirit" (83).

10   Pierre D. Chantepie de la Saussaye, *Manual of the Science of Religion*, trans. Beatrice S. Colyer-Fergusson (née Max Müller) (London: Longmans, Green, and Co., 1891), 4. In the French version, Henri Hubert, who was close to Mauss and Durkheim, also specifies that the material of the Phenomenology of Religion and that of the History of Religions are, in reality, the same: "These two studies have two ways of ordering the same facts. Phenomenology must present separately the classes of phenomena that history exposes concurrently by era and by country" ("Introduction à la traduction française," in *Manuel d'histoire des religions* [Paris: Armand Colin, 1904], xxiii).

11   Jean Hering, *Phénoménologie et philosophie religieuse: Étude sur la théorie de la connaissance religieuse* (Paris: Librairie Félix Alcan, 1926). Contained in the work is a summary of Scheler's theses.

12	Dominique Janicaud, *Le Tournant théologique de la phénoménologie française* (Combas: Éditions de l'éclat, 1991).

13	Hering, *Phénoménologie et philosophie religieuse*, 43.

14	Ibid., 49. See also Jean-François Lyotard, *Phenomenology*, trans. Brian Beakley (Albany, NY: State University of New York Press, 1991), 47–54.

15	In support of this affirmation, Hering cites two passages from Husserl's *Ideas* (§49), according to which (a) the *Ego cogitans* is without doubt the Absolute Being; and (b) the world of transcendental *res* is absolutely dependent upon the conscience.

16	Hering, *Phénoménologie et philosophie religieuse*, 64.

17	Ibid., 61. One needs to specify that this 'object' is not necessarily concrete: "The 'intentional' object does not necessarily exist in an ontological sense" (62). But, in every case, these objects never exist in the conscience, as subjective representation, for they only exist as the object of an intentional target.

18	Ibid., 68.

19	Ibid., 52–53.

20	Ibid., 65.

21	Ibid., 118. On Schleiermacher, see above, note 26, Chapter 3, and note 41, Chapter 3, with corresponding paragraphs in the main text.

22	See also Hering, *Phénoménologie et philosophie religieuse*, 100, where, a propos the teleological order existing in the world, he admits that the thesis would imply the existence of a God who "would clearly be transcendent, not just relative to the conscience but also to the world. That is why he would not be found in the Universe." It would be hard to be more orthodox or less unforeseeable.

23	Ibid., 140. We have seen above, at note 9, Chapter 5, that Hegel held this prejudice, as did Pascal, Kant, and so many others.

24	On these *reinventions* of Jesus, see above, note 15, Chapter 1, with the corresponding paragraph in the main text.

25	I reserve the examination of the notion of *sui generis* that Hering uses several times for the chapter devoted to Eliade (who makes systematic use of this).

26	Hegel, *Lectures on the Philosophy of Religion*, 33 and 46.

27	van der Leeuw, *Religion in Essence and Manifestation*, 678.

28	Ibid., 684.

29	Ibid., 674 (all three phrases cited).

30	Hans H. Penner, quoted by Guilford Dudley, *Religion on Trial: Mircea Eliade and His Critics* (Philadelphia, PN: Temple University Press, 1977), 39. On the frequent use of the word "mystery" in the work of Eliade, see the assembled quotations in my *Twentieth Century Mythologies*.

31	van der Leeuw, *Religion in Essence and Manifestation*, 680.

32	"We put out of action the general position which belongs to the essence of the natural attitude; we parenthesize everything which that position encompasses with respect to being: thus the whole natural world which is continually 'there for us,' 'on hand,' and which will always remain there according to consciousness as an 'actuality' even if we choose to parenthesize it. [...] Thus I exclude all sciences relating to this natural world no matter how firmly they stand there for me, no matter how much I admire them, no matter how little I think of making even the least objection to them" (Husserl, *Ideas Pertaining to a Pure Phenomenology and to a Phenomenological Philosophy. First Book. General Introduction to a Pure Phenomenology*, trans. F. Kersten [The Hague: Martinus Nijhoff, 1983], 61).

33	van der Leeuw, *Religion in Essence and Manifestation*, 684.

34   The first edition of Otto's *The Idea of the Holy* appeared fifteen years before the major work of van der Leeuw.

35   Otto, *The Idea of the Holy*, 7th ed., trans. John Harvey (Oxford: Oxford University Press, 1936), 89.

36   This metaphysical point of view is contradicted by what linguistics tells us (cf. Benveniste, *Indo-European Language and Society*, 444–68). The conclusions of Benveniste hold in three points: 1) there is no common term in Indo-European to render the notion of "holy"; 2) in several languages (Latin, Greek, Avestan), the notion is translated by a double expression ("*sacer*" and "*sanctus*" in Latin, for example); and 3) "but we are not in a position to construct a single model on the basis of these coupled terms" (468). Now, these negative conclusions only concern the one, Indo-European linguistic prehistory. It could thus be thought that one would observe an even larger heterogeneity and dispersion, at a more universal level.

37   In 1909, Otto had published two critical essays in which he opposed, respectively, Kant to the theologian Heinrich Fries, and Goethe to Darwin.

38   Otto, *The Idea of the Holy*, 2nd ed., 29.

39   van der Leeuw, as we have seen, will take up this theme that inverts the direction of the framework put in place by Husserlian phenomenology.

40   Otto, *The Idea of the Holy*, 2nd ed., 9.

41   Ibid., 9–10.

42   Ibid., 26. The old opposition made by Arnobious ("*nostra religio*" versus "*vestrae religiones*") is therefore still current despite the passage of several centuries.

43   Ibid., 109.

44   Ibid., 110.

45   Ibid., 111.

46   Ibid.

47   Ibid., 83.

48   Wach's *Sociology of Religion* certainly must not be understood as a sociological explanation of religion in the style of Durkheim or Weber. For Wach, it is religion that explains society, and not the other way around. Indeed, he speaks of it as a force that transcends history: "We like to think that the desired agreement among students of society could be reached on the basis of the formula that perfect integration of a society never has been nor can be achieved without a religious basis." But, he adds immediately, provided additionally that one considers religion "as that profoundest source from which all human existence is nourished and upon which it depends in all its aspects: man's communion with God" (383). A critique of Wach's positions is found in McCutcheon's *Manufacturing Religion* and *The Discipline of Religion* (index, *s.v.* "Wach").

49   A surprising example of this is found in Mircea Eliade, *Occultism, Witchcraft and Cultural Fashions: Essays in Comparative Religions* (Chicago: University of Chicago Press: 1978), 54–57, where Eliade associates, in the name of common religious inspiration, alchemy, yoga, shamanism, Gnosticism, Kabbalah, esotericism, hermeticism, and tantrism.

50   Cf., among many others, *Myths, Dreams and Mysteries*, trans. Philip Mairet (New York: Harper and Row, 1975), 33.

51   His reputation as Indianist and Sanskritist does not emerge faultless from attentive scrutiny, as I have shown in *Impostures et pseudo-science: L'oeuvre de Mircea Eliade* (Villeneuve d'Ascq: Presses universitaires du Septentrion, 2005), 35–36.

52   Eliade, *Occultism, Witchcraft and Cultural Fashions*, 47.

53　Mircea Eliade, *The Sacred and the Profane*, trans. Willard Trask (New York: Harcourt Brace and World, 1959), 18.

54　I have analyzed the major characteristics of this style in "The Poetical and Rhetorical Structure of the Eliadean Text: A Contribution to Critical Theory and Discourses on Religions," in Wedemeyer and Doniger, *Hermeneutics, Politics and the History of Religions*, 133–46. See also McCutcheon, *The Discipline of Religion*, 5–8, on the rhetorical techniques used by the History of Religions.

55　On this, one may consult the indispensable synthesis by Kocku von Stuckrad, *Western Esotericism: A Brief History of Secret Knowledge* (London: Equinox, 2013); but also, more specifically concerning Eliade, Richard Noll, *The Jung Cult: Origins of a Charismatic Movement* (London: Fontana, 1996); and my own work, *Twentieth Century Mythologies: Dumézil, Lévi-Strauss, Eliade*: "Addendum III: Esotericism and Fascism," 243–58. There, I establish that most of the symbols beloved of Eliade (symbolism of the center, the cosmic tree, the ladder, the labyrinth, the bridge, light, knots, waters, initiation) were borrowed from Guénon, giving me cause to specify that, if one is to understand the work of Eliade alongside his official university work, one must also take account of his political, Romanian, esoteric, Gnostic, and Jungian influences, for they are fundamental.

56　Mircea Eliade, *The Portugal Journal*, trans. Mac Linscott Ricketts (Albany, NY: SUNY Press, 2010).

57　Ibid., 68–69. Elsewhere (86), he expresses regret that Hitler had not been a sailor (being afraid of shipwrecks), since otherwise he would have defeated the English in 1940.

58　Wach and Eliade were intellectually close, as McCutcheon points out in *The Discipline of Religion*, 60.

59　For some of Eliade's precursors, see Adrianna Berger, "Mircea Eliade: Romanian Fascism and the History of Religions in the United States," in *Tainted Greatness*, 2nd ed., ed. Nancy A. Harrowitz (Philadelphia: Temple University Press, 1994), 51–74. (A first version was published in 1989.)

60　Mircea Eliade, *Mephistopheles and the Androgyne: Studies in Religion, Myth and Symbol* (New York: Sheed and Ward, 1965), 202.

61　Eliade, *The Sacred and the Profane*, 116 and 117.

62　Mircea Eliade, *Myth and Reality*, trans. Willard R. Trask (Long Grove, IL: Waveland, 1998), 144. Eliade will accord the same "religious" — or rather, "eschato-logical" — justification to the massacres of millions committed by the SS in the camps (cf. Dubuisson, *Impostures et pseudo-science*, 92.)

63　Eliade, *Myth and Reality*, 171–72.

64　Ibid., 14–143. For a semiotically inspired criticism (Saussure and Barthes) of the Eliadean conceptions of the symbol, see Darlene M. Juschka, "Deconstructing the Eliadean Paradigm: Symbol," in *Introducing Religion: Essays in Honor of Jonathan Z. Smith*, ed. Willi Braun and R. T. McCutcheon (New York: Routledge, 2014), 162–77.

65　Eliade, *The Quest: History and Meaning in Religion* (Chicago: University of Chicago Press, 1969), 36.

66　For example, in the *Portugal Journal*, 15 and 206.

67　Eliade, *Journal II, 1957–1969*, trans. Fred H. Johnson, Jr. (Chicago: University of Chicago Press, 1989), 69, 179, and 189.

68　On this specific point, see my *Twentieth Century Mythologies*: "Addendum III: Esotericism and Fascism," 243–58, reproduced (in its French version) in *Imposture et pseudo-science*, esp. 123–25 [English version, 253–56], where all the texts are cited in which Eliade, reflecting the ancient Gnostics like Valentin, whom he admired, incriminates the Jews and Judaism for having desacralized the Cosmos, thus committing a kind of ontological crime—a crime against Being. It is clear that Eliade's "metaphysical anti-Semitism," following the nice formulation of Scholem, citing Wasserstrom (*Religion after Religion*, 178 and 179), is not vulgar or popular anti-Semitism in the Nazi image. This metaphysical version of anti-Semitism is more frightening in that it advances hidden under the appearances of a quite erudite discussion of specialists. "Camouflage" is a term often used by Eliade to designate the disguises under which the Holy manifests itself to men. Thus, what is returned to the latter is the task of "decoding" them. One may also refer to the analyses and documents assembled by Steven M. Wasserstrom, *Religion after Religion: Gershom Scholem, Mircea Eliade and Henry Corbin at Eranos* (Princeton: Princeton University Press, 1999); Alexandra Laignel-Lavastine, *Cioran, Eliade, Ionesco: L'oubli du fascisme* (Paris: Presses universitaires de France, 2002); Leon Volovici, *Nationalist Ideology and Antisemitism: The Case of Romanian Intellectuals in the 1930s* (Oxford: Pergamon Press, 1991); McCutcheon, *Manufacturing Religion*, 83–88 and 94–96; Carlo Ginzburg, "Mircea Eliade's Ambivalent Legacy," in Wedemeyer and Doniger, *Hermeneutics, Politics and the History of Religions*, 307–23. For his part, Moshe Idel, in *Mircea Eliade: From Magic to Myth* (New York: Peter Lang, 2014), has shown that the Eliadean approach to Judaism and the Kabbalah was quite often inexact. The origin of these errors is, as always, looking into Eliade's will to enter facts, at any price, into the predefined metaphysical frameworks of his system when these frameworks are anachronistic and arbitrary.

69   Dubuisson, *Impostures et pseudo-science*, 180n87.

70   Eliade, *Myth and Reality*, 146.

71   Eliade, *Journal II*, 159.

72   Julien Ries, "*Homo religiosus*," in *Dictionnaire des religions*, 3rd ed., ed. Paul Poupard (Paris: Presses universitaires de France, 1984), 1:863.

Chapter 6

1   Cf. Craig Martin, "Delimiting Religion," 157.

2   See, for example, McCutcheon, *Manufacturing Religion*, 9 and 183, where we find the expression "essentialist thinking"; also King, *Orientalism and Religion*, 7–9, 11 and 112, for the idea of an "endemic essentialism" that for him belongs to Oriental Studies.

3   A very good example of this is found in Wiebe, *The Politics of Religious Studies*, 203, regarding the above-cited essay by Douglas Allen, "Phenomenology of Religion." One may also look to McCutcheon's *The Discipline of Religion*, 204–8, in Robert Ellwood, *The Politics of Myth: A Study of C. G. Jung, Mircea Eliade, and Joseph Campbell* (Albany: State University of New York Press, 1999).

4   Gregory Alles, "Toward a Genealogy of the Holy: Rudolf Otto and the Apologetics of Religion," *Journal of the American Academy of Religion* 69, no. 2 (2001): 326.

5   Fitzgerald, *The Ideology of Religious Studies*, 47 and 202–3.

6   Strenski, *Four Theories of Myth*, 102.

7   John A. Saliba, '*Homo Religiosus' in Mircea Eliade: An Anthropological Evaluation* (Leiden: Brill, 1976). See also J. Z. Smith, *To Take Place: Toward Theory in Ritual* (Chicago: University of Chicago Press, 1987), 1–6; and Russell T. McCutcheon, *Critics*

Not Caretakers: Redescribing the Public Study of Religion (Albany: State University of New York Press, 2001), 46–47.

　8　Otto, *The Idea of the Holy*, 2nd ed., 5. Numerous critiques of Otto's positions are found in Fitzgerald, *The Ideology of Religious Studies*; King, *Orientalism and Religion*; and McCutcheon, *Manufacturing Religion* (index, s. v. "Otto").

　9　For example, in Max Scheler's *On the Eternal in Man* (New York: Harper and Brothers, 1960), 170 and 268.

　10　Hering, *Phénoménologie et philosophie religieuse*, 23, 25, 45, 62 and 94. The expression is also found in Durkheim (see note 20, Chapter 3, with the corresponding paragraph in the main text), but with no metaphysical claim. In the same way, Durkheim ascribes a classifying function to the opposition sacred–profane, for whom there is no implication of an ontology of the Holy.

　11　McCutcheon, *Manufacturing Religion,* 26.

　12　McCutcheon, *The Discipline of Religion*, 54–55. As indicated by the title, Chapter IV of this work ("Methods, Theories, and the Terrors of History: Closing the Eliadean Era with Some Dignity," 191–212) is devoted to a clear criticism of Eliade and his principal disciples (B. Rennie, D. Cave, C. Olson, R. Ellwood). See also *Manufacturing Religion*, 3, 16, 26, 135, 189, and 197; Lincoln, *Theorizing Myth*, 21–24; King, *Orientalism and Religion*, 11 and 61; Fitzgerald, *The Ideology of Religious Studies*, 41. The position of Douglas Allen (in "Recent Defenders of Eliade: A Critical Evaluation," *Religion* 24 [1994]: 333–51) is ambiguous, as with all compromise.

　13　In the eyes of Eliade, religious meanings are to be chosen from such qualifiers as deep, superior, total, cosmic, complete, higher, etc., as I have ironically pointed out in "Poetical and Rhetorical Structure," 138. Is it possible to choose any hollower epithets?

　14　In addition to these textbooks one must also cite the often-collected works destined for advanced students and offering a much more critical approach to the notions and concepts utilized in Religious Studies. For example, among many others: Taylor, *Critical Terms for Religious Studies*; John R. Hinnells, ed., *The Routledge Companion to the Study of Religion* (London: Routledge, 2007); Braun and McCutcheon, *Guide to the Study of Religion*; Strenski, *Thinking about Religion: A Reader* (Malden: Blackwell, 2006); and von Stuckrad and Segal, eds., *Vocabulary for the Study of Religion*, 3 vols. (Leiden: Brill, 2015).

　15　Mark MacWilliams, Joanne Punzo Waghorne, Deborah Sommer, Cybelle Shattuck, Kay A. Read, Selva J. Raj, Khaled Keshk, Deborah Halter, James Egge, Robert M. Baum, Carol S. Anderson, and Russell T. McCutcheon, "Religion/s between Covers: Dilemmas of the World Religions Textbook," *Religious Studies Review* 31, nos. 1–2 (2005): 1–36. On page 1 we find a list of the fifteen principal textbooks that were consulted (*Religions*; *World Religions Today*; *Living Religions*; *Religions of the World*; *Experiencing the World's Religions: Tradition, Challenge, and Change*; *Patterns of Religion*, etc.). One may also refer to McCutcheon, "The Poverty of Theory in the Classroom," in *Manufacturing Religion*, 101–26, as well as pages 203–5, where he stresses both the paradoxes in the teaching of Religious Studies in the United States and the profound difference that exists between simple introductory, or "bread-and-butter" courses, and more substantial courses. In the same volume (139–44), McCutcheon provides a critique of the monumental, sixteen-volume *Encyclopedia of Religion* under the editorial direction of Eliade (New York: MacMillan, 1987).

　16　Joanne Punzo Waghorne, "Revisiting the Question of Religion in the World Religions Textbooks," *Religious Studies Review* 31, nos. 1–2 (2005): 3.

17 Deborah Sommer, "Chinese Religions in World Religions Textbooks," *Religious Studies Review* 31, nos. 1–2 (2005): 5–6.

18 Kay A. Read, "World Religions and the Miscellaneous Category," *Religious Studies Review* 31, nos. 1–2 (2005): 11. These indigenous cultures are also, for the most part, former colonial possessions that were considered primitive for a long time (absence of writing or science; ignorance of monotheism, etc.). The questions raised by this heritage are apparently too embarrassing for the textbooks that prefer to neglect this historical dimension, despite its cruciality.

19 Selva J. Raj, "The Quest for a Balanced Representation of South Asian Religions in World Religions Textbooks," *Religious Studies Review* 31, nos. 1–2 (2005): 14–16.

20 Sommer, "Chinese Religions in World Religions Textbooks," 4.

21 James Egge, "Buddhism in World Religions Textbooks," *Religious Studies Review* 31, nos. 1–2 (2005): 26–27. Cf. note 25, Chapter 7, with corresponding paragraph in the main text.

22 Robert M. Baum, "The Forgotten South: African Religions in World Religions Textbooks," *Religious Studies Review* 31, nos. 1–2 (2005): 27–30. In contrast to Buddhism, one may say about African religions and traditions that, since the nineteenth century, in one way or another, they have always been left on the sidelines of the great civilizations.

23 Khaled Keshk, "Islam in World Religions Textbooks," *Religious Studies Review* 31, nos. 1–2 (2005): 20–23. On this prejudice, see note 9, Chapter 3, and notes 30-32, Chapter 3.

24 Ibid., 23.

25 To have an idea of the semantic richness of the English word "God," see, for example, Francis Schüssler Fiorenza and Gordon D. Kaufman, "God," in Taylor, *Critical Terms for Religious Studies*, 136–59.

26 McCutcheon, *Critics Not Caretakers*, 53–55.

27 Stereotypes such as the reassuring one of the believer or the faithful, borrowed from the image imposed by Christian religions, and denounced by McCutcheon in "The Perils of Having One's Cake and Eating It Too: Some Thoughts in Response," *Religious Studies Review* 31, nos. 1–2 (2005): 33.

28 Waghorne ("Revisiting the Question of Religion in the World Religions Textbook," 4) situates this, for this reason, in the "metanarrative of world religions" — that is, on the level of the deep structures that organize the story which, thanks to them, becomes canonical.

29 Ibid., 3–4.

30 Ibid., 3. Situations that not all textbooks seem to appreciate much.

31 Mark MacWilliams, "Introduction," *Religious Studies Review* 31, nos. 1–2 (2005): 2.

32 McCutcheon, "The Perils of Having One's Cake and Eating It Too," 34.

Chapter 7

1 Nicolas Bancel, Pascal Blanchard, and Françoise Vergès, *La République coloniale* (Paris: Hachette, 2003), 56.

2 The London Missionary Society, which brought together several Protestant churches, had been founded in London in 1795. It sent missionaries to China, India, Africa, Australia, Oceania, and Madagascar in particular. Its most famous representative was, no doubt, David Livingstone (1813–1873).

3 Raoul Girardet, *L'Idée coloniale en France de 1871 à 1962* (Paris: Hachette, 1972), 254–55.

4 Formulation taken from the *Moniteur de Rome* (July 7, 1887), cited by Claude Prudhomme, in *Stratégie missionnaire du Saint-Siège sous Léon XIII (1878–1903)* (Rome: École Française de Rome, 1994), 600–601. Leo XIII was Pope from 1878 until his death in 1903.

5 The *Congregatio de Propaganda Fide* (Sacred Congregation of Propaganda) had been created in 1622 by Pope Gregory XV in order to extend Catholicism and manage ecclesiastical affairs in non-Catholic countries. Cf. Umberto Benigni, "Sacred Congregation of Propaganda" in *The Catholic Encyclopedia* (New York: Robert Appleton, 1911), also available at: http://www.newadvent.org/cathen/12456a. htm.

6 From *La Réforme intellectuelle et morale* in *Œuvres complètes*, Vol. 1 (Paris: Calmann-Lévy, 1947), quoted by Raoul Girardet, *L'Idée coloniale en France de 1871 à 1962*, 420.

7 Lucien de Montagnac, Letter to Leuglay, January 1, 1843, in *Lettres d'un soldat, neuf ans de campagne en Afrique* (Paris: Librairie Plon, 1885), 334.

8 Dubuisson, *The Western Construction of Religion*, 154–55, and *Religion and Magic*, 123–30.

9 In particular, McCutcheon, in *The Discipline of Religion*, 42–43; and Chidester, in *Savage Systems*, whose rather radical program is announced as early as page xiii.

10 Chidester, *Empire of Religion*, 2.

11 The ethnology of land, endowed with its specific methodology, would not be developed until the beginning of the twentieth century, with Bronislaw Malinowski. Previously, information was provided by missionaries, travelers, and explorers. Tylor, Frazer, Mauss, and Durkheim never themselves conducted physical/personal research in these lands.

12 Chidester, *Empire of Religion*, 42.

13 Pascal Blanchard et al., *Human Zoos: The Invention of the Savage*, trans. Deke Dusinberre et al. (Paris: Musée du Quai Branly, 2011).

14 Concerning India, Kapil Raj has drawn attention to what could be a fourth type of mediation, taking place "from the top," in urban centers, between the native elite and the British administration: "Colonial Encounters, Circulation and the Co-construction of Knowledge and National Identities: Great Britain and India, 1760–1850," in *Social History of Science in Colonial India*, ed. S. Irfan Habib and Dhruv Raina (Delhi: Oxford University Press, 2007), 83–101; and "Régler les Différends, Gérer les Différences: Dynamiques Urbaines et Savantes à Calcutta au XVIIIe siècle;" *La Revue d'Histoire Moderne et Contemporaine* 55, no. 2 (May, 2008) (special issue: "Sciences et Villes-Mondes," ed. Stéphane Van Damme and Antonella Romano): 70–100.

15 Asad correctly sees in the Western and modern conception of the notion of religion, elaborated from the eighteenth century onward, a "concept of a transhistorical essence" (*Genealogies of Religion*, 29).

16 Chidester (*Savage Systems*, 11–15, 36–38, 234–36, 253–54; and *Empire of Religion*, 22–23) has strongly stressed this point. He also reminds us that the massacre of the Herero allowed the Ethnological Museum of Berlin to enrich its collection of human skulls and skeletons (*Empire of Religion*, 29–30).

17 Said, *Orientalism*, 79; Asad, *Genealogies of Religion*, 1. The latter recalls that the history of the West is itself written based on its own categories. This is not the case for the Orient. There is thus nothing astonishing about the fact that our native

history is written at the center of the history of humanity — a notion that we also invented — nor that other histories gravitate around it. There, as well, the opposition between center and peripheries is patently clear.

18 These expressions are taken (respectively) from Fitzgerald, *The Ideology of Religious Studies*, 22; Chidester, *Savage Systems*, 16; and King, *Orientalism and Religion*, 4.

19 On this idea of recycling, see the important theoretical contribution of Yves Jeanneret, *Penser la trivialité*, Volume 1: *La Vie triviale des êtres culturels* (Paris: Lavoisier, 2008).

20 King, *Orientalism and Religion*, 204–5.

21 In their "General Introduction" to *The Post-Colonial Studies Reader*, 2nd ed. (London: Routledge, 2006), 1, Bill Ashcroft, Gareth Griffiths, and Helen Tiffin insist on the fact, just as Edward Said (*Orientalism*, 5–15), that the notions of power, knowledge, culture, religion, and politics do not go back to impermeable and autonomous notions which would be as galaxies living self-sufficiently. Even if they seem far apart from each other, the ideas circulate and recycle there permanently.

22 This geographical tripartition corresponds as well to the division made by comparative linguistics in the nineteenth century between Semitic, Aryan or Indo-European, and Oriental or Turanian languages. Cf. Masuzawa, *The Invention of World Religions*, 3.

23 Ibid., 265–74.

24 Cf. note 2, Chapter 3. See also Masuzawa, *The Invention of World Religions*, 259–65.

25 On this, see Philip Almond, *The British Discovery of Buddhism* (Cambridge: Cambridge University Press, 1988); Donald S. Lopez Jr. ed., *Curators of the Buddha: The Study of Buddhism under Colonialism* (Chicago: University of Chicago Press, 1995); King, *Orientalism and Religion*, 143–60; and Masuzawa, *The Invention of World Religions*, 121–46. See also Judith Snodgrass, *Presenting Japanese Buddhism to the West: Orientalism, Occidentalism, and the Columbian Exposition* (Chapel Hill, NC: University of North Carolina Press, 2003). The author of the latter book recalls that, in spite of its proclaimed ecumenism, the 1893 Parliament, which was just a part of the Chicago World's Fair and the Chicago Columbian Exposition (known also by the shortened name "Chicago Columbian Exposition"), was dominated by the idea of the superiority of American Protestantism. She even speaks of it as an "aggressively Christian event" (1).

26 Cf. note 23, Chapter 6. Masuzawa devotes a chapter to this, entitled "Islam, a Semitic Religion" (*The Invention of World Religions*, 179–206). The accusation is unjust, in her view, since Islam, with Christianity and Buddhism, is the only religion deserving to be called "universal".

27 Ibid., 205.

28 It is also used by Masuzawa (*The Invention of World Religions*), Fitzgerald (*The Ideology of Religious Studies*), McCutcheon ("'Man Is the Measure of All Things': On the Fabrication of Oriental Religions by European History of Religions," in *Working Papers on Method and Theory from Hannover*, ed. Steffan Führding [Leiden: Brill, 2017], 93–94, note 5: "... the European invention of these so-called Oriental religions, such as Hinduism..."), and Jason Ânanda Josephson, *The Invention of Religion in Japan* (Chicago: University of Chicago Press, 2012). King evokes "the modern construction of 'Hinduism' as a single world religion" (*Orientalism and Religion*, 100); see as well Gauri Viswanathan, "Colonialism and the Construction of Hinduism," in *The Blackwell Companion to Hinduism*, ed. Gavin Flood (Malden, MA:

Blackwell, 2003): 23–44. On this same topic, Isomae Jun'ichi prefers to speak of "The Conceptual Formation of the Category 'Religion' in Modern Japan: Religion, State, Shintô," *Journal of Religion in Japan* 1, no. 3 (2012): 226–45. He had published prior to that "Deconstructing 'Japanese Religion': A Historical Survey," *Japanese Journal of Religious Studies* 32, no. 2 (2005): 235–48. From the first page of his earlier essay, he points out that the first mention of the English expression "Japanese religion" was made in 1907 by Anesaki Mahasaru, as meaning, for him, "the religion particular to Japan." In contrast to China, Japan has closely followed the progress of Western Religious Studies; cf. Satoko Fujiwara, "Japan," in Alles, *Religious Studies*, 191–217.

29 Smith, "Religion, Religions, Religious," 186–87.

30 See the entry in the Oxford English Dictionary, but Geoffrey A. Oddie argues for 1787 in his *Imagined Hinduism: British Protestant Missionary Constructions of Hinduism, 1793–1900* (New Delhi: Sage, 2006), 71–72. See also King, *Orientalism and Religion*, 100.

31 Smith, "Religion, Religions, Religious," 187.

32 See, for example, King, *Orientalism and Religion*, 100ff.

33 Nonetheless, see T. H. Barrett, "Chinese Religion in English Guise: The History of an Illusion," *Modern Asian Studies* 39 (2005): 509–33; Sommer, "Chinese Religions in World Religions Textbooks." In *Before Religion*, Nongbri recalls (25) that the word used in modern Chinese to translate very approximately the word "religion" (*zongjiao*; in Japanese, *shûkyô*), was invented at the end of the nineteenth century by Japanese translators of European texts before being reintroduced in China. The two terms, both composites, stress the notion of traditional teaching. From Guanghu He, in "China: The Prehistory, Emergence, and Disappearance of Religious Studies in China" (in Alles, *Religious Studies*, 160–75), it emerges that Chinese Religious Studies came about quite late and remain tributaries of the Western works translated there. Now, these latter works (by, for example, Tillich, Dawson, Berger, Otto, Müller, Smart) belong to an era that, today, is over. He notes, for example (174), that, in China, the phenomenology of religion has yet to arrive… But he is doubtless correct in recalling on the following page that Religious Studies can only develop in a climate of freedom and tolerance.

34 King, *Orientalism and Religion*, 110. I take advantage of this fact to recall that the word "hindu" corresponds to the Persian pronunciation of the Sanskrit word "*sindhu*," designating "river" (especially the Indus) and the area it traverses (the Sindh). Thus, originally, it has no religious connotation whatsoever. But the ambiguity has to be dispelled at every occasion. One example is found in Joseph T. O'Connell, "The Word 'Hindu' in Gaudîya Vaishnava Texts," *Journal of the American Oriental Society* 93, no. 3 (1973): 340–44. The texts in question were composed between the beginning of the sixteenth century and the end of the eighteenth. See also the valuable information provided by Robert Eric Frykenberg, "Constructions of Hinduism at the Nexus of History and Religion," in *Defining Hinduism: A Reader*, ed. J. E. Llewellyn (London: Equinox, 2005), especially 126–27.

35 The best current synthesis, and therefore the best introduction to these questions, is no doubt found in Esther Bloch, Marianne Keppens, and Rajaram Hegde, eds., *Rethinking Religion in India: The Colonial Construction of Hinduism* (Abingdon: Routledge, 2010). Bloch and Keppens were students of S. N. Balagangadhara at Ghent University, but their work fits without difficulty into this wave of Critical Studies. See also King, *Orientalism and Religion*; Oddie, *Imagined Hinduism*; Fitzgerald, *The Ideology of Religious Studies*; Sharada Sugirtharajah, *Imagining Hinduism: A Postcolonial Perspective* (London: Routledge, 2003); Llewellyn, *Defining Hinduism*; S.

N. Balagangadhara, *Reconceptualizing India Studies* (New Delhi: Oxford University Press, 2012); and Sushil Mittal and Gene Thursby, eds., *Religions of South Asia: An Introduction* (London: Routledge, 2006).

36 Richard King, "Colonialism, Hinduism and the Discourse of Religion," in Bloch, Keppens, and Hegde, *Rethinking Religion in India*, 103–4.

37 They will be found again later; see note 4, Chapter 8.

38 See note 32, Chapter 1 and its corresponding paragraph in the main text.

39 Cf. W. Sweetman, "Unity and Plurality: Hinduism and the Religions of India in Early European Scholarship," *Religion* 31 (2011): 209–24; and G. Viswanathan, "Colonialism and the Construction of Hinduism," in Flood, *The Blackwell Companion to Hinduism*, 23–44

40 Bloch, Keppens, and Hegde, *Rethinking Religion in India*, 9.

41 Especially David N. Lorenzen, "Hindus and Others," in Bloch, Keppens, and Hegde, *Rethinking Religion in India*, 25–40, and "Who Invented Hinduism?" in Llewellyn, *Defining Hinduism*, 52–80.

42 Cf. note 34, Chapter 7. See also Oddie, "Hindu Religious Identity with Special Reference to the Origin and Significance of the Term 'Hinduism,' c. 1787–1947," in Bloch, Keppens, and Hegde, *Rethinking Religion in India*, 41–55.

43 A synthetic presentation of the "Hindu dharma," "Jaina Dharma," "Bauddha dhamma," and "Sikh Dharma" can be found in Mittal and Thursby, *Religions of South Asia*. See also Michel Picard, "What's in a Name? An Enquiry about the Interpretation of Agama Hindu as 'Hinduism,'" *Jurnal Kajian Bali* 22, no. 2 (2012): 122–23; Michel Picard, *Kebalian La Construction dialogique de l'identité balinaise*, Cahier d'Archipel 44 (Paris: EHESS, 2017), 20–23. In these latter two articles, Picard recalls that it was the Christian missionaries who, in 1801, with their translation of the Bible, chose to render the word "religion" by "*dharma*," Christianity becoming *ipso facto* "the true *dharma*" (*satyadharma*). This has not prevented certain Hindus from considering their indigenous *dharma* as a superior and universal principle, thereby englobing all religions. In these Buddhist areas of Sri Lanka, the word "âgama" ("canonical text") was retained to translate the same word.

44 I refer to the oldest missionary sources (Nobili; Ziegenbalg), cited by Sweetman ("Unity and Plurality," 85–59) and Oddie (*Imagined Hinduism*, 53 and 57), which confirm that the number of different sects is too large to allow evoking the existence of a single religion bringing them all together.

45 Wilhelm Halbfass, "The Idea of the Veda and the Identity of Hinduism," in Llewellyn, *Defining Hinduism*, 17–18.

46 I have addressed this question in my *Religion and Magic*, 71–84.

47 Cf. note 11, Chapter 4, and note 43, Chapter 7.

48 Oddie, "Hindu Religious Identity," 46–47.

49 I borrow this list from King, *Orientalism and Religion*, 105. Buddhism, for its part, in the eyes of Westerners, possessed a founder, sacred texts, and a clergy (if one can use this new anachronism to describe its "monks" [*bhikshu*], who in fact renounce worldliness and live in poverty).

50 The result being, for example, the small book by D. S. Sarma, *Essence of Hinduism* (Bombay: Bharatiya, 1971). The Table of Contents rolls out the following chapters which can only look familiar to the Western mind: "Hindu Scriptures," "Hindu Rituals and Myths," "Hindu Ethics," "Hindu Theism," and "Hindu Philosophy." See also King, "The Modern Myth of Hinduism," in *Orientalism and Religion*, 96–117; and Fitzgerald, *The Ideology of Religious Studies*, 134–55.

51 Balagangadhara ("Orientalism, Postcolonialism and the 'Construction' of Religion," in Bloch, Keppens, and Hegde, *Rethinking Religion in India*, 135–63) also thinks that this Hinduism does not correspond to anything real, and that it offers an inexact description of India. It concerns an imaginary entity, at most a "pattern" that brings coherence and readability to Westerners' experience of India (137). In *Reconceptualizing India Studies*, 52–53, he adds that the creation of Hinduism is a translation into a religious key of Indian facts as presented by Westerners. In the same volume (at page 87), Balagangadhara notes that the notion of religion offers no explanation for the caste-system, when in fact it is probably the major structuring factor of Hindu society, itself organized around the opposition of "pure" and "impure". Let us remember that a single class, or *varna*, can be represented on the Indian scale by a large number of castes. Although pan-Indian, the caste-system is sub-divided into a great number of local or regional variations. Now, as Fitzgerald for his part remarks (*The Ideology of Religious Studies*, 154–55 and 159), taking up an idea of Chris J. Fuller (*The Camphor Flame: Popular Hinduism and Society in India* [Princeton: Princeton University Press, 1992]), the divinities, be they superior or local, are inseparable from the caste-system and its functioning. They are constantly associated with and implicated in it. The autonomy of the religious, as an instance independent of the social world, and thus existing in a *sui generis* way, is consequently an error or a fallacy formulated by *a priori* religionists.

52 King, *Orientalism and Religion*, 102.

53 Oddie, *Imagined Hinduism*, 99 and 345–46; Oddie, "Hindu Religious Identity," 46–51; Frykenberg, "Constructions of Hinduism," 127–29; Brian K. Smith, "Questioning Authority: Constructions and Deconstructions of Hinduism," in Llewellyn, *Defining Hinduism*, 111; and Halbfass, "The Idea of the Veda and the Identity of Hinduism," 23.

54 This story should also be read in the light of the epistemological debates started up by Indian theoreticians of "post-colonial studies." Cf. note 21, Chapter 7, and King, "Beyond Orientalism? Religion and Comparativism," Chapter 9 of *Orientalism and Religion*, 187–218.

55 King, "Colonialism, Hinduism and Religion," 102–3.

56 John Zavos shares this opinion in "Representing Religion in Colonial India," in Bloch, Keppens, and Hegde, *Rethinking Religion in India*, 57–58, where he speaks of "processes of interaction." So too does Will Sweetman, "Unity and Plurality," 93.

57 Bloch, Keppens, and Hegde, *Rethinking Religion in India*, 12–14, to which I add the impertinent but so very essential question raised by Jakob de Roover and Sarah Claerhout at the end of this same volume: "The Colonial Construction of What?" (164–83).

58 Cf. note 2, Chapter 1 and the corresponding paragraph.

59 On this term, see Julius J. Lipner, "Ancient Banyan: An Inquiry into the Meaning of 'Hinduness'," in Llewellyn, *Defining Hinduism*, 33–34 (originally published in 1996). King recalls that Lipner suggests using the term "Hinduism" to designate a culture rather than the idea of a unique religion (*Orientalism and Religion*, 108).

60 The discussion is summarized in Jun'ichi, "The Conceptual Formation of the Category 'Religion' in Modern Japan," 229–30. See also Fitzgerald, "The Religion-Secular Dichotomy: A Response to Responses," *Electronic Journal of Contemporary Japanese Studies* (April 6, 2004), accessible at www.japanesestudies.org.uk/discussionpapers/Fitzgerald2.html; and George Lazopoulos, "Japanese History, Post-Japan," *Cross-Currents: East Asian History and Culture* 10 (2014): 95.

61   Fitzgerald, "The Religion-Secular Dichotomy," 10–12.

62   See note 33, Chapter 7.

63   Beside the work of Jun'ichi and Fitzgerald already cited, one may attempt to grasp the subtleties of this history by referring to Fujiwara, "Japan," in Alles, *Religious Studies*, 191–218; and Susumu Shimazono, "State Shinto and the Religious Structure of Modern Japan," *Journal of the American Academy of Religion* 73, no. 4 (2005): 1077–98. The latter makes clear that even the Japanese understanding of their own religious traditions tends to be "vague and confusing."

64   Isomae Jun'ichi, "Deconstructing 'Japanese Religion,'" *Japanese Journal of Religious Studies* 32, no. 2 (2005): 240.

65   Fujiwara, "Japan," in Alles, *Religious Studies*, 195.

66   Ibid., 192.

67   See note 35, Chapter 3 and the corresponding paragraph in the main text. See also Smith, "Religion, Religions, Religious" and "A Question of Class," in *Relating Religion*, 189–91 and 160–78 respectively.

68   See Chidester, *Empire of Religion*, 27.

69   Smith, "A Matter of Class," 169.

70   McCutcheon, *Manufacturing Religion*, 164.

71   Masuzawa, *The Invention of World Religions*, xi and 20. She also notes (292) that French science was absent from the debates relative to the invention of World Religions.

72   Smith, "A Matter of Class," 169.

Chapter 8

1   We must not forget that for men at the beginning of the nineteenth century, such as Abbé J. A. Dubois (*Hindu Manners, Customs and Ceremonies*, 6th ed., trans. Henry K. Beauchamp [Delhi: Oxford University Press, (1816) 1989], 10), there was only one religion at the origin of humanity: "Unfortunately human passion gained the upper hand. Whole nations were corrupted, and men made for themselves a religion more suited to the depravity of their own hearts." It was thus inevitable that they would try to recover it from among all the human *religions* of their time. See also note 2, Chapter 1, and Picard, "What's in a Name?," 113–40, esp. 123, for the misunderstandings harbored by the word "hindu" (as well as note 34, Chapter 7). The Indonesian multi-layer cake that stacks together indigenous culture, local traditions, Hindu influences, Muslim conquest, and Western holdings makes the use of the word "religion" even more delicate and problematic, as is stressed by the same author in *Kebalian La Construction dialogique de l'identité balinaise* (Paris: Cahier d'archipel 44, 2017), 7–345.

2   Elsewhere, I have criticized this point of view defended by Eliade, among others. See "The Reconstruction of Prehistoric Religions," Addendum IV of *Twentieth Century Mythologies*, 259–66.

3   In this case, the inverted commas signify that the word "religion" does not designate a province of ancient reality, but rather a heuristic function. Cf. Smith, *Relating Religion*, 207–9; and Nongbri, *Before Religion*, 157–59.

4   But even for these, as has been noted, the solution does not seem perfectly adequate. One may refer to Craig Martin, among many other authors, "Delimiting Religion," *Method and Theory in the Study of Religion* 21 (2009): 157–76; followed by his *A Critical Introduction to the Study of Religion*, 1–6; also Thomas A. Tweed, *Crossing*

and Dwelling: A Theory of Religion (Cambridge, MA: Harvard University Press, 2006), 33–53; Chidester, *Empire of Religion*, 11–18; William E. Arnal, "Definition," in Braun and McCutcheon, *Guide to the Study of Religion*, 21–34; and Ernst Feil, "The Problem of Defining and Demarcating 'Religion,'" in *On the Concept of Religion* (Albany, NY: State University of New York Press, 2000), 1–35. Arnal concludes his introductory chapter by writing that it is a very good thing that the object "religion" does not exist; for, he adds, that provides the indispensable precondition for studying its practices without any of those *a prioris* that we moderns have a tendency to qualify as "religious". I recently re-examined other insoluble paradoxes in "Definitions of Religion," in *Vocabulary for the Study of Religion*, ed. K. von Stuckrad and R. Segal (Leiden: Brill, 2015), 3:392–96.

   5   Fitzgerald, *The Ideology of Religious Studies*, 6.

   6   Ibid., 15.

   7   Barthes, *Mythologies*, 254–55.

   8   Fitzgerald, *The Ideology of Religious Studies*, 6.

   9   Ibid., 22.

  10   Ibid., 13.

  11   Ibid., 13–14.

  12   Ibid., 244. See also Fitzgerald's article, "A Response to Kevin Schilbrack," *Method and Theory in the Study of Religion* 25, no. 1 (2013): 101–6, where he specifies that, in his view, there are no essential differences between religious and non-religious domains, but that the latter are imagined and represented as though there were, by a contemporary market ideology that uses this dichotomy in order itself to appear modern and rational by comparison (with religion being traditional and nostalgic).

  13   Cf. note 34, Chapter 7, and note 51, Chapter 7.

  14   In his *Discourse on the First Decade of Titus Livius*, Book I, Chapters 11 and 12, Machiavelli makes use of the Critias Fragment by Sextus Empiricus, *Adversos Mathematicos*, I, 54.

  15   According to Edward B. Tylor, in *Primitive Culture: Research into the Development of Mythology, Philosophy, Religion, Language, Art, and Custom*, 2 vols., 2nd ed. (London: John Murray, 1873), 1, culture is a complex whole that brings together all elements that he himself included in the title of his work, without forgetting, as a supplement, knowledge, beliefs, morality, and laws, as well as all of the aptitudes acquired by people living in society.

  16   Masuzawa, "Culture," in Taylor, *Critical Terms*, 70–93. See as well Nye, *Religion: The Basics*, 23–56; and Bruce Lincoln, "Culture," in Braun and McCutcheon, *Guide to the Study of Religion*, 409–22.

  17   Cf. Raymond Williams, *Culture and Society, 1780–1950* (New York: Columbia University Press, 1958); also, and especially, Christopher Herbert, *Culture and Anomie: Ethnographic Imagination in the Nineteenth Century* (Chicago: University of Chicago Press, 1991). Herbert stresses this paradox, recalling the one that is raised by the use of the word "religion": if the notion of culture is so necessary, why is it at the same time so difficult to define (see pages 3 and 300)? He resolves in the end to admit that the "persuasiveness" of the modern idea of culture is perhaps just a supplementary illusion, to be accredited to … our culture.

  18   For Masuzawa ("Culture," 78), even if culture is more than a simple aggregate of discrete elements, it is not for all something that one perceives immediately.

  19   Maurice Bloch, who also shares the scepticism of numerous anthropologists concerning the possibility of isolating a distinct phenomenon called "religion," has

proposed the term "transcendental social" to designate the roles, status, etc., that exist independently of the individuals who embody them at a particular moment. They represent in some way an ideal superstructure (see "Why Religion Is Nothing Special, but Is Central," *Philosophical Transactions of the Royal Society* 363 [2008]: 2055–61). In this sense, he runs counter to A. R. Radcliffe-Brown (*Structure and Function in Primitive Society* [London: Cohen and West, 1952]), for whom "social structure" is something tangible and mixes with what can be observed in the real world. For Bloch, the "religious-like phenomena" ("Why Religion Is Nothing Special," 2055) belong to the transcendent level.

20 Dubuisson, *The Western Construction of Religion*, 199–213, and taken up again, in summary-form, in *Religion and Magic*, 93–96.

21 I borrow this expression from Borgeaud (*L'histoire des religions* [Gollion: Infolio éditions, 2013], 175), for it translates very well my own notion of "cosmographic formation".

22 I am referring clearly to the classic and perhaps most original work of Smith, *To Take Place*. Following Smith (110), who cites J. C. Heestermann (*The Inner Conflict of Tradition: Essays in Indian Ritual, Kingship and Society* [Chicago: University of Chicago Press, 1985], 3), I would be tempted to establish a parallel between my "cosmographic formation" and their conception of rituals in the sense that both create or attempt to create definitive worlds that are closed, finished, and sealed into themselves. Rituals present the enormous advantage of being miniature cosmographic practices: pure, localized, delimited on the temporal level, and subject to the inflexible authority of the *Maîtres du désordre* (Masters of Disorder; I take here the title of the collective work published by Jean de Loisy and Bertrand Hell [Paris: Musée du quai Branly, 2011]). Controlling chaos and the unforeseen is much easier. As is the reparation of potential accidents.

23 Dumézil, *Loki*, cited in Dubuisson, *Twentieth Century Mythologies*, 68.

24 Jonathan Z. Smith, "In Comparison a Magic Dwells," in *Imagining Religion: From Babylon to Jonestown* (Chicago: University of Chicago Press, 1982), 19–25 (20).

25 Ibid., 35.

26 Discussed in my *Twentieth Century Mythologies*, 5–102.

27 See my "A Critical Survey of Claude Lévi-Strauss's and the Structural Study of Myth" in *Cambridge History of Mythology and Mythography*, ed. R. Woodard (Cambridge: Cambridge University Press, forthcoming [2020]).

Conclusion

1 Cf. note 40, Chapter 4.

2 This exact history is the subject of my *Dictionnaire des grands thèmes de l'histoire des religions, de Pythagore à Lévi-Strauss*.

3 I am thinking of the work of Philippe Hamon, Gérard Genette, François Recanati, Pierre Macherey, Tzvetan Todorov, Dan Sperber, Jean-Pierre Dupuy, Maurice Godelier, Bernard Lahire, Bruno Latour, Wiktor Stoczkowski, Jean-Pierre Richard, Joseph Courtés, Francis Affergan, and Mondher Kilani, amongst others.

4 This expression is borrowed from Daniel Gold, *Aesthetics and Analysis in Writing on Religion: Modern Fascinations* (Berkeley, LA: University of California Press, 2003). On this subject (note 54, Chapter 5, and note 13, Chapter 6), which is much more important than it may seem, see also Kocku von Stuckrad, *The Scientification of Religion: An Historical Study of Discursive Change, 1800–2000* (Berlin: de Gruyter, 2015.)

Bibliography

Acosta, José de. *Natural and Moral History of the Indies*, vol. 1. Translated by Frances López-Morillas. Durham: Duke University Press, 2002.

———. *Natural and Moral History of the Indies*, vol. 2. Translated by Edward Grimston. London: The Haklyut Society, 1880. Originally published as *Historia natural y moral de las Indias*. Seville: Juan de Leon, 1590.

Adams, Charles Joseph. "Classification of Religions." In *Encyclopaedia Britannica. Ultimate Reference Suite*, 2007. Accessible at: https://www.britannica.com/topic/classification-of-religions.

Allen, Douglas. "Phenomenology of Religion." In *The Encyclopedia of Religion*, vol. 11, edited by M. Eliade, 272–85. New York: Macmillan, 1987.

———. "Recent Defenders of Eliade: A Critical Evaluation." *Religion* 24 (1994): 333–51.

Alles, Gregory D. "Toward a Genealogy of the Holy: Rudolf Otto and the Apologetics of Religion." *Journal of the American Academy of Religion* 69, no. 2 (2001): 323–41.

Alles, Gregory D., ed. *Religious Studies: A Global View*. London: Routledge, 2010.

Almond, Philip. *The British Discovery of Buddhism*. Cambridge: Cambridge University Press, 1988.

Althusser, Louis. *For Marx*. Translated by Ben Brewster. London: Allen Lan, 1969. Originally published as *Pour Marx*. Paris: François Maspero, 1975.

———. "Idéologie et appareils idéologiques d'État (Notes pour une recherche)." In *Positions (1964–1975)*, 67–125. Paris: Les éditions sociales, 1976.

Arnal, William E. *The Symbolic Jesus: Historical Scholarship, Judaism and the Construction of Contemporary Identity*. London: Equinox, 2005.

———. "Definition." In Braun and McCutcheon, *Guide to the Study of Religion*, 21–34.

———. "The Origins of Christianity Within, and Without, 'Religion': A Case Study." In Arnal and McCutcheon, *The Sacred is the Profane*, 134–70.

Arnal, William E., and McCutcheon, Russell T., eds. *The Sacred is the Profane: The Political Nature of "Religion"*. New York: Oxford University Press, 2013.

Asad, Talal. *Genealogies of Religion: Discipline and Reasons of Power in Christianity and Islam*. Baltimore: Johns Hopkins University Press, 1993.

———. *Formations of the Secular: Christianity, Islam, Modernity*. Stanford, CA: Stanford University Press, 2003.

Ashcroft, Bill, Gareth Griffiths, and Helen Tiffin. *The Post-Colonial Studies Reader*. 2nd ed. London: Routledge, 2006.

Augustine. *City of God.* Translated by David S. Wiesen. Cambridge, MA: Harvard University Press, 1968.

Balagangadhara, S. N. "Orientalism, Postcolonialism and the 'Construction' of Religion." In Bloch, Keppens, and Hegde, *Rethinking Religion in India,* 135–63.

———. *Reconceptualizing India Studies.* New Delhi: Oxford University Press, 2012.

Bancel, Nicolas, Pascal Blanchard, and Françoise Vergès. *La République coloniale.* Paris: Hachette, 2003.

Barrett, T. H. "Chinese Religion in English Guise: The History of an Illusion." *Modern Asian Studies* 39 (2005): 509–33.

Barthes, Roland. *Mythologies. The Complete Edition, in a New Translation.* 2nd ed. Translated by Richard Howard and Annette Lavers. New York: Hill and Wang, 2012. Originally published as *Mythologies.* Paris: Éditions du Seuil, 1957.

Baslez, Marie-Françoise. *Comment les chrétiens sont devenus catholiques Ier-Ve siècle.* Paris: Tallandier, 2019.

Baum, Robert M. "The Forgotten South: African Religions in World Religions Textbooks." In "Religion/s between Covers: Dilemmas of the World Religions Textbook," special issue, *Religious Studies Review* 31, no. 1–2 (2005): 27–30.

Benavides, Gustavo. "North America." In Alles, *Religious Studies,* 242–68.

Benigni, Umberto. "Sacred Congregation of Propaganda." In *The Catholic Encyclopedia.* New York: Robert Appleton, 1911. Accessible at: http://www.newadvent.org/cathen/12456a.htm.

Benveniste, Émile. *Indo-European Language and Society.* Translated by Jean Lallot. Miami, FL: University of Miami Press, 1973. Originally published as *Le Vocabulaire des institutions indo-européennes, vol. 2, Pouvoir, droit, religion.* Paris: Les éditions de minuit, 1969.

Bergamo, Mino. *L'Anatomie de l'âme: De François de Sales à Fénelon.* Translated by M. Bonneval. Grenoble: J. Million, 1994. Originally published as *L'anatomia dell'anima: da François de Sales a Fénelon.* Bologna: Il Mulino, 1991.

Berger, Adriana. "Mircea Eliade: Romanian Fascism and the History of Religions in the United States." In *Tainted Greatness,* edited by Nancy A. Harrowitz, 51–74. Philadelphia: Temple University Press, 1994.

Blanchard, Pascal, Nicolas Bancel, Gilles Boëtsch, and Sandrine Lemaire. *Zoos humains et exhibitions coloniales: 150 ans d'invention de l'Autre.* Paris: La Découverte, 2011.

Bloch, Esther, Marianne Keppens, and Rajaram Hegde, eds. *Rethinking Religion in India: The Colonial Construction of Hinduism.* Abingdon: Routledge, 2010.

Bloch, Maurice. "Why Religion Is Nothing Special but Is Central." *Philosophical Transactions of the Royal Society* 363 (2008): 2055–61.

Bobineau, Olivier. *L'Empire des papes: Une sociologie du pouvoir dans l'Église.* Paris: CNRS *édition,* 2013.

Borgeaud, Philippe. *Aux origines de l'histoire des religions.* Paris: Éditions du Seuil, 2004.

———. *L'histoire des religions.* Gollion: Infolio éditions, 2013.

Bossuet, Jacques-Bénigne. *A Discourse on the History of the Whole World*. n.t. London: Matthew Turner, 1868. Originally published as *Discours sur l'histoire universelle*. Paris: Librairie Hachette, 1686.

_____. *A Universal History, from the Beginning of the World, to the Empire of Charlemagne*. 2 vols. Translated by Mr. Elphinston. London: David Steel, 1767. Originally published as *Discours sur l'histoire universelle*. Paris: Librairie Hachette, 1686.

Bourdieu, Pierre. "Genèse et structure du champs religieux." *Revue française de sociologie* XII, no. 3 (1971): 295–334.

Braun, Willi. "Colloquium on Method and Theory." *Method and Theory in the Study of Religion* 28, no. 1 (2016): 1–38.

Braun, Willi, and Russell T. McCutcheon, eds. *Guide to the Study of Religion*. London: Continuum, 2007.

_____. *Introducing Religion: Essays in Honor of Jonathan Z. Smith*. New York: Routledge, 2014.

Burnouf, Émile. *The Science of Religions*. Translated by Julie Liebe. London: S. Sonnenschein, Lowrey and Co., 1888. Originally published as *La Science des religions*. Paris: Maisonneuve et Cie., 1872.

Chantepie de la Saussaye, Pierre Daniel. *Manual of the Science of Religion*. Translated by Beatrice S. Colyer-Fergusson (née Max Müller). London: Longmans, Green, and Co., 1891. Originally published as *Lehrbuch der Religionsgeschichte*. 2 vols. Freiburg: Mohr, 1887–1889.

Chidester, David. *Savage Systems: Colonialism and Comparative Religion in South Africa*. Charlottesville: University Press of Virginia, 1996.

_____. *Christianity: A Global History*. New York: Harper Collins, 2000.

_____. *Empire of Religion: Imperialism & Comparative Religion*. Chicago: University of Chicago Press, 2014.

Constant, Benjamin. *On Religion: Considered in Its Source, Its Forms, and Its Developments*. Translated by Peter Paul Seaton Junior. Carmel, IN: Liberty Fund, 2017. Originally published as *De la religion considérée dans sa source, ses formes et ses développements*. Paris: Pichon, 1830–1831.

Cuchet, Guillaume. *Faire de l'histoire religieuse dans une société sortie de la religion*. Paris: Publications de la Sorbonne, 2013.

Demoule, Jean-Paul. *Mais où sont passés les Indo-Européens?* Paris: Éditions du Seuil, 2014.

Derrida, Jacques. "Faith and Knowledge: The Two Sources of 'Religion' at the Limits of Reason Alone." Translated by Samuel Weber. In *Religion: Cultural Memory in the Present*, edited by Jacques Derrida and Gianni Vattimo, 1–78. Stanford, CA: Stanford University Press, 1998. Originally published as "Fede e sapere. Le due fonti della religione." In *La religione. Annuario filosofico europeo*. Rome: Laterza, 1995.

Dubuisson, Daniel. "Présentation." *Strumenti critici* 85. *Poétique et rhétorique des saviors dans les sciences humaines*. (September, 1997): 354–60.

_____. *The Western Construction of Religion*. Translated by William Sayers. Baltimore: Johns Hopkins University Press, 2003. Originally published as *L'Occident et la religion: Mythe, pensée, idéologie*. Brussels: Éditions Complexe, 1998.

_____. *Dictionnaire des grands thèmes de l'histoire des religions: De Pythagore à Lévi-Strauss*. Brussels: Éditions Complexe, 2004.

_____. *Twentieth Century Mythologies: Dumézil, Lévi-Strauss, Eliade*. Translated by Martha Cunningham. London: Equinox, 2006. Originally published as *Mythologies du XXᵉ siècle Dumézil, Lévi-Strauss, Eliade*. Lille: Presses universitaires de Lille, 1993.

_____. "The Poetical and Rhetorical Structure of the Eliadean Text: A Contribution to Critical Theory and Discourses on Religions." In Wedemeyer and Doniger, *Hermeneutics, Politics and the History of Religions*, 133–46.

_____. "Definitions of Religion." In *Vocabulary for the Study of Religion*. Vol. 3, edited by K. von Stuckrad and R. Segal, 392–96. Leiden: Brill, 2015.

_____. *Religion and Magic in Western Culture*. Translated by Martha Cunningham. Leiden: Brill, 2016.

_____. "Critical Thinking and Comparative Analysis in Religious Studies." *Method and Theory in the Study of Religion* 28, no. 1 (2016): 26–30.

Dubuisson, Daniel, ed. "Poétique et rhétorique des savoirs dans les sciences humaines." Special issue, *Strumenti critici* 85 (September, 1997).

Dubuisson, Daniel, and Sophie Raux. "L'histoire de l'art et les Visual Studies: Entre mythe, science et idéologie." *Histoire de l'art* 70 (2012): 13–21.

Dudley, Guilford. *Religion on Trial: Mircea Eliade and his Critics*. Philadelphia: Temple University Press, 1977.

Dumézil, Georges. *Archaic Roman Religion: With an Appendix on the Religion of the Etruscans*. 2 vols. Translated by Philip Krapp. Chicago, IL: University of Chicago Press, 1970. Originally published as *La Religion romaine archaïque*. Paris: Payot, 1966.

_____. *Loki*. 3rd ed. Paris: Flammarion, 1985.

Durkheim, Émile. *The Elementary Forms of the Religious Life*. 2nd ed. Translated by Joseph Ward Swain. London: Allen & Unwin, 1976. Originally published as *Les Formes élémentaires de la vie religieuse: le système totémique en Australie*. Paris: F. Alcan, 1912.

_____. Review of Antonio Labriola, "Essais sur la conception matérialiste de l'histoire." Translated by W. D. Halls. In *Durkheim on Politics and the State*, edited by Anthony Giddens, 128–36. Cambridge: Polity Press, 1986. Originally published in *Revue philosophique de la France et de l'étranger* xliv (1897): 645–51.

Eagleton, Terry. *The Ideology of the Aesthetic*. Cambridge, MA: Blackwell, 1990.

Egge, James. "Buddhism in World Religions Textbooks." In "Religion/s between Covers: Dilemmas of the World Religions Textbook," special issue, *Religious Studies Review* 31, nos. 1–2 (2005): 26–27.

Ehrman, Bart D. *After the New Testament: A Reader in Early Christianity*. Oxford: Oxford University Press, 1999.

Eliade, Mircea. *Myths, Dreams and Mysteries*. Translated by Philip Mairet. London: Harvill, 1960. Originally published as *Mythes, rêves et mystères*. Paris: Gallimard, 1957.

_____. *The Sacred and the Profane*. Translated by Willard Trask. New York: Harcourt, Brace and World, 1959. Originally published as *Le sacré et le profane*. Paris: Gallimard, 1965.

_____. *Myth and Reality*. Translated by Willard Trask. New York: Harper and Row, 1963. Originally published as *Aspects du mythe*. Paris: Gallimard, 1963.

_____. *Mephistopheles and the Androgyne*. Translated by J. M. Cohen. New York: Sheed and Ward, 1965. Originally published as *Méphistophélès et l'androgyne*. Paris: Gallimard, 1962.

_____. *The Quest. History and Meaning in Religion*. Chicago: University of Chicago Press, 1969.

_____. *Fragments d'un journal I: 1945–1969*. Paris: Gallimard, 1973.

_____. *Occultism, Witchcraft and Cultural Fashions*. Chicago: University of Chicago Press, 1978.

_____. *The Portugal Journal*. Albany: SUNY Press, 2010.

Encrevé, René. "Histoire." In *Encyclopédie du protestantisme*. 2nd ed., edited by Pierre Gisel, 586–605. Paris: Presses universitaires de France, 2006.

Eusebius of Caesarea. *Preparation of the Gospel*. Translated by E. H. Gifford. Oxford: Clarendon Press, 1903. Originally published as *Praeparatio Evangelica*.

_____. *Préparation évangélique*. Translated by E. des Places. 7 vols. Paris: Éditions du Cerf, 1974–1987. Originally published as *Praeparatio Evangelica*.

Eyl, Jennifer. "Semantic Voids, New Testament Translation, and Anachronism: The Case of Paul's Use of 'Ekklêsia.'" *Method and Theory in the Study of Religion* 26, nos. 4–5 (2014): 315–39.

Feil, Ernst. "The Problem of Defining and Demarcating 'Religion.'" In *On the Concept of Religion*, edited by E. Feil, 1–35. Albany, NY: State University of New York Press, 2000.

Finley, Moses I. "Foreword." In *Greek Religion and Society*, edited by P. E. Easterling and J. V. Muir, xiii–xx. Cambridge: Cambridge University Press, 1985.

Fitzgerald, Timothy. *The Ideology of Religious Studies*. New York: Oxford University Press, 2000.

_____. "The Religion-Secular Dichotomy: A Response to Responses." *Electronic Journal of Contemporary Japanese Studies* (April 6, 2004). Accessible at: www.japanesestudies.org.uk/discussionpapers/Fitzgerald2.html

_____. "A Response to Kevin Schilbrack." *Method and Theory in the Study of Religion* 25, no. 1 (2013): 101–6.

Foucault, Michel. *The Archaeology of Knowledge: And the Discourse on Language*. Translated by A. M. Sheridan Smith. New York: Pantheon Books, 1972. Originally published as *L'Archéologie du savoir*. Paris: Gallimard, 1969.

Frykenberg, Robert Eric. "Constructions of Hinduism at the Nexus of History." In Llewellyn, *Defining Hinduism*, 125–46.

Fujiwara, Satoko. "Japan." In Alles, *Religious Studies*, 191–208.

Gaillard, Gérald. *Dictionnaire des ethnologues et des anthropologues*. Paris: Armand Colin/Masson, 1997.

Gelasius I, Pope. "Epistle 13." Translated by Karl F. Morrison. In *Tradition and Authority in the Western Church 300–1140*. Princeton: Princeton University Press, 1969.

Ginzburg, Carlo. "Mircea Eliade's Ambivalent Legacy." In Wedemeyer and Doniger, *Hermeneutics, Politics and the History of Religions*, 307–23.

Girardet, Raoul. *L'Idée coloniale en France de 1871 à 1962*. Paris: Hachette, 1972.

Gold, Daniel. *Aesthetics and Analysis in Writing on Religion: Modern Fascinations.* Berkeley, LA: University of California Press, 2003.

Greenblatt, Stephen. *The Swerve: How the World Became Modern.* New York: W. W. Norton, 2011.

Guyot, M. T. *Dictionnaire universel des hérésies, des erreurs et des schismes.* Lyon: Périsse Frères, 1847.

Halbfass, Wilhelm. "The Idea of the Veda and the Identity of Hinduism." In Llewellyn, *Defining Hinduism,* 16–29.

Halter, Deborah. "Christianity in World Religions Textbooks." In "Religion/s between Covers: Dilemmas of the World Religions Textbook," special issue, *Religious Studies Review* 31, nos. 1–2 (2005): 23–26.

Hamilton, Peter. "The Enlightenment and the Birth of Social Science." In *Formations of Modernity,* edited by Stuart Hall and Bram Gieben, 17–70. Oxford: Open University and Polity Press, 1992.

Haussig, Hans-Michael. *Der Religionsbegriff in den Religionen: Studien zum Selbst- und Religionsverständnis in Hinduismus, Buddhismus, Judentum und Islam.* Berlin: Philo, 1999.

He, Guanghu. "China: The Prehistory, Emergence, and Disappearance of Religious Studies in China." In Alles, *Religious Studies,* 160–75.

Heestermann, J. C. *The Inner Conflict of Tradition: Essays in Indian Ritual, Kingship and Society.* Chicago: University of Chicago Press, 1985.

Hegel, Georg W. F. *Introduction to Aesthetics.* Translated by Martha Cunningham. Originally published as *Einleitung to Vorlesungen* über *die* Ästhetik. Berlin: Dunker und Humblot, 1835–1838.

———. *Lectures on the Philosophy of Religion. Together with a Work on the Proofs of the Existence of God.* 2nd ed. Translated by E. B. Spiers and J. Burdon Sanderson. London: Routledge, 1962.

Hell, Bertrand, and Jean de Loisy. *Les Maîtres du désordre.* Paris: Musée du quai Branly, 2011.

Herbert, Christopher. *Culture and Anomie: Ethnographic Imagination in the Nineteenth Century.* Chicago: University of Chicago Press, 1991.

Hinnells, John R., ed. *The Routledge Companion to the Study of Religion.* London: Routledge, 2007.

Hughes, Aaron W. "The Study of Islam Before and After September 11: A Provocation." *Special Feature on Islamic Studies Symposium, Method and Theory in the Study of Religion* 24, nos. 4–5 (2012): 314–36.

———. *Theorizing Islam: Disciplinary Deconstruction and Reconstruction.* London: Equinox, 2012.

———. "How to Theorize with a Hammer, or, On the Destruction and Reconstruction of Islamic Studies." In Ramey, *Writing Religion,* 172–93.

Janicaud, Dominique. *Le Tournant théologique de la phénoménologie française.* Combas: Éditions de l'éclat, 1991.

Jeanneret, Yves. *Penser la trivialité.* Volume 1: *La Vie triviale des* êtres *culturels.* Paris: Lavoisier, 2008.

Josephson, Jason Ânanda. *The Invention of Religion in Japan.* Chicago: University of Chicago Press, 2012.

Jun'ichi, Isomae. "Deconstructing 'Japanese Religion': A Historical Survey." *Japanese Journal of Religious Studies* 32, no. 2 (2005): 235–48.

_____. "The Conceptual Formation of the Category 'Religion' in Modern Japan: Religion, State, Shintô." *Journal of Religion in Japan* 1, no. 3 (2012): 226–45.

Juschka, Darlene M. "Deconstructing the Eliadean Paradigm: Symbol." In Braun and McCutcheon, *Introducing Religion*, 162–77.

Kane, Pandurang Vaman. *History of Dharmashāstra. Ancient and Medieval Religions and Civil Law in India.* 5 vols. Poona: Bandarkar Oriental Research Institute, 1930–1962.

Kant, Emmanuel. *Critique of Pure Reason.* Translated by J. M. D. Meiklejohn. London: Henry G. Bohn, 1855. Originally published as *Critik der reinen Vernunft.* Riga: J. F. Hartknoch, 1781.

Keshk, Khaled. "Islam in World Religions Textbooks." In "Religion/s between Covers: Dilemmas of the World Religions Textbook," special issue, *Religious Studies Review* 31, nos. 1–2 (2005): 20–23.

Kindt, Julia. *Rethinking Greek Religion.* Cambridge: Cambridge University Press, 2012.

King, Richard. *Orientalism and Religion: Postcolonial Theory, India and "The Mystic East."* London: Routledge, 1999.

_____. "Colonialism, Hinduism and the Discourse of Religion." In Bloch, Keppens, and Hegde, *Rethinking Religion in India*, 95–113.

King, Richard, ed. *Religion Theory Critique: Classic and Contemporary Approaches and Methodologies.* New York: Columbia University Press, 2017.

Kippenberg, Hans Gerhard. *Discovering Religious History in the Modern Age.* Princeton: Princeton University Press, 2002. Originally published as *Die Entdeckung der Religionsgeschichte. Religionswissenschaft und Moderne.* Munich: C. H. Beck, 1997.

Klutz, Todd. "*Christianos.* Defining the Self in the Acts of the Apostles." In *Religion, Language, and Power,* edited by Nile Green and Mary Searle-Chatterjee, 167–85. New York: Routledge, 2008.

Labarrière, P. J. "Phénoménologie de l'Esprit." In *Encyclopédie philosophique universelle. Vol. III. Les oeuvres philosophiques,* edited by Jean-François Mattéi, 1824–25. Paris: Presses universitaires de France, 1992.

Laignel-Lavastine, Alexandra. *Cioran, Eliade, Ionesco: L'oubli du fascisme.* Paris: Presses universitaires de France, 2002.

Lazopoulos, George. "Japanese History, Post-Japan." *Cross-Currents: East Asian History and Culture* 10 (2014): 93–99.

Levine, Amy-Jill. "De-Judaizing Jesus: Theological Need and Exegetical Execution." In Ramey, *Writing Religion*, 148–71.

Lincoln, Bruce. *Myth, Cosmos, and Society: Indo-European Themes of Creation and Destruction.* Cambridge, MA: Harvard University Press, 1986.

_____. *Theorizing Myth: Narrative, Ideology, and Scholarship.* Chicago: Chicago University Press, 1999.

_____. *Holy Terrors: Thinking About Religion after September 11.* 2nd ed. Chicago: University of Chicago Press, 2006.

_____. "Culture." In Braun and McCutcheon, *Guide to the Study of Religion*, 409–22.

Lipner, Julius J. "Ancient Banyan: An Inquiry into the Meaning of 'Hinduness.'" In Llewellyn, *Defining Hinduism*, 30–47.

Littleton, Scott C. *The New Comparative Mythology: An Anthropological Assessment of the Theories of Georges Dumézil.* Berkeley, LA: University of California Press, 1966.

Llewellyn, J. E., ed. *Defining Hinduism: A Reader.* London: Equinox, 2005.

Loisy, Jean de, and Bertrand Hell. *Les Maîtres du désordre.* Paris: Musée du quai Branly, 2011.

Lopez, Donald S., Jr., ed. *Curators of the Buddha: The Study of Buddhism under Colonialism.* Chicago: University of Chicago Press, 1995.

Lorenzen, David N. "Who Invented Hinduism?" In Llewellyn, *Defining Hinduism*, 52–80.

_____. "Hindus and Others." In Bloch, Keppens, and Hegde, *Rethinking Religion in India*, 25–40.

Lubbock, John A. *The Origin of Civilization and the Primitive Condition of Man.* New York: Appleton, 1871.

Lyotard, Jean-François. *Phenomenology.* Translated by Brian Beakley. Albany, NY: State University of New York Press, 1991. Originally published as *La Phénoménologie*. Paris: Presses universitaires de France, 1954.

MacWilliams, Mark. "Introduction." In "Religion/s between Covers: Dilemmas of the World Religions Textbook," special issue, *Religious Studies Review* 31, nos. 1-2 (2005): 1–3.

Magnin, É. "Religion." In *Dictionnaire de théologie catholique.* Vol. 13. No. 2, edited by Alfred Vacant et Eugène Mangenot, col. 2286. Paris: Letouzey et Ané, 1937.

Martin, Craig. "Delimiting Religion." *Method and Theory in the Study of Religion* 21 (2009): 157–76.

_____. *A Critical Introduction to the Study of Religion.* London: Routledge, 2012.

Marx, Karl Frederick Engels. *The German Ideology. Part One. With Selections from Parts Two and Three and Supplementary Texts,* edited by C. J. Arthur. New York: International Publishers, 2004.

_____. *On Colonialism.* n.t. Moscow: Foreign Languages Publishing House, n.d.

Masuzawa, Tomoko. "Culture." In Taylor, *Critical Terms for Religious Studies*, 70–93.

_____. *The Invention of World Religions.* Chicago: University of Chicago Press, 2005.

_____. "Regarding Origin: Beginnings, Foundations, and the Bicameral Formations of the Study of Religion." In Ramey, *Writing Religion*, 131–48.

Mauss, Marcel. "A Sociological Assessment of Bolshevism (1924-5)." Translated by Ben Brewster. *Economy and Society* 13, no. 3 (1984): 331–74. Originally published as "Appréciation sociologique du bolchevisme." *Revue de métaphysique et de morale* 31 (1924): 103–32.

McCutcheon, Russell T. *Manufacturing Religion: The Discourse on Sui Generis Religion and the Politics of Nostalgia.* New York: Oxford University Press, 1997.

_____. *Critics not Caretakers: Redescribing the Public Study of Religion.* Albany: State University of New York Press, 2001.

_____. *The Discipline of Religion: Structure, Meaning, Rhetoric.* London: Routledge, 2003.

_____. "The Perils of Having One's Cake and Eating It Too: Some Thoughts in Response." In "Religion/s between Covers: Dilemmas of the World

Religions Textbook," special issue, *Religious Studies Review* 31, no. 1–2 (2005): 32–36.

_____. "The Resiliency of Conceptual Anachronism: On Knowing the Limits of 'The West' and 'Religion.'" *Religion* 36, no. 3 (2006): 154–65.

_____. "'Man Is the Measure of All Things': On the Fabrication of Oriental Religions by European History of Religions." In *Working Papers on Method and Theory from Hannover*, edited by Steffan Führding, 82–107. Leiden: Brill, 2017.

Miller, Dean A. *The Epic Hero*. Baltimore: Johns Hopkins University Press, 2000.

Mittal, Sushil, and Gene Thursby, eds. *Religions of South Asia: An Introduction*. London: Routledge, 2006.

Montagnac, Lucien de. *Lettres d'un soldat. Neuf ans de campagne en Afrique*. Paris: Librairie Plon, 1885.

Müller, Friedrich Max. *Lectures on the Origin and Growth of Religion, as Illustrated by the Religions of India*. London: Longmans, Green and Co., 1878.

Noll, Richard. *The Jung Cult: Origins of a Charismatic Movement*. London: Fontana Press, 1996.

Nongbri, Brent. *Before Religion: A History of a Modern Concept*. New Haven: Yale University Press, 2013.

Nye, Malory. *Religion: The Basics*. 2nd ed. London: Routledge, 2008.

O'Connell, Joseph T. "The Word 'Hindu' in Gaudîya Vaishnava Texts." *Journal of the American Oriental Society* 93, no. 3 (1973): 340–44.

Oddie, Geoffrey A. *Imagined Hinduism: British Protestant Missionary Constructions of Hinduism, 1793–1900*. New Delhi: Sage, 2006.

_____. "Hindu Religious Identity with Special Reference to the Origin and Significance of the Term 'Hinduism', c. 1787–1947." In Bloch, Keppens, and Hegde, *Rethinking Religion in India*, 41–55.

Otto, Rudolf. *The Idea of the Holy*. Translated by John Harvey. New York: Oxford University Press, 2nd ed. 1952. Originally published *as Das Heilige: Über das Irrationale in der Idee des Göttlichen und sein Verhältnis zum Rationalen*. Breslau: Trewendt and Granier, 1917.

Pagels, Elaine. *The Gnostic Gospels*. New York: Random House, 1979.

Picard, Michel. "What's in a Name? An Enquiry about the Interpretation of Agama Hindu as 'Hinduism.'" *Jurnal Kajian Bali* 22, no. 2 (2012): 113–40.

_____. *Kebalian La Construction dialogique de l'identité balinaise*. Cahier d'Archipel 44. Paris: EHESS, 2017.

Poliakov, Léon. *History of Antisemitism*. 4 vols. Translated by Richard Howard (I; NY: Vanguard, 1965); Natalie Gerardi (II; NY: Vanguard, 1975); Miriam Kochan (III; Abingdon: Routledge, 1975); and George Klin (IV; Philadelphia: University of Philadelphia Press, 1977). Originally published as *Histoire de l'antisémitisme*. 4 vols. Paris: Calman-Lévy, 1955, 1961, 1968, 1977.

Prudhomme, Claude. *Stratégie missionnaire du Saint-Siège sous Léon XII (1878–1903)*. Rome: École Française de Rome, 1994.

Radcliffe-Brown, A. R. *Structure and Function in Primitive Society*. London: Cohen and West, 1952.

Raj, Kapil. "Colonial Encounters, Circulation and the Co-construction of Knowledge and National Identities: Great Britain and India, 1760–1850." In

Social History of Science in Colonial India, edited by S. Irfan Habib and Dhruv Raina, 83–101. Delhi: Oxford University Press, 2007.

_____. "Régler les différends, gérer les différences: dynamiques urbaines et savantes à Calcutta au XVIIIe siècle." In "Sciences et Villes-Mondes," edited by Stéphane Van Damme and Antonella Romano, special issue, *Revue d'Histoire Moderne et Contemporaine* 55, no. 2 (May, 2008): 70–100.

Raj, Selva J. "The Quest for a Balanced Representation of South Asian Religions in World Religions Textbooks." In "Religion/s between Covers: Dilemmas of the World Religions Textbook," special issue, *Religious Studies Review* 31, nos. 1–2 (2005): 14–16.

Ramey, Steven W. "Introduction." In Ramey, *Writing Religion*, 1–13.

Ramey, Steven W., ed. *Writing Religion: The Case for the Critical Study of Religion.* Tuscaloosa: University of Alabama Press, 2015.

Read, Kay A. "World Religions and the Miscellaneous Category." In "Religion/s between Covers: Dilemmas of the World Religions Textbook," special issue, *Religious Studies Review* 31, nos. 1–2 (2005): 10–13.

Reinach, Salomon. *Manuel de philologie*. Paris: Hachette, 1880.

Renan, Ernest. *Nouvelles études d'histoire religieuse*. Paris: Calmann Lévy, 1884.

_____. *Studies of Religious History and Criticism*. Translated by O. B. Frothingham. New York: Carleton, 1864. Originally published as *Études d'histoire religieuse*. Paris: Michel Lévy, 1857.

_____. *La Réforme intellectuelle et morale in Œuvres complètes, Vol. 1*. Paris: Calmann-Lévy, 1947.

Ries, Julien. "*Homo religiosus.*" In *Dictionnaire des religions*, vol. 1. 3rd ed., edited by Paul Poupard, 860–65. Paris: Presses universitaires de France, 1984.

Robert, Fernand. *La Religion grecque*. Paris: Presses universitaires de France, 1981.

Robertson, Paul. "De-Spiritualizing *Pneuma*: Modernity, Religion, and Anachronism in the Study of Paul." *Method and Theory in the Study of Religion* 26, nos. 4–5 (2014): 365–83.

Roover Jakob de, and Sarah Claerhout. "The Colonial Construction of What?" In Bloch, Keppens, and Hegde, *Rethinking Religion in India*, 164–83.

Rousseau, Jean-Jacques. *Profession of Faith of a Savoyard Vicar*. n.t. Rockville, MD: Wildside Press, 2008. Originally published as part of Book IV of *Emile, ou De l'éducation*. Amsterdam: Jean Neaulme [false information for Paris: Nicolas Bonaventure Duchesne], 1762.

Saliba, John A. *'Homo Religiosus' in Mircea Eliade: An Anthropological Evaluation*. Leiden: Brill, 1976.

Sarma, D. S. *Essence of Hinduism*. Bombay: Bharatiya Vidya Bhavan, 1971.

Scheid, John. *An Introduction to Roman Religion*. Translated by Janet Lloyd. Edinburgh: Edinburgh University Press, 2003. Originally published as *La Religion des Romains*. Paris: Armand Colin, 1998.

Scheler, Max. *On the Eternal in Man*. Translated by Bernard Noble. New York: Harper and Brothers, 1960. Originally published as *Vom Ewigen im Menschen*. Leipzig: Der Neue-Geist-Verlag, 1921.

Schlegel, August Wilhelm von. n.t. *Transactions of the Royal Society of Literature of the United Kingdom 1835*. Bonn: Édouard Weber, 1842.

Schleiermacher, Friedrich Daniel Ernst. *On Religion: Speeches to Its Cultured Despisers.* Translated by John Oman. New York: Harper and Brothers, 1958. Originally published as *Über die Religion. Reden an die Gebildeten unter ihren Verächtern.* Berlin: Unger Verlag, 1799.

Schüssler Fiorenza, Francis, and Gordon D. Kaufman. "God." In Taylor, *Critical Terms for Religious Studies,* 136–59.

Segal, Robert A. *Theorizing about Myth.* Amherst: University of Massachusetts Press, 1999.

Sergent, Bernard. *Les Indo-Européens: Histoire, langues, mythes.* Paris: Éditions Payot & Rivages, 1995.

Shattuck, Cybelle; "Judaism in World Religions Textbooks." In "Religion/s between Covers: Dilemmas of the World Religions Textbook," special issue, *Religious Studies Review* 31, nos. 1–2 (2005): 8–10.

Shepard, Robert. *God's People in the Ivory Tower: Religion in the Early American University.* New York: Carlson, 1991.

Shimazono, Susumu. "State Shinto and the Religious Structure of Modern Japan." *Journal of the American Academy of Religion* 73, no. 4 (2005): 1077–98.

Smart, Ninian. *Worldviews: Cross-Cultural Explorations of Religious Beliefs.* New York: Scribner, 1983.

Smith, Brian K. "Questioning Authority: Constructions and Deconstructions of Hinduism." In Llewellyn, *Defining Hinduism,* 102–24.

Smith, Jonathan Z. *Imagining Religion: From Babylon to Jonestown.* Chicago: University of Chicago Press, 1982.

_____. *To Take Place: Toward Theory in Ritual.* Chicago: University of Chicago Press, 1987.

_____. "'Religion' and 'Religious Studies': No Difference at All." *Soundings* 71 (1988): 231–44.

_____. "Religious Studies: Whither (Wither) and Why?" *Method and Theory in the Study of Religion* 7 (1995): 407–13.

_____. "Religion, Religions, Religious." In *Relating Religion: Essays in the Study of Religion.* Chicago: University of Chicago Press, 2004, 169–96. Originally published in Taylor, *Critical Terms for Religious Studies,* 269–84.

_____. "Classification." In Braun and McCutcheon, *Guide to the Study of Religion,* 35–44.

Snodgrass, Judith. *Presenting Japanese Buddhism to the West: Orientalism, Occidentalism, and the Columbian Exposition.* Chapel Hill, NC: University of North Carolina Press, 2003.

Sommer, Deborah. "Chinese Religions in World Religions Textbooks." In "Religion/s between Covers: Dilemmas of the World Religions Textbook," special issue, *Religious Studies Review* 31, nos. 1–2 (2005): 4–7.

Spiro, Melford I. "Religion: Problems of Definition and Explanation." In *Culture and Human Nature.* London: Transaction, 1994, 187–98.

Stausberg, Michael. "Western Europe." In Alles, *Religious Studies,* 14–49.

Stoczkowski, Wiktor. "Essai sur la matière première de l'imaginaire anthropologique: Analyse d'un cas." *Revue de synthèse* IV, nos. 3–4 (1992): 439–57.

Strenski, Ivan. *Four Theories of Myth in Twentieth-Century History: Cassirer, Eliade, Lévi-Strauss and Malinowski.* Iowa City: University of Iowa Press, 1987.

_____. *Thinking about Religion: A Reader.* Malden, MA: Blackwell, 2006.

Stroumsa, Guy G. *A New Science: The Discovery of Religion in the Age of Reason.* Cambridge, MA: Harvard University Press, 2010.

Stuckrad, Kocku von. *The Scientification of Religion: An Historical Study of Discursive Change, 1800–2000.* Berlin: de Gruyter, 2015.

_____. *Western Esotericism: A Brief History of Secret Knowledge.* London: Equinox, 2013.

Sugirtharajah, Sharada. *Imagining Hinduism: A Postcolonial Perspective.* London: Routledge, 2003.

Sweetman, Will. "Unity and Plurality: Hinduism and the Religions of India in Early European Scholarship." *Religion* 31 (2011): 209–224; reprinted in Llewellyn, *Defining Hinduism*, 81–98.

Taylor, Mark, ed. *Critical Terms for Religious Studies.* Chicago: University of Chicago Press, 1998.

Tiele, Cornelis Petrus. *Outline of the History of Religion to the Spread of Universal Religions.* London: Trübner, 1877.

Tillich, Paul. *Theology of Culture.* Translated by Robert C. Kimball. Oxford: Oxford University Press, 1959.

Tweed, Thomas A. *Crossing and Dwelling: A Theory of Religion.* Cambridge, MA: Harvard University Press, 2006.

Tylor, Edward B. *Primitive Culture: Research into the Development of Mythology, Philosophy, Religion, Language, Art, and Custom.* 2 vols. 2nd ed. London: John Murray, 1873.

Urbanski, Sébastien. *L'enseignement du fait religieux: École, république, laïcité.* Paris: Presses universitaires de France, 2016.

Van der Leeuw, Gerardus. *Religion in Essence and Manifestation: A Study in Phenomenology*, translated by J. E. Turner. London: Allen & Unwin, 1938.

Viswanathan, Gauri. "Colonialism and the Construction of Hinduism." In *The Blackwell Companion to Hinduism*, edited by Gavin D. Flood, 23–44. Malden, MA: Blackwell, 2003.

Volovici, Leon. *Nationalist Ideology and Antisemitism: The Case of Romanian Intellectuals in the 1930s.* Oxford: Pergamon Press, 1991.

Wach, Joachim. *Sociology of Religion.* Chicago: University of Chicago Press, 1947. Originally published as *Einführung in die Religionssoziologie.* Tübingen: Mohr Siebeck, 1931.

Waghorne, Joanne Punzo. "Revisiting the Question of Religion in the World Religions Textbooks." *Religious Studies Review* 31, nos. 1–2 (2005): 3–4.

Wasserstrom, Steven M. *Religion after Religion: Gershom Scholem, Mircea Eliade and Henry Corbin at Eranos.* Princeton: Princeton University Press, 1999.

Wedemeyer, Christian K., and Wendy Doniger, eds. *Hermeneutics, Politics and the History of Religions: The Contested Legacies of Joachim Wach and Mircea Eliade.* New York: Oxford University Press, 2010.

Whimster, Sam, ed. *The Essential Max Weber: A Reader.* 2nd ed. London: Routledge, 2006.

Wiebe, Donald. *The Irony of Theology and the Nature of Religious Thought.* Montreal: McGill-Queen's University Press, 1991.

_____. *The Politics of Religious Studies: The Continuing Conflict with Theology in the Academy.* New York: St. Martin's Press, 1999.

Williams, Raymond. *Culture and Society, 1780–1950*. New York: Columbia University Press, 1958.

Yelle, Robert. "Criticism and Critique (in, among and of Religions)." In *Vocabulary for the Study of Religion*, edited by Robert A. Segal and Kocku von Stuckrad. 2016. http://dx.doi.org/10.1163/9789004249797_vsr_COM_00000253

Zavos, John. "Representing Religion in Colonial India." In Bloch, Keppens, and Hegde, *Rethinking Religion in India*, 56–68.

Person and Author Index

Subject Index

AAR (American Academy of Religion) 47, 56–57, 58, 59–60, 107, 109
anachronisms 12, 128, 177n49
Anthropology
    Christian 19, 162–63n11
    general *vii*, 14, 33–34, 39, 56, 89, 103, 136, 143, 144, 147, 148, 151–52, 180–81n19
    popular 9
archetypes 53
Aryans 20, 31, 123, 159n8, 175n22
atheism 3, 24, 26, 35, 53, 54, 74, 88, 123
Aztecs 108, 112, 142

Brahman 112, 128, 129–30
Brahmanism 38, 42, 127, 132
Buddhism 38, 42, 51, 57, 65, 107, 108, 109–110, 113, 121, 122–23, 124, 125, 134, 135, 136, 138, 141, 146, 173n22, 175n26, 177n49

Capitalism 137, 145, 158n6
Catholic Church
    Catholicism 2, 36, 125, 174n5
    institutions 49, 50, 51, 57
    religion 40, 115
    theology 39
censorship 17–19
Christian religion 10, 11, 12, 14, 15, 16, 23, 24, 25, 27, 49, 83, 84, 85, 89, 93, 103, 108, 110, 124, 127, 134, 142, 144, 155n9, 173n27
christianos 13
Code of Canon Law, the 17, 19, 157nn21–22, 157n26

cognitive imperialism 116, 119, 145, 151
colonialism/colonial conquest 9, 33, 70, 72, 73, 113, 114–18, 121, 127, 131, 132, 136–37, 141, 151, 173n18
comparativism 41, 149–50
Confucianism 38, 108, 121, 123, 134, 135, 138
cosmic religion 96–98, 103, 172n13
Critical Studies 2–3, 4, 9, 43, 47, 62, 63, 71, 72, 74, 101, 103, 105, 110, 113, 114, 116, 142, 143, 149, 152, 153, 156n18, 176n35
cultural imperialism 3, 114, 119
culture
    Christian 1, 7–9, 10, 14, 15, 21, 29, 53, 64, 81, 110–11, 150
    Indian 127, 129, 130, 146
    general 8, 9, 14, 33, 48, 66, 102, 107, 111, 138, 146–48, 175n21, 180n15, 180nn17–18
    popular 26, 48
    Western 8, 9, 19, 22, 24, 32, 56, 60, 67, 70, 101, 110–11, 117, 152

Darwinism 32, 33
dharma 13, 53, 127, 128–29, 130, 143, 162n11, 177n43
domination 9, 15–16, 34, 52, 54, 61, 64, 68, 70, 72–73, 114, 117, 119, 120, 133. *See also* power
doxa 8, 34, 50, 52, 153, 162n9

ecumenism 40, 55, 102–3, 137, 175n25
eidos 78, 82, 100
ekklêsia 13
Enlightenment, the 23, 26

CPSIA information can be obtained
at www.ICGtesting.com
Printed in the USA
LVHW042112090223
739117LV00004B/154